Uses of the Past in the Novels of William Faulkner

Studies in Modern Literature, No. 37

A. Walton Litz, General Series Editor

Professor of English
Princeton University

Joseph Blotner

Consulting Editor for Titles on William Faulkner
Professor of English
University of Michigan

Other Titles in This Series

Uses of the Past in the Novels of William Faulkner

by
Carl E. Rollyson Jr.

UMI RESEARCH PRESS
Ann Arbor, Michigan

Copyright © 1984
Carl Edmund Rollyson Jr.
All rights reserved

Produced and distributed by
UMI Research Press
an imprint of
University Microfilms International
A Xerox Information Resources Company
Ann Arbor, Michigan 48106

Library of Congress Cataloging in Publication Data

Rollyson, Carl E. (Carl Edmund)
    Uses of the past in the novels of William Faulkner.

    (Studies in modern literature ; no. 37)
    Revision of thesis—University of Toronto, 1975.
    Bibliography: p.
    Includes index.
    1. Faulkner, William, 1897-1962—Knowledge—History.
2. History in literature. 3. Time in literature. 4. Memory
in literature. 5. Historical fiction, American. I. Title.
II. Series.
PS3511.A86Z962 1984   813'.52   84-2745
ISBN 0-8357-1554-X

To Lisa

Contents

Acknowledgments

My study of William Faulkner began in high school in 1963 with a puzzled but exhilarating reading of *The Sound and the Fury*. At Michigan State University in 1966 Professor M. Thomas Inge, who has remained in so many ways my teacher and my guide, introduced me to "The Bear" at a time when I was also engaged in learning about the philosophy of history and historiography. This book had its inception in 1970 as a graduate paper for Professor Michael Millgate's class on Wessex and Yoknapataw-pha at the University of Toronto. Under his astute and assiduous supervision I expanded the paper and completed it in 1975. Now, nearly ten years later, I have revised and updated *Uses of the Past in the Novels of William Faulkner*, omitted a chapter, rearranged and augmented material within chapters, and expanded the introduction, conclusion, and bibliography. For permission to reprint parts of articles previously published in journals, I would like to thank the editors of *Mississippi Quarterly* 29 (1976):361–74, *Dalhousie Review* 56 (1976–77): 671–81, *Literature and History* 5 (1977): 45–54, *The Markham Review* 7 (1978):31–36, and *Massachusetts Studies in English* 7 (1980):34–39. Grateful acknowledgment is made as well to Random House, Inc., to include selections from copyrighted works of William Faulkner and to A. D. Peters & Co. Ltd. to include selections from copyrighted work of Herbert Butterfield.

1

Introduction

I

This book attempts to define both the uniqueness of Faulkner's uses of the past and the extent to which those uses derive from, or are comparable to, the work of historians and historical novelists. In many respects, of course, his novels are not historical at all. Most of them are set in or near his own lifetime, none in the distant past, so that when we speak of the past in his work we are usually thinking of a time no more than three to four generations from his own, a time that was still partially present for him in the minds of old people or of the descendants of the white and black inhabitants of the antebellum South. Faulkner's novels are historical in the sense that their concern is frequently with characters who are obsessed with a personal, family, or regional past. The chief reasons for the predominance of the past in the minds of Faulkner's characters, for the tremendous historical depth which that predominance gives to his fiction, and for what he sees as the inherent limitations of regarding the past as the sole determinant of man's history are perhaps illuminated by Ortega y Gasset's suggestion:

> The past is man's moment of identity...nothing besides is inexorable and fatal. But, for the same reason, if man's only Eleatic [immutable] being is what he has been, this means that his authentic being, what in effect he is—and not merely "has been"—is distinct from the past, and consists precisely and formally in "being what one has not been," in non-Eleatic being.[1]

In *Flags in the Dust*, for example, there are a number of moments in Miss Jenny's, old Bayard's, and old man Falls's accounts of the Civil War which make the past actions of the Sartorises seem "inexorable and fatal."[2] Young Bayard's life is blighted by his constant recurrence to the moment when his brother John jumped out of his plane and thumbed his nose at him, and in *Light in August* Hightower's present is silenced by the thundering of galloping horses out of his grandfather's past. But precisely because man

tends to identify himself with his past and to see his past as the sole determinant of his being, the novels imply — and Faulkner himself has said — that
man should rather see life as motion, change: to immerse one's self entirely
in the past is to remain what one "has been," and once anything "stops,
abandons motion, it is dead."[3] Thus for Faulkner, too, "authentic
being...consists precisely and formally in 'being what one has not been.'"

Even though this book is not specifically concerned with Faulkner's
view of time, his nonfiction statements on the subject are obviously of crucial importance in determining the ways in which he uses the past and the
extent to which his uses differ from those of his characters. Faulkner told
Malcolm Cowley that "my ambition...is to put everything into one sentence — not only the present but the whole past on which it depends and
which keeps overtaking the present, second by second."[4] On the face of it,
this statement may seem to endorse Sartre's notion that in Faulkner's fiction
"the past takes on a sort of super-reality; its contours are hard and clear,
unchangeable."[5] Sartre demonstrates very well that in *The Sound and the
Fury* the past overtakes Quentin's present and that Quentin sees the present
only in terms of the past. But, as several critics have pointed out, it is dangerous to equate the author's views with a particular character's perceptions,[6] especially since other characters in other novels, such as Charles
Bon in *Absalom, Absalom!*, express the opposite view of time: *"What
WAS is one thing, and now it is not because it is dead...and therefore
what IS...is something else again because it was not even alive then."*[7]
Clearly, more needs to be said about the exact way in which Faulkner sees
the past as overtaking the present.

At the University of Virginia Faulkner stated:

> To me, no man is himself, he is the sum of his past. There is no such thing really as was
> because the past is. It is a part of every man, every woman, and every moment. All of
> his and her ancestry, background, is all a part of himself and herself at any moment.
> And so a man, a character in a story at any moment of action is not just himself as he is
> then, he is all that made him, and the long sentence is an attempt to get his past and
> possibly his future into the instant in which he does something.[8]

The past is an inescapable part of the present — but this notion is quite different from the one which suggests that all man has is his past. Faulkner
believes that the present grows out of the past and that the present is part
of the continuum of time.[9] But his statement presupposes that there is a
valid distinction to be made between past and present even though both are
a part of the "instant" in which a character "does something."

In his most elaborate explanation of his conception of time Faulkner
used the idea of a machine which could demonstrate in physical terms the
relationship of past, present, and future to each other:

Well, a man's future is inherent in that man — I — in the sense that life, A.D. 1957, is not the end of life, that there'll be a 2057. That we assume that. There may not be, but we assume that. And in man, in man's behavior today is nineteen fifty — two thousand and fifty-seven, if we just had a machine that could project ahead and could capture that, that machine could isolate and freeze a picture, an image, of what man will be doing in 2057, just as the machine might capture and fix the light rays showing what he was doing in B.C. 28. That is, that's the mystical belief that there is no such thing as *was*. That time *is*, and if there's no such thing as *was*, then there is no such thing as *will be*. That time is not a fixed condition, time is in a way the sum of the combined intelligences of all men who breathe at that moment.[10]

Faulkner sees time as a fluid and malleable medium. Not just the past but all of time is present in the "combined intelligences of all men who breathe at that moment." If he believed otherwise — that time is a fixed condition — then all of time would be past, would be *was*, and there would be no such thing as *is*. In considering this alternate possibility, Faulkner said: "If *was* existed there would be no grief or sorrow."[11] The past does not exist as a separate entity in the present but as part of the continuum of time. Thus we know the past only from our own vantage point in time, from our present moment. In a rare endorsement of another thinker's ideas, Faulkner admitted: "I agree pretty much with Bergson's theory of the fluidity of time. There is only the present moment, in which I include both the past and the future, and that is eternity. In my opinion time can be shaped quite a bit by the artist; after all, man is never time's slave."[12] With this and Faulkner's other statements in both his fiction and nonfiction in mind, Robert Hemenway has succinctly summarized the author's thesis:

one can only live in that present tense, . . . although the past may inform the present, or sometimes even explain a part of that present, it does not and must not "exist" in the present; it cannot be permitted to determine present reality.[13]

Much of the Faulkner criticism of the past two decades would support Hemenway's interpretation.[14] In particular, two books by Warren Beck and Richard P. Adams focus on the author's dynamic conception of time and show the various ways in which the novels call for man to break out of the stultifying patterns of the past or, indeed, out of any abstract formulation which clouds his response to the concrete reality of the present.[15] This study attempts to build on Beck and Adams and to demonstrate how Faulkner's definition of life as "man in motion" relates to his uses of the past. His novels are treated as representations of what in the broadest sense may be called historical process — a process in which change continues to deepen and widen the differences between past and present but in which the fundamental repetitions and ironies of history tie together all periods of time into the continuum that Faulkner and his critics have spoken of.

II

Faulkner's conception of time — and of the past in particular — prevents him from writing anything like a conventional historical novel in the manner of Scott and his successors. Since no part of time's continuum exists entirely in and for itself, a novel set completely in the past is virtually an impossibility, for the past can be imagined only in its relationship to the present and future, just as the present and future have to be created in Faulkner's writing with reference to the past. If time is a fluid condition, then none of its constituents — and certainly not the past — can stay fixed long enough to justify what is commonly termed an historical novel.

In his evaluation of *All The King's Men* Faulkner makes clear his profound wariness of the novelist's hold on the past. In praising the Cass Mastern episode, in which the narrator, Jack Burden, digresses from his present into the nineteenth-century past, Faulkner notes:

> It's fine the way Warren caught not only the pattern of their acts but the very terms they thought in of that time.... He should have taken the Cass story and made a novel. Though maybe no man 75 years from that time could have sustained that for novel length.[16]

Perhaps the past can be captured momentarily in all of its fullness and intactness, but as a rule, Faulkner seems to say, it is unapproachable as a world in itself. We get glimpses, insights, into the past but not the past as such because we are always moving further away from it.

This is why Faulkner makes excursions into the past that are inextricably fused with his characters' sense of the present. Even in *The Unvanquished*, his most sustained narrative of the past, the chapters are more like episodes, historic moments, rather than like the continuous, integral composition of an historical period of the kind we get in *The History of Henry Esmond*.[17] In other words, Faulkner essays an approach to the past knowing full well that the whole of it cannot be recaptured. In this regard, he acts very much like the twentieth-century historian relying on partial evidence — like Oscar Handlin, who concentrates on turning points in history where the past can be evoked concisely and dramatically in chapter-length studies.[18]

Divisions in point of view are so prevalent in Faulkner's treatment of the present that it is no wonder that the past should be recreated in a series of segments, distinct from each other, although capable of connection in the continuum of time. Hugh M. Ruppersburg reminds us of Faulkner's emphasis on "distance itself — between individuals...generations...and different modes of experience...."[19] Faulkner also enforces this consciousness of distance, or discreteness, or disunity by beginning each chapter in

Absalom, Absalom! "as a seemingly new narrative, with no apparent relationship to any other...."[20] The awareness of a new narrative or story is even greater in *Go Down, Moses,* and variations on this kind of fragmented structure occur throughout his career.[21]

Another way to understand Faulkner's avoidance of historical fiction per se while he remains very much concerned with the past is to realize how strenuously he explores an open-ended view of the past, especially of his own past as fiction-maker. Thus Lisa Paddock notes that in his three short story collections he rearranges old material in a new context to bring out different meanings and to give rise "to an entirely new literary creation." Moreover, he "implicitly insists upon the connections that exist between seemingly unrelated components, transforming what appear to be discrete fragments into organically unified wholes."[22] The past as a self-contained narrative closed off from the present does not interest Faulkner and is not possible for him to conceive because, as Paddock puts it, the fragmented form of his fiction "attests his denial of the finality of any given work."[23] Each novel, and Faulkner's entire output, seems designed to resist the idea of placing a perimeter around the past, codifying and documenting it in the manner of a consistent historical fiction. Part of the past can be documented, as *Go Down, Moses* demonstrates, but as a part of history the past's boundaries blur, become very ambiguous, and far more flexible than the past in the historical novels of Faulkner's predecessors.

Just how flexible the past can be is revealed in the title chapter of *Go Down, Moses.* As Wesley Morris observes, "Was" "opens for the reader, almost without his being aware of it, a series of questions about origins."[24] After a full reading of the novel, events in "Was" can be dated and human motivations deciphered, but Morris is correct in remarking that the title of the first chapter suggests an indefiniteness about what exactly happened and when. The one-word title suspends or deters our immediate effort to place the story in time, in the chronology of an historical fiction, for we are not sure of what came before or after; we are thrust into the middle of "Was." The story is open at both ends, so to speak, yet it has, in Morris's words, an "Aristotelian wholeness," and an "adequate structure of its own." "In its seeming internal wholeness the story presents itself, therefore, as a privileged moment, an objectified fragment of the past, but the suggestion of infinite regression in the title denies this moment, and any moment, privileged status," Morris concludes. The past has no privileged status, for, as *Requiem for a Nun* shows, there is no past but rather a succession of pasts. The implication of "Was" is that "not only the pattern of their acts but the very terms they thought in of that time" can be summoned, but not in novel-length narrative.

When Faulkner in *The Unvanquished* tries to string together as chapters his discrete, story-like excursions into the past, he invites our search for transitions from one part of an historical period to another that we have come to expect in a continuous historical fiction, and he fails to provide them clearly enough. *Go Down, Moses*, on the other hand, eschews transitions by abruptly naming Ike at the beginning of the novel without clearly indicating how his story figures into "Was." Thus the very act of making transitions is refused, and we have to make leaps from one period of time to another, eventually learning to construct a continuum out of disparate pieces of narrative and of time.

There are still other ways in which Faulkner probably finds historical fiction inimical to the development of his dynamic idea of history. Historical fiction, after all, is an aspect of that actual world he sublimates into Yoknapatawpha County, a fictional world of self-made boundaries and histories. Before he created Yoknapatawpha, "he says he commenced with the idea that novels should deal with imaginary scenes and people," Malcolm Cowley reports.[25] In the writing that came before his first novels Faulkner avoids, for the most part, a realistic depiction of his native region and aims, on the contrary, for symbolic, poetical evocations of feelings and various states of mind that are all too vaguely rendered in many instances. It is as if he tries to get as far away from the factual as possible while taking to its extreme Aristotle's notion that "poetry is more philosophical and of higher value than history; for poetry universalizes more, whereas history particularizes."[26] With the emergence of Yoknapatawpha, Faulkner would draw upon actual places and persons for his fiction, and with the writing of his essay "Mississippi," he would bring together aspects of his home state, his apocryphal county, and his own history, yet there is always the principle dramatized in his fiction and enunciated in his nonfiction statements that he is an independent and autonomous creator, and not an historian of the South, or of any realm outside of the one he creates.[27]

Faulkner's imagination, in other words, is primary; facts, sources, evidence of the sources of his creations are secondary. From this elevation of the artist's world above its roots in reality Faulkner criticizes Sherwood Anderson:

> I think when a writer reaches the point when he's got to write about people he knows, his friends, then he has reached the tragic point. There seems to me there's too much to be written about, that needs to be said, for one to have to resort to actual living figures.[28]

In other words, actuality, documented history, real living figures (even if disguised), are all part of what has already been said, already been experienced. Fiction, on the other hand, is what is genuinely new, independent, and original.

One has to probe and, to some extent, stretch Faulkner's talk in interviews to ascertain the underlying assumptions of his fictional methodology, for he often spoke, as Millgate says, "in a kind of basic Model T English that was utterly unlike his characteristic written style."[29] In another way, however, the statements "can be made the texts of quite intricate critical discussions"[30] because, like the fiction, the statements are highly compressed perceptions. Art, Faulkner surely believes, evades excessive explicitness, and an historically oriented art should do no less. In *The Sound and the Fury, As I Lay Dying, Absalom, Absalom!, Requiem for a Nun*, and in a few other works, he employs words like time, the past, and history as abstractions or concepts, but he does so sparingly and never in the manner of an historical novelist, or of Jack Burden: "Soon now we shall go out of the house and go into the convulsion of the world, out of history into history and the awful responsibility of Time."[31] As Millgate suggests, in his own work Faulkner avoids this kind of "summarised message." The Cass Mastern episode, on the other hand, is a "a deeply imagined and richly worked moral fable embedded — separate, complete, intact, powerful — in the heart of the novel, enforcing without overt commentary the message which the central first-person narrative articulates, a little too self-consciously, on the author's behalf."[32] Millgate calls the Cass Mastern story a fable that is akin to "the story of the bear and the dog in *Go Down, Moses,* the transcendent love story of Ike and the cow in *The Hamlet,* the story of the crippled racehorse in *A Fable,*"[33] and, I would add, the story of the French architect and Thomas Sutpen in *Absalom, Absalom!.* All such fables universalize and crystallize history, at once stripping and condensing it to its essential meaning.[34] In this respect, I argue in Chapter 3, Faulkner shares much with historical fiction as it was practiced by Scott.

Faulkner's fierce commitment to the primacy of his art precludes his direct use of the plots of history or of politics. He writes, instead, what Joseph Turner calls an "invented historical novel" that rejects the documented past or even elements of that same past disguised in fiction.[35] "Faulkner, for example, can tell us that Rosa Coldfield never bore children, and there is the end to the question. But if a novelist were to write about Queen Elizabeth, the reader would expect from the very first that Elizabeth bore no legitimate children and that the crown was passed on to James I."[36] It is the prior purchase history would have on his fiction that Faulkner cannot countenance as the sole owner and proprietor of Yoknapatawpha. The originality of his voice, and of his vision of history, comes out of both a time and a place of his own making.

Robert Penn Warren calls Faulkner an apolitical novelist and wonders why

in his vast panorama of society in a state where politics is the blood, bone, sinew and passion of life, and the most popular sport, Faulkner has almost entirely omitted not only a treatment of the subject, but references to it. It is easy to be contemptuous of politics anywhere, and especially easy in Jackson, Mississippi, but it is not easy to close one's eyes to the cosmic comedy enacted in that State House; and it is not easy to understand how Faulkner with his genius for the absurd, even the tearfully absurd, could have rejected this subject.[37]

From Faulkner's point of view, however, it is not for him to provide commentary on political or on any other kind of already recorded history but to fashion one of his own, for unlike some authors who view their writing as one of the "many creative roles within or without established society," he tends to view writing as *the* creative role, *the* prop, and *the* pillar of civilization.[38]

Warren also suggests that Faulkner may simply have contempt for politics, and this certainly seems to be the case in *The Mansion* and in his view of Willie Stark:

> As I read him, he wanted neither power for the sake of his pride nor revenge for the sake of his vanity; he wanted neither to purify the earth by obliterating some of the population from it nor did he aim to give every hillbilly and redneck a pair of shoes. He was neither big enough nor bad enough.[39]

Only someone like Ahab or like Thomas Sutpen, a character larger than life, can be the subject of a great novel, in Faulkner's estimation. Stark, on the other hand, is for Faulkner a particularization of history, not its embodiment. Stark does not move him enough because he is "second-rate"[40] —as, I suspect, much of the political world was for Faulkner. By cutting himself off from politics he simultaneously severs himself from the kind of material that might bring him closer to historical fiction. From Melville he learned about the grandiosity of design that gave the greatest life to fiction. "Melville, in fact, was the master who taught Faulkner most clearly and emphatically that the forms of fiction were not fixed but truly protean, capable of infinite evolution in response to evolving creative needs, and who showed that a writer with sufficient ability and courage could do almost anything with the novel and get away with it. . . ."[41] A narrative of Willie Stark's life could not be truly protean, endlessly evolving, and capable of "almost anything." Faulkner rather brutally told an interviewer that he would have kept the Cass Mastern story "and thrown the rest of the book away."[42]

Like other writers of his time, Faulkner regarded historical fiction as a degenerate form and reacted against its sentimentalization of the past. After Scott, much of Victorian historical fiction concentrated on the past as pageant and spectacle. Historical novels were escapist exercises in nostalgia and antiquarianism, and forays into the quaintness of the past, into its manners and mores. As a result, precise attention to matters of esthetic form, style, and characterization were slighted in favor of unthinking entertainment. And to some extent, Scott, the daring originator of the genre, might be charged with starting its decline, since he professed not to take his own novels very seriously.[43] In a letter Faulkner alludes to his disrespect for the historical novel by briefly explaining his efforts to get more out of *Absalom, Absalom!* "than a historical novel would be. To keep the hoop skirts and plug hats out, you might say."[44]

In spite of all these reasons for keeping Faulkner well on the remote side of historical fiction, I have attempted to show in Chapters 2 and 3, and in the Conclusion, that his novels share a certain continuity with nineteenth-century historical novels by Scott and Thackeray. Michael Millgate notes that "Faulkner may have been too conscious of standing in opposition to the historical traditions associated with Scott to have recognized him as a master...[and] there is little specific evidence of Faulkner's familiarity with [Thackeray's] work," but my judgment is that their novels formed a part of his reading until at least his sixteenth year,[45] a year he mentions when remembering a quotation from the Polish historical novelist Henryk Sienkiewicz.[46] The events of eighteenth- and nineteenth-century Poland, Scotland, and England surely fascinated the young Southerner and even contributed to the shaping of his vision of history. All these foreign societies had the South's concern with "concrete, highly personal relationships," with the centrality of the family and clan obligations, and with "manners *and* violence," nurtured and tested by "the old code of honor."[47] Faulkner's novels inevitably grow out of the broad cultural ties between the South and Europe that he makes explicit in the *Compson Appendix*, where it is shown that man has repeatedly been dispossessed of his land and of his past—both of which he attempts to recover through memory. Certainly Faulkner radically modified what he received from his sources, but the very nature of his region oriented him toward a wider vision of history—as Cleanth Brooks suggests:

> Faulkner's culture was basically agricultural, traditional, and steeped in history. Unlike the non-Southern areas of the United States, it had lost a war. It had experienced at first hand war's ravages and the consequences, economic and political, of military and political defeat. The memories of the defeated are always long memories, whether in Ireland or Dixie.[48]

Faulkner is as critical of the Sartorises for their vain heroics as Thackeray is of history's political heroes. Indeed, Faulkner extends Thackeray's exploration of the private life, the personal consciousness through which history is always filtered. Faulkner follows Scott part of the way by positioning Quentin Compson, Bayard Sartoris, and Ike McCaslin as passive heroes who are receptive to competing versions of the past. But that past exists only in their memories and speculations. Consequently, no past event in Faulkner can be over in quite the way events like the Jacobite rebellion are over at the end of *Waverley*. History is a permanently unsettling pheno-menon in Faulkner.

As his career progressed toward *Requiem for a Nun*, Faulkner's sense of the historical became more pronounced in his fiction and was stimulated by his acute consciousness of change, and of the need to interpret and to live with that change. This is a cardinal concern of the greatest historical fiction[49] that he may have first absorbed in his childhood reading.[50] In an earlier version of my remarks on Faulkner and historical fiction, I stressed far more parallels in plot and characters between his novels and those of Scott, Thackeray, and Conrad and left the impression, perhaps, that he was directly indebted to his predecessors.[51] I have suggested fewer parallels in this book because the extended comparisons between novels tended to blur the significant differences between them and to dilute the point of my comparison: Although *Redgauntlet* and *Absalom, Absalom!*, *Henry Esmond* and *The Unvanquished*, *Nostromo* and *Go Down, Moses* employ different structures and modes of narration, these pairs of novels are com-parable in the ways in which they force us to follow and to participate in the characters' reinterpretations of past events. All of them show how such reinterpretations stem not only from the characters' steadily increasing awareness and knowledge of past events, but also from their developing awareness of themselves as the products and extensions of those past events.

Yet it is precisely here, in the process of reinterpretation, that Faulk-ner's novels differ from those of Thackeray and Scott, in that they do not offer a permanent resolution of conflicting views of the past. As I suggest in Chapter 6, Conrad perhaps prepared the way for Faulkner's open-ended view of the past, since *Nostromo* often injects us into the flow of past events even as they are being described from the particular perspective of one of the novel's character-narrators. In this way we have not the one or (at the most) two versions of a single sequence of events given by Scott and Thackeray,[52] but several versions of several different sequences of events, so that it becomes extremely difficult to separate the character-narrator or "historian" from the sequence of events he describes. We depend upon a character like Captain Mitchell, for example, for many of the crucial "facts" of the novel. Of course we can check Mitchell's reliability by recur-ring to the narrator's judgment of him, by referring to the way others regard him, or by applying to his interpretation our knowledge of Costa-guana's history gained from other parts of the novel, yet it remains true that we experience important parts of that history in the making through his point of view. The beginning and end of the Montero revolt are encompassed in his monologues just as the revolt itself is summarized in Decoud's letters. As a result, we, very much like the modern historian, must engage in the task of criticizing the very sources that provide us with our "history." Indeed Conrad seems intent on demonstrating that his characters' uses of the word "fact" reveal their determined if unsuccessful efforts to transform their individual points of view into *the* view of Costaguana's history. The word "fact" by and of itself makes their observations sound more substantial and more objective than they really are.

In Faulkner the process of challenging his characters' "facts" is even more extreme, for some of the events to which the "facts" are supposed to relate may never have happened, or may not be known to have happened until they are recreated or, perhaps, invented by Quentin Compson and Shreve McCannon in *Absalom, Absalom!*, by Ike McCaslin in *Go Down, Moses*, and by Gavin Stevens in *Requiem For a Nun*. Thus it appears that the central question in Faulkner's "historical" novels is what the characters *think* happened in the past. What actually happened may never be entirely resolved, although our compulsion to achieve such resolution stimulates us to scrutinize the structures of the novels in order to determine which of the characters or narrative sequences is closest to the truth.

III

Flags in the Dust, The Unvanquished, Absalom, Absalom!, Go Down, Moses, The Sound and the Fury and the *Compson Appendix*, and *Requiem For a Nun* have been selected for special scrutiny in order to explore the historical dimensions of the fictional world of Yoknapatawpha and to determine that world's relationship to the history of Faulkner's region. While other novels such as *As I Lay Dying* and *Sanctuary* might have been examined for what they reveal of Faulkner's general conception of time, these six novels were chosen as representative of the author's different and distinctive uses of the past in both the early and later works of the Yoknapatawpha series. Novels which have a significant historical content—such as *Light in August* (which ranges widely over several periods of time and points of view), *Intruder in the Dust* (which speculates on the meaning of Southern history in the form of a dialogue between two main characters), and *The Reivers* (which narrates the events of a specific personal past)—do not receive attention because they do not significantly modify the basic reading of the comparable historical content of the novels here discussed.

The *Snopes* trilogy might have been given special treatment as a unique study of history in that it portrays the development of a single

family and the development of Yoknapatawpha County in a three-volume
work presumably intended to have a higher degree of unity in its presentation of historical details than the Yoknapatawpha series as a whole, but in
an introductory note to *The Mansion* Faulkner rejects this kind of unity
and calls attention to the fact that he has not corrected the contradictions
and inconsistencies of his "chronicle," thereby seeming to imply that each
novel of the trilogy must be taken on its own terms. Furthermore, various
critics have shown how the novels of *Snopes* are individual works bearing
as much resemblance in style and structure to the other Yoknapatawpha
novels as to the remainder of the trilogy of which they are a part. Warren
Beck, in particular, has analyzed *Snopes* as an extension of *Absalom,
Absalom!*'s exploration of conflicting interpretations of present and past
events,[53] while Robert Penn Warren has distinguished the Snopeses from
the Compsons, the Sartorises, and the McCaslins in a way that reveals the
trilogy's inappropriateness to a study of this kind:

> In Faulkner's myth of the Snopeses, the tribe descends from bushwhackers, those who
> had no side in the Civil War and merely exploited it. That is, the modern Snopeses,
> being descended from people who had no commitment to moral reality in the past, can
> recognize no commitment in the present. They have, in the moral sense, no identity, no
> history.[54]

The questions that young Bayard Sartoris, Quentin Compson, and Ike
McCaslin confront in regard to the past and its relationship to their present
identity are simply not confronted by the Snopeses. These three characters
may differ greatly in their efforts to ignore, embrace, or repudiate their
family pasts, but all three are caught up in some kind of relationship with
the past whether they wish to understand that relationship or not.

Chapter 2 analyzes *Flags in the Dust* and *The Unvanquished* in order
to show how the interpretation of historical process grows out of
Faulkner's different attempts to deal with the past as family legend and as
personal reminiscence. Though *Flags* is set primarily in the South just after
World War I and is concerned with more than exploring the Sartoris past,
the novel nevertheless represents Faulkner's first portrayal of the historical
dimensions of his characters' lives. The figure of Colonel Sartoris continues to dominate the memories of the old generation — of old man Falls,
old Bayard and Miss Jenny — but more as a legend than as an historical
fact. It is clear that young John and Bayard Sartoris have emulated the
romantic and sometimes foolhardy exploits of their ancestors, but the
parallels between past and present patterns of actions are suggestive rather
than definite and sometimes vague and ambiguous. As a result, this first
novel of the Yoknapatawpha series adumbrates but does not thoroughly

explore the complex relationship between past and present which characterizes historical process in Faulkner's mature fiction.

The Unvanquished attempts to present a clearer and more comprehensive view of historical process than was possible in *Flags* by concentrating on a mature Bayard Sartoris's recollections of his youth and early manhood during the Civil War and Reconstruction period. Bayard searches the past in an attempt to recover the stages by which he developed into the person he has become. Unlike young Bayard (his grandson), Quentin Compson, and Ike McCaslin, Bayard gives an intimate and immediate view of a past in which he himself has participated. But there are many points at which it is difficult to detect the perspective of the older Bayard, so that we feel directly immersed in the past events themselves; and it is often at these very points that the novel is least convincing in its portrayal of historical process, for we cannot establish the meaning those past events now have for Bayard. *The Unvanquished* succeeds as a reading of historical process only at those times when Bayard Sartoris, like so many of Faulkner's characters in his major fiction, reverts to the past in search of the sources of his own identity in the present.

Chapters 3 and 5 analyze in depth the structures of *Absalom, Absalom!* and *Go Down, Moses*, Faulkner's most complex studies of historical process. In these two novels the way in which the characters approach the recreation of the past is inseparable from the identity which they simultaneously fashion for themselves. Chapters 4 and 6 explore certain analogies which can be drawn between Faulkner's methods and those of historians who believe that an understanding of the past grows out of the interaction between the historian and his evidence—that, indeed, the interpretative process itself (as exemplified in the exchanges between Quentin and Shreve, and between Ike and Cass) is precisely what constitutes historical knowledge. Chapter 4, in particular, considers and evaluates the large body of criticism that has focused on *Absalom, Absalom!* as a work of historical interpretation, while Chapter 6 shows how *Go Down, Moses* places more emphasis than *Absalom, Absalom!* on what happened in the past, offering even closer analogies between Faulkner's methods and those of historians—though few critics have treated in any detail the ways in which Faulkner here adopts an historical approach to the past. Because there is more concrete evidence of past life (for example, the commissary books in the fourth section of "The Bear"), Ike's reconstruction of the past can be compared with the historian's analysis of his documents. Even so, *Go Down, Moses*, like most of Faulkner's novels, is noteworthy for its concentration on contemporary life, and for its projections into the future as well as into the past.

IV

Because each of these books appears to be an inquiry into the whole problem of knowing the past from the viewpoint of the present, Chapter 7 suggests that the Yoknapatawpha novels do not stand in relation to some "history" outside themselves, as do most historical novels which profess to be a specific record of a particular period of time, but rather offer a rendering of "history" itself, with the various characters' conflicting versions of what may have happened held together in a dialectical tension. As we shall see when the *Compson Appendix* is examined, Faulkner was not very concerned about the inconsistencies that Malcolm Cowley had detected in comparing the "facts" of the *Appendix* with *The Sound and the Fury*. Faulkner implied that there was no established Yoknapatawpha history, no saga, and that *The Sound and the Fury* itself was not a definitive statement against which other later works must be measured. There was, for Faulkner, only the individual work he was engaged in creating, and many of the "inconsistencies" were to be attributed to his having revised the "facts" or created them anew in response to the urgency of the present moment. Faulkner, then, is primarily interested in the recreation of history as a contemporary event, occurring *now,* as the author, the characters, and all of us probe a problematic past.

That problematic past is most often examined through the form of a dialogue. In *Absalom, Absalom!, Go Down, Moses,* and *Requiem for a Nun* the dialogue becomes a formal principle that makes explicit the implicit dialogues between the sections or chapters of his other books, as each of the four parts of *The Sound and the Fury*, for example, represents a peculiar way of integrating past and present that qualifies and defines all the other parts. The participants in each of these dialogues—Quentin and Shreve, Ike and Cass, Stevens and Temple Drake—interact and evolve their points of view in response to each other. Not only do their points of view clash, but they themselves are aware of the clash and must confront it.

Although Faulkner's experiments with point of view are taken to be signs of his modernity, it is important that we recognize the resemblances between his dialogues and Plato's, in which:

> On the one hand, the individual's own point of view on a problem only emerges as it comes into conflict with the points of view expressed by the other individuals participating in the dialogue. On the other hand, each participant expresses his point of view as it merges with the moral character he manifests in his actions, so that the conflict does not remain merely verbal and intellectual. The drama of these dialogues is this movement of a problem through different minds and into different lives. The participants are at cross-purposes and collide because the point of view each states is not something he

happens to have thought about; it is the direction in which the life he has been leading points.[55]

Nowhere is this function of the dialogue clearer or more completely explored than in *Absalom, Absalom!*, where Shreve's attitude toward the past, as he himself realizes, is conditioned by the life he has been leading as a Canadian, so that he comes to the Sutpen story with a mind that is very different from Quentin's. The collisions here between different individuals, cultures, and minds occur on a large historical scale.

It is natural to feel frustrated by such a dialogue, since it never seems to reach a definitive conclusion. As Euthyphro said to Socrates: "I really don't know how to explain to you what is in my mind. Whatever statement we put forward always somehow moves round in a circle, and will not stay where we put it."[56] Faulkner's dialogues also end on an indeterminate point in the present, so that we must "move round in a circle" always reinterpreting the past; for contemporary man, in Faulkner's view, is forever recapitulating and reforming the past in new ways and in new contexts that accord with his present sense of himself. As in the Platonic dialogues, ideas in Faulkner's novels are inseparable from the dramatic form in which they appear, and it is the dramatic form which above all creates and sustains the tensions out of which Faulkner's sense of history emerges.

2

The Presentation of the Past and of Historical Process as Legend and Fact in *Flags in the Dust* and *The Unvanquished*

I

The question of how one should respond to historical process, and to the complex interaction of past and present, is central to our evaluation of the actions of the main characters in Faulkner's major fiction. It is a question adumbrated in the plight of young Bayard Sartoris in *Flags in the Dust*, the first novel of the Yoknapatawpha series. From the first time that we see him in Part One of the novel, we realize that he is governed by an obsession with what is past, specifically with his brother's death. He acts as if he were fated to repeat his twin's demise, but it is not entirely clear to us whether that obsession derives from his family's tendency to memorialize and glorify its dead or from some other source. He seems outraged at the stupid and futile manner in which John died, but his constant retelling of John's final moments also reflects his sense of personal responsibility and guilt and perhaps his anguish over having lost "a double of himself."[1] Just as Miss Jenny tends to alternate between a critical and celebratory view of the Sartorises, so young Bayard tends to alternate between a critical and celebratory view of his brother's death. Unlike the usually clear-headed Miss Jenny, however, young Bayard is confused and immature. He does not seem content either to accept or reject the model of Sartoris behavior which his brother represents, and he cannot live with an ambivalence whose true nature he shrinks from recognizing or analyzing. As a result, he lives in a tormented state of isolation from his family and its past, from his wife and his friends, and, it appears, from his true self. Unfortunately, Faulkner's potentially fascinating characterization of young Bayard is, in some ways, a failure in that young Bayard is also isolated from us—to such an extent that it is not always possible to believe in his emotions and not always clear how his reactions to his brother's death are meant to reflect upon his family's past and its relationship to the present.[2]

Miss Jenny tells Narcissa that young Bayard is a "cold brute'" who "'never cared a snap of his fingers for anybody in his life except Johnny'" (48). Then Narcissa herself begins to remember and to compare the behavior of the two brothers before the war: "Bayard's was a cold, arrogant sort of leashed violence, while in John it was a warmer thing, spontaneous and merry and wild" (64). Toward the end of the novel the MacCallum episode corroborates Narcissa's distinction between John's warmth and spontaneity and Bayard's coldness and arrogance (309, 323–24). The narrator, too, treats Bayard as an alienated figure who engages in futile attempts to come to terms with death itself, and with "the dark and stubborn struggling of his heart" (39, 238, 325). In none of these respects does he seem to have much in common with the other Sartorises of the past or the present.

Certainly his brother John has been much more successful in following the example of Miss Jenny's Jeb Stuart and the Carolina Bayard, those "two flaming stars garlanded with Fame's burgeoning laurel and the myrtle and roses of Death, incalculable and sudden as meteors in General Pope's troubled military sky" (13). World War I was a godsend for John as the Civil War had been for the Carolina Bayard: they have the same lack of political convictions, the same disregard for discipline, and the same futile but dazzling and engaging recklessness. It may be said that like his predecessor John's "brief career swept like a shooting star across the dark plain" of his family's "mutual remembering and suffering, lighting it with a transient glare like a soundless thunder-clap, leaving a sort of radiance when it died" (19). The air war can be seen, then, as John's attempt to carry on his family's impulse to fix an image of itself upon the skies, making aviation the romantic side of war that cavalry once had been.[3]

In spite of the differences between himself and his brother, young Bayard has also been influenced by Miss Jenny's romantic rhetoric, for he speaks "not of combat, but rather of a life peopled by young men like fallen angels, and of a meteoric violence like that of fallen angels" (113). He already sees the World War—as the older generation sees the Civil War—in mythic rather than factual terms, portraying it and his brother as things "high-pitched as a hysteria, like a glare of fallen meteors on the dark retina of the world" (114). It appears that John III is being transformed into something like the legendary embodiment of the Sartoris past his great-grandfather has long become. For while the spirit of Colonel John Sartoris continues to brood over and dominate old Bayard's room at the bank, his great-grandson, another John, has died in another war and been similarly "freed of time." The violent end and active afterlife of these two

Sartorises make them strikingly complementary figures, as though their shared names have marked them — and the old and young Bayards who are obsessed with them — for fatality and doom.

Evidently young Bayard has subconsciously attached himself to the Sartoris legend by becoming obsessed with his brother's fate, for it is a curious fact that he never confronts directly his family's past. Indeed he rejects Miss Jenny's analogies between the behavior of the Sartorises in both wars and scorns the Carolina Bayard's participation in a "'two-bit war'" (220). It is only the members of the older generation who show an active and conscious interest in preserving ancestral history. As children young Bayard and his brother are pictured as shunning the past which seems shut up in the tomb-like parlor of the Sartoris house:

> Occasionally young Bayard or John would open the door and peer into solemn obscurity in which the shrouded furniture loomed with a sort of ghostly benignance, like albino mastodons. But they did not enter; already in their minds the room was associated with death. (51)

As a way of explaining Bayard's lack of interest in the past and his solitariness, several critics have remarked on his resemblance to a whole "lost generation" of young men — men like Fitzgerald's Anthony Patch who felt that "In justification of his manner of living there was first, of course, The Meaninglessness of Life."[4] It is suggested that Bayard is a wasteland figure transferred to a Southern setting[5] and, more specifically, that he resembles those wartime aviators Faulkner wrote about in "All The Dead Pilots," who were already dead in the sense that they were mentally exhausted and incapable of coping with the world after the war.[6] Similarly, young Bayard is indeed "unfitted for the world," worn out, and incapable of choosing anything other than death. His attempts in Parts Three and Four of *Flags* to incorporate himself into the rhythms of the land — through farming, his marriage to Narcissa, and even his final trip to the MacCallums, where he returns to his boyhood haunts as a hunter — all fail to restore equilibrium to his restless soul. He suffers from an appalling deracination that makes it impossible for him to see any connection between himself and the world he inhabits.

After a confusing day in which he has frightened Simon half to death with his automobile, gone drinking with Rafe MacCallum, ridden a wild stallion until it viciously throws and kicks him, indulged in further drinking with Suratt, and serenaded Narcissa, young Bayard ends up on the sheriff's bed at the jail, as the moonlight seeps into his room "refracted and sourceless," suggesting a dimension-less sky in what Bayard sees as a meaningless universe that holds no intelligence capable of understanding or justifying his suffering. To Bayard this is a world where his bleak face reveals his very life center becoming numb, his "nerves radiated like threads of ice" (143). Thus he defines or values his life in quantitative terms and waits for death, having exhausted "not much more than" one third of his normal life span (144).

But even in scenes like this, in which Bayard's despair is explicitly revealed, very little of his inner life is presented: he lacks the self-consciousness of most wasteland figures. His despair is described but does not seem to emerge from himself, from his mental and spiritual condition, and so seems, as Edmond Volpe points out,

> disproportionate and imposed from without. For example, when Bayard is released by the approach of summer from the absorbing routine of farm work, Faulkner describes him as "coming dazed out of sleep, out of the warm, sunny valleys where people lived into a region where cold peaks of savage despair stood bleakly above the lost valleys, among black and savage stars" (183). Neither Bayard's personality nor his situation can dramatically support such an expression of cosmic despair.[7]

Similarly, Melvin Backman concludes that "Bayard's malaise seems in excess of its cause, and its effect upon the novel is oppressive."[8] Bayard's actual experience seems too far removed from the abstract authorial language which is used to describe it, so that we have difficulty in believing that his feelings have been accurately rendered.

Even if we grant that Bayard is, in part, a figure from the First World War and the generation of the Twenties, we are still faced with his recurring guilt over his brother's death and with the clearly established fact that the differences between himself and his brother were noticed and commented upon before the war. There is also young Bayard's tendency to envelop himself, so to speak, in the atmosphere of the past, to dwell on the experiences which he and his brother shared. Just after his automobile accident, he goes to his room and picks up his brother's canvas hunting coat, buries his face in it, and smells its "fading stale acridity," as he whispers "'Johnny...Johnny'" (204). He burns the coat and other mementoes of John's childhood and youth (204–5) in a futile effort to destroy the hold his brother's memory has over him. Here in his clutching of the dead matter of the past he most resembles Quentin Compson and Gail Hightower, and Richard P. Adams's description of Bayard might also serve as an apt summary of what prevents all three of these characters from living completely in the present:

> He is trying to loop back in time, to enter the moving stream of life and change its course at a point in the past. Of course he cannot, and his efforts to do so keep him from moving with the stream in the present. He exists in a kind of living death, from which the only release possible for him is death itself.[9]

In the MacCallum episode it seems clear that Bayard will never be able to rid himself of the past's death-like grip:

> For an instant he saw the recent months of his life coldly in all their headlong and heedless wastefulness; saw it like the swift unrolling of a film, culminating in that which any fool might have foreseen. Well, dammit, suppose it had: was he to blame? had he insisted that his grandfather ride with him? had he given the old fellow a bum heart? And then, coldly: You were scared to go home. You made a nigger sneak your horse out for you. You, who deliberately do things your judgment tells you may not be successful, even possible, are afraid to face the consequences of your own acts. Then again something bitter and deep and sleepless in him blazed out in vindication and justification and accusation; what he knew not, blazing out at what, Whom, he did not know: You did it! You caused it all: you killed Johnny. (306-7)

Bayard's rare act of self-evaluation, in which he sees "the recent months of his life coldly in all their headlong and heedless wastefulness," is very like the army major's criticism of Jeb Stuart for acting with the "rashness of a heedless and headstrong boy" (18), and like the narrator's description of Jeb Stuart and the Carolina Bayard as "two heedless and reckless boys wild with their own youth" (12). But unlike these two "boys" Bayard is able, for a moment, to confront the consequences of his immature behavior, even though he never again attempts to analyze or ameliorate his actions.

Young Bayard has fragmented himself into multiple personalities and suffers from the "psychic division" Margaret Yonce finds in all of Faulkner's wounded aviators.[10] In the passage quoted above concerning Bayard's self-appraisal, she calls attention to several ambiguities that reveal his indeterminate character:

> Notice the shift from third person to second, which might be explained easily enough as a shift in authorial perspective from omniscient observer to first-person narrator, or as a report of an internal monologue without use of quotation marks. Yet even if one gets past this technical difficulty, he still has to explain why Bayard would refer to himself as "You" rather than "I". A possible explanation is that he recognizes in himself a deep duality, a "self" which is virtually autonomous, over which he has no control. To confuse the issue still further, however, one must decide the implication of the capital letters at the end of the passage. If the "Whom" is directed towards some kind of deity (the "Player" referred to at the end of the novel?), then are the final "You"'s also directed to this Being — or is Bayard addressing himself once more? The matter is not easily resolved.[11]

Yonce shrewdly identifies how difficult it is in this novel to track young Bayard's consciousness; since the language of the self keeps shifting uncertainly neither Bayard nor the reader know precisely "Whom" they are addressing, or if Bayard is truly confronting or escaping his responsibilities.

Perhaps, as Faulkner once suggested, young Bayard never clears up his confusion about who and what is responsible for his fate because he never admits to himself what he really knows, that he has never been able either to conform to or to break away from the demands of the Sartoris legend.[12] After his grandfather's death, Bayard feels that he has no place to stay and no reason to live, and he thus remains, to the end of his life, caught up in a tumult of "vindication and justification and accusation" (306).

The conclusion of *Flags in the Dust* emphasizes the glamorous and disastrous exploits of the Sartorises and, by implication, young Bayard's part in those exploits, speaking of them as a "game outmoded and played with pawns shaped too late and to an old dead pattern" (369–70). The deadness of that pattern is suggested in the last pages of the novel when Miss Jenny visits the Sartoris graves and is reminded of the arrogant headstones which glorify the often needless deaths of the family's males. The names, dates, and inscriptions on the graves recall the similar genealogical parade that old Bayard witnessed in the family Bible when he went up to the attic to record the deaths of Bayard's wife and brother (79–83).

The Carolina Bayard and John III responded instinctively to the situations in which they met their deaths as if they were merely acting out their parts in some preestablished design. Young Bayard, on the other hand, does not respond instinctively to that design but is tormented and destroyed by his halfhearted commitment to it, although to say this is to attribute to him an attitude that we are never sure he really has. Ultimately Bayard's place in the Sartoris tradition seems to be determined not by how he regards himself and his connection to it but by the pervasive and sometimes ambiguous influences of the tradition on all members of the family. In this early novel Faulkner is already very clear about the necessity of *not* living in the past, but Bayard's confusion about the relationship of past and present, and his lack of interest in the operation of the family tradition in his own lifetime perhaps reflect a similar confusion—or lack of curiosity—on Faulkner's part, a failure to grasp or even identify the subject itself in all its richness. Yoknapatawpha, past and present, is spread out in this diffuse novel as if its author had not yet learned to discipline his point of view toward it.

For Doreen Fowler "the Sartoris myth is the novel's [*Sartoris's*] most elaborate example of the substitution of a man-made fiction for an unsatisfactory reality."[13] In support of her thesis she quotes Horace Benbow observing "little puny man's way of dragging circumstance about to fit his preconception of himself as a figure in the world."[14] She shows how Belle Mitchell, Narcissa Benbow, Caspey and many other characters romanticize and otherwise embellish their self-images, and how the narrator exposes their ruses.[15] True enough, but the extravagance of the narrator's language sometimes overwhelms his realism and he seems to partake of a Sartoris voice, of an unregenerate romanticism — as Cleanth Brooks reminds us in quoting this sentence from the conclusion of *Flags in the Dust*: "For there is death in the sound of it [the Sartoris name], and a glamorous fatality, like silver pennons downrushing at sunset, or a dying fall of horns along the road to Roncevaux" (370).[16]

Such sentences tend to wind back upon themselves and curl up like the coiling images of Byron Snopes's lust (249). This is a repetitive — one might say incestuous — style, operating as the perfect analogue for the incest and doubling that Irwin finds so prevalent in Faulkner's fiction. In his later, maturer novels, however, Faulkner mixes his styles, so that his characters' experiences are cycled through many different points of view; thus he avoids rehearsing the hermetic prose of *Flags*, as if he realized the dangers to his writing in having it mirror, without counterpoint, his characters' consciousnesses. As Irwin suggests, doubling and incest are "both images of the self-enclosed — the inability of the ego to break out of the circle of self and of the individual to break out of the ring of the family."[17] If Faulkner was to escape from the solipsistic tendencies of *Flags* taken over perhaps, from his depiction of "the South after the Civil War...a region turned in upon itself,"[18] he had to engage in the juxtapositions and dialogues — the contrapuntal rhythms of his great novels, beginning with *The Sound and the Fury*.[19]

II

The Unvanquished, with its concentration on the mature Bayard Sartoris's recollections of his youth and early manhood during the Civil War and Reconstruction, seems to attempt a clearer and more comprehensive view of historical process than *Flags in the Dust*, where the Sartoris past is not probed very deeply as historical fact but is presented as legend or myth. Bayard (the old Bayard of *Flags*) is presented as searching the past in an effort to recover the stages by which he developed into the person he has become. *The Unvanquished* seems, in fact, to be a reworking of the Sartoris story in which the past events that are described as a "dead time" and a "dead pattern" at the beginning and end of *Flags* are recreated in their original vitality and in chronological order. Episodes which old man Falls remembered in *Flags* — the Colonel's capture of the Yankee camp, his flight from the Yankees who come to look for him, his killing of the carpetbaggers, his death at the hands of Redmond — are now placed in their contemporary context and in relation to Bayard's own biography. As a result, we get a more direct portrayal of the past and an account of the development from childhood to manhood of one of the family's more durable members. Bayard refers to himself in *The Unvanquished* as "The Sartoris,"[20] a title which suggests that he is the head of the family and the embodiment of family tradition.

A brief comparison of some of the scenes which appear in both *Flags in the Dust* and *The Unvanquished* may help to clarify their different uses of the past. As Olga Vickery has observed, in old man Falls's version of the Colonel's flight from the Yankees, his "parting words [to Bayard] become less truthful in the factual sense but more dramatic": "'And then he tole you to tell yo' aunt he wouldn't be home for supper.'" Bayard, on the other hand, remembers his father saying: "'Take care of Granny'" (82). Professor Vickery concludes that in old man Falls's narrative "the historical context becomes largely irrelevant; the Colonel's adventure has become a part of folk literature."[21] Obviously in *Flags* the legendary aspect of the past predominates over the strictly historical.

Perhaps the most significant difference between the past as legend in *Flags* and the past as historical or, at least, autobiographical fact in *The Unvanquished* is found in old man Falls and Bayard's focus upon the Colonel's killing of the carpetbaggers. Old man Falls creates an elaborate scene concentrating upon the daring and the nonchalance of the Colonel's deed (225). Bayard sparingly evokes a sober Sartoris, raising a hand to prevent his followers from cheering him and asking whether any man wishes to call him to account. The Colonel's attitude is the opposite of a cavalier's; he is personally responsible before the whole community.[22]

Bayard is intimately aware of his father's frustrations and failures and knows him not only as the legend we hear of in *Flags* but as the corpse in *The Unvanquished* who is, like all men, "just clay" (270). The pipe "which Ringo said [Bayard's father] was smoking," and which "slipped from his hand as he fell" (252) and died, is the same pipe that old man Falls gives to old Bayard in *Flags in the Dust*. In *Flags* the pipe symbolizes the recurrent and seemingly omnipotent power of the past, of the Colonel who was a "far more definite presence in the room" than the two old men (5). But in *The Unvanquished* the "smoking pipe" is linked with the expiration of life, the end of human aspiration. Bayard sees the steady decline of his father's principles and energies and knows only too well that his father is both fallible and mortal.

Because *The Unvanquished* firmly sets out a direct, chronological view of the past, specifically of that Civil War period which is an important but shadowy presence in *Flags*, the sources of the Colonel's legendary power and its effect upon Bayard are also explored. Thus while the Colonel's mortality is emphasized, so also is his ability to transcend the normal limitations of reality. Even as a child Bayard knew that his father was not a large man (10), yet there was something in his carriage that stimulated Bayard and his black playmate Ringo to regard him as being larger than he was:

> He could have stood on the same level with Granny and he would have only needed to bend his head a little for her to kiss him. But he didn't. He stopped two steps below her, with his head bared and his forehead held for her to touch her lips to, and the fact that Granny had to stoop a little now took nothing from the illusion of height and size which he wore for us at least. (11)

In *Flags* the Colonel's heroic and mythic dimensions grow primarily out of the characters' imaginations, but here in *The Unvanquished* those very same dimensions develop not only out of Bayard's youthful perceptions, but also out of the Colonel's own actions, so that human imagination and historical fact are brought into closer coherence.

Similarly, the war itself is not just remembered as part of an anecdote or tale as in *Flags* but is seen close-up as it affects the Sartoris family. In "Raid" the apparently isolated events of the first two chapters — the invasion of the Yankees and the burning of the Sartoris house — are grouped with similar events occurring all over the South. As Granny, Bayard, and Ringo travel along the road to Memphis, they see a "burned house like ours" (93): "We just looked quitely at the same mound of ashes, the same four chimneys standing gaunt and blackened in the sun like the chimneys at home" (98). Loosh's defection from the Sartoris fold is many times multiplied by the masses of slaves who have left their masters, acting by

> impulses inexplicable yet invincible which appear among races of people at intervals and drive them to pick up and leave all security and familiarity of earth and home and start out, they don't know where, empty-handed, blind to everything but a hope and a doom. (92)

All the familiar patterns and routines of Southern life have been disrupted, so that what has happened to the Sartorises is representative of a complex social disintegration on a large scale. The Sartorises themselves are placed directly within the context of actual historical events.

Like so many of the heroes of nineteenth-century European historical fiction, Bayard earns our trust by appreciating the humanity on both sides of an historic conflict.[23] He perceives and sometimes participates in the virtues and vices of his family, friends, and foes; and at the same time he attempts to preserve the best and destroy the worst qualities of the past in order to create and prepare for a just and peaceful present and future. *The Unvanquished* bears a distinct resemblance to Thackeray's *Henry Esmond*, a copy of which is in Faulkner's library.[24] In *Esmond*, a child grows to manhood, and is thrust into the midst of historic events (England during the Glorious Revolution and the reign of Queen Anne) which he gradually comes to understand. Henry Esmond becomes the transitional figure capable of transforming the family's loyalties to a lost cause into a recognition of the need for change, for a new form in which to carry on the family's traditional values. In both novels the continuity of history is expressed in the form and content of the individual hero's life.[25]

The Unvanquished as a whole appears to adopt *Esmond's Bildungsroman* approach to historical fiction. As G. Robert Stange explains in his introduction to the Rinehart edition of *Esmond*, "the typical subject of both these literary forms is social change, the theme they have in common is the relation of the individual to the life of society. The historical novel is concerned with public action, the *Bildungsroman* traces a private career."[26] The point of combining both literary forms into one novel is to show "how an individual is shaped by social conflict; and [to offer] us a reading of history, in the light of which the destinies of [the author's] characters are interpreted."[27]

Like Henry Esmond, Bayard Sartoris is "less an active hero than he is an observer," and both of them apparently derive from Scott's device of the "weak hero" who functions as a convenient intermediary between contending sides of an historical controversy. Or as John Pikoulis puts it, Bayard is a narrator who "contains within himself several competing points of view."[28] Unfortunately, *The Unvanquished* does not provide sufficient evidence of the bearing of these competing points of view upon Bayard himself. It is not as consistent as *Henry Esmond* in its development of an intimately viewed individual consciousness through periods of time, a mind that not only lives through the immediate historical commotion but lives on into periods in which retrospect is possible, when the consequences of those events of the war period can be more clearly seen.

Esmond writes about himself in the third person and in the past tense but often shifts into the first person and the present tense—as if to suggest that the "I" of the memoirs is a Henry Esmond who is looking back at his earlier and somewhat different self. Indeed Esmond frequently compares and contrasts the passions and prejudices of his youth in England with the tranquillity and maturity of his old age in Virginia as he writes his memoirs. He speaks as a man of experience giving his grandchildren the benefit of his thoughts, seasoned by the trials and errors of a lifetime. Sometimes he stops to wonder over the vividness of certain memories and the lasting impressions that certain people have made on him. As he draws near the end of his memoirs, his references to his grandchildren become more frequent, and we become more and more conscious of an old man keenly involved in passing on his story to another generation.

The process by which Bayard matures and manages to modify his family's code of violence is not fully dramatized in the chapters leading up to "An Odor of Verbena." As Michael Millgate observes:

We may accept the reassessment of Sartoris values within the limited context of "An Odor of Verbena" itself, but it is more difficult to accept that reassessment as retroactively effective, as enforcing also a revaluation of those episodes in Bayard's childhood and youth which have been previously described.[29]

For example, Bayard offers no explicit judgment of his father's or his family's failings until "An Odor of Verbena." In his account of his father's confrontation with the McCaslins, who threaten to use their "solid bloc of private soldier white trash votes" (56) to demote the Colonel, Bayard reveals only his conception of his father's personality: "he probably wouldn't have minded being demoted even to private by God Himself; it was the idea that there could be latent within the men he led the power, let alone the desire, to so affront him" (56). Here we are forewarned of what Bayard calls in "An Odor of Verbena" the Colonel's "will to dominate" (258), but Bayard himself is curiously reticent about his own reactions to the events he describes. Indeed, other than in his role as narrator, he says relatively little. He seems by nature an observer rather than an actor. Even though he is obviously implicated in his family's swindle of the Yankees, and we have no reason to interpret his silence as disapproval, his role is nevertheless passive and largely overshadowed by that of his loquacious and extremely shrewd black companion, Ringo. Bayard's detachment is perhaps a way of preparing us for his ability to evaluate his heritage from a somewhat removed stance in the novel's last chapter, but his detachment also makes it difficult for us to follow his development from innocence to experience, as we follow Charles Mallison's development in *Intruder in the Dust*.

Bayard's passive role in much of the novel is perhaps partially justified by the distinctions he makes between himself and Ringo. He mentions in both "Raid" and in "Riposte in Tertio" that "Father always said that Ringo was a little smarter than I was" (91, 142), and he refers to Ringo's superior adaptability to the changing circumstances of war in "An Odor of Verbena." Ringo is "smarter" than Bayard in the sense that he is always able to select with great alacrity the expedient thing to do, and then is clever and mature enough to compete with adults forcefully and vigorously. Thus in "Riposte in Tertio" Bayard notes that he was "just past fifteen then" (156), while it seemed that Ringo and Granny "were the same age instead of him and me" (143). Indeed the conversation between Granny and Ringo at the end of Part One of this chapter captures precisely what Bayard means:

"Well, I reckon that completes that," Ringo said. "Anyway, we handled two hundred and forty-eight head while the business lasted."

"Two hundred and forty-six," Granny said. "We have lost the team." (152)

Next to these very precise "businessmen" Bayard does seem like a bewildered teenager. He does not even know where Ringo got the Union

Army letterheads on which the names of Union generals are forged (144), and he is not active in the procurement of the mules, even though he shares Ringo's knowledge that Ab Snopes, the middleman who sells back to the army its own mules, is not to be trusted.

It is not until the conclusion of "Riposte in Tertio" that we are given even the slightest idea of Bayard's sense of responsibility for Granny's death at the hand of Grumby: "I was just fifteen, and for most of my life her face had been the first thing I saw in the morning and the last thing I saw at night, but I could have stopped her, and I didn't" (174). Bayard believes that he could not be expected to overrule Granny, who had always overruled him, yet he feels that he should have done so. This one sentence is almost the only preparation we have for Bayard's struggle with the problem of responsibility for his own actions when he confronts his father's killer at the novel's conclusion.

In the next chapter, "Vendée," we see Bayard fulfilling the revenge code of his society by hunting down and killing Grumby, but the adult Bayard does not comment on his own actions, and gives no indication of what he now thinks of them. Cleanth Brooks argues that Bayard is too young to think of or to accept any other alternative to revenge, especially since "the country is absolutely lawless; there are no constituted authorities to whom he could appeal had he wished."[30] But in "An Odor of Verbena" Bayard suggests that the guilt he suffers from having taken a human life is part of what motivates him to reject the use of violence. If we are to accept *The Unvanquished* as a retrospective narrative in which Bayard searches the past to recover the stages by which he developed into the person he has become, then there should surely be some indication in "Vendée," or in the chapter that follows it, of the changes in his character, but there is no such indication, and the transitions between the chapters are not specifically related to the transitions presumably taking place in Bayard's mind.

"Skirmish at Sartoris" does prepare us for "An Odor of Verbena" in the sense that Drusilla and Bayard engage in a kind of rehearsal for their competing roles as interpreters of the Colonel's legacy by attempting to accompany him to his confrontation with the Burdens (235). As usual, we have no precise idea of Bayard's attitude toward his father's actions, though his wish to accompany the Colonel is arguably indicative of a growing sense of personal responsibility for the family's actions, first expressed at the conclusion of "Riposte in Tertio." That Bayard in "Skirmish at Sartoris" is prevented from joining his father (237), and so is again isolated from the main action, is perhaps a way of preserving him, so to speak, for "An Odor of Verbena," where he must take all of the responsibility for protecting the family and community upon himself, making his individual deed stand for the meaning of a whole tradition, as Uncle Buck at the end of "Vendée" had implied it must.

As already suggested, "An Odor of Verbena," in contrast to the other chapters of *The Unvanquished*, is reflective both of Bayard's past experiences and of his attempt to view them against the background of his mature judgment. In Part One, just after he has learned that his father has been shot and killed, the adult Bayard (now twenty-four) is conscious of a duty to himself which may seem in conflict with his heritage but actually grows out of what he has been taught as much as out of what he has learned for himself (247–48). Bayard knows that his beliefs are truly no more than academic if they are not applicable to the community in which he has grown up. The deliberateness of his position — standing on the very ground of his family's tradition, having defended it in the past, and now having to confront it in order to gain a full understanding of himself — is in marked contrast to his grandson's confusing vacillation between "vindication and justification and accusation" (306) in *Flags in the Dust,* and it is plainly part of the purpose of *The Unvanquished* to define the Sartoris tradition precisely, to see it as a whole, and to portray it in action.

Bayard has dissociated himself from Ringo's eager, precocious participation in the corruption of Granny's moral scruples by observing that Ringo "had changed so much that summer while he and Granny traded mules with the Yankees that since then I had had to do most of the changing just to catch up with him" (248). But since "that day when we nailed Grumby's body to the door of the old compress" (243), Ringo had "changed even less than" Bayard because he had fully accepted the revenge code; he now in "An Odor of Verbena" appears before Bayard "with weariness (or maybe it was more than just weariness)" (248), fatalistically anticipating the need for another killing to avenge another Sartoris. Because Bayard cannot accept this fatalism, he concludes: "I would never catch up with him" (248).

Like Ringo, Drusilla has failed to revalue the Sartoris code. Her attitudes have hardened, have become formal and fatalistic, so that Bayard knows exactly how she will appear to him when he meets her: her figure embodies, in succinct fashion, the Sartoris past. Drusilla, "not tall, not slender as a woman is but as a youth, a boy is," remains caught up in those war adventures which she related to Bayard with so much gusto nine years before (252).

In Part Two of "An Odor of Verbena" Bayard recalls a scene from four years earlier in which Drusilla had defended the Colonel's violence as necessary to the fulfillment of his "dream" (252) of raising the whole country "by its bootstraps" (256). Bayard had quickly replied that no "dream" was worth the sacrifice of human life, any human life. In this argument with Drusilla, Bayard had recalled Grumby's death and distinguished between his killing and his father's for he and Ringo "had had to perform" in completely lawless times "more than should be required of children because there should be some limit to the age, the youth at least below which one should not have to kill" (254). Now, as if aware that her husband has exhausted his ruthless will to dominate (258), Drusilla makes love to Bayard, hoping to convince him of his own deep involvement in the Colonel's dream. But the Colonel himself underlines the uselessness of Drusilla's love of violence and sets a nonviolent example for his son:

> "Yes. I have accomplished my aim, and now I shall do a little moral housecleaning. I am tired of killing men, no matter what the necessity nor the end. Tomorrow, when I go to town and meet Ben Redmond, I shall be unarmed." (266)

At the moment when Bayard himself confronts Redmond, the past that his father, Drusilla, and Ringo justify and celebrate is dead; Bayard destroys the pattern of a "succinct and formal violence" by a succinct and formal act of his own. After a confused moment, even his father's lieutenant George Wyatt understands that "'maybe you're right, maybe there has been enough killing in your family'" (289). In effect, Wyatt and later Drusilla, who leaves a sprig of verbena in tribute to his courage before she leaves the house, ratify Bayard's deed as worthy of a gentleman, of a Sartoris.

Indeed Bayard himself does not discount the value that his father's life will have for him, so that in the final pages of *The Unvanquished* we again glimpse something of that respectful attitude toward the Colonel which informs Bayard's character in *Flags in the Dust*. After all, no matter how successful Bayard has been in breaking the cycle of violence, he has also taken on the burden of being "The Sartoris," of inheriting his father's legacy—as he realized before he left the house to face Redmond. He had started to look at his father's corpse again,

> but I did not, I did not see him again and all the pictures we had of him were bad ones because a picture could no more have held him dead than the house could have kept his body. But I didn't need to see him again because he was there, he would always be there; maybe what Drusilla meant by his dream was not something which he possessed but something which he had bequeathed us which we could never forget, which would even assume the corporeal shape of him whenever any of us, black or white, closed our eyes. (291)

Like Old Carothers McCaslin's legacy to his heirs, the Colonel's bequest is ineradicable and unforgettable. In fact, the passage just quoted from *The Unvanquished* seems deliberately to evoke the opening pages of *Flags in the Dust*, where the Colonel almost takes a "corporeal shape," and where his "dream" is mentioned:

> As usual old man Falls had brought John Sartoris into the room with him. Freed as he was of time, he was a far more definite presence in the room than the two of them

cemented by deafness to a dead time and drawn thin by the slow attenuation of days.
He seemed to stand above them, all around them, with his bearded, hawklike face and
the bold glamor of his dream. (5)

At the end of *The Unvanquished* it appears that the direct sources of the
Colonel's peculiar power over the Sartorises are being revealed. The
Colonel who sits before his "cold hearth" with a "dead cigar" (264) in *The
Unvanquished* reminds us of Bayard himself in *Flags*, an old man who has
not only inherited his father's title but has also come to resemble him, and
especially of the scene between Bayard and his grandson, where his cold
cigar is symbolic of his exhaustion, worn out by time and approaching
death (37-38). In this same scene the continuity between generations of
Sartorises is also emphasized by the "hawklike planes" of young Bayard's
face, which resemble the Colonel's "hawklike face" (5). In *The Unvanquished* we read the description of the Colonel's library, note his set of
Dumas (18), and recall that Dumas is Bayard's favorite reading in *Flags*.
Even the Colonel's habit of sitting with his muddy boots in the library (18)
reappears as a part of the aging Bayard's routine in *Flags* (30-32).

The Unvanquished, then, clearly goes beyond *Flags in the Dust* in its presentation of the past in both its legendary and factual aspects. "An Odor of
Verbena" and, less successfully, *The Unvanquished* as a whole use Bayard
Sartoris as the focal point of historical process, for he has been formed by
the code of the Sartoris past yet manages to change that code and prepare
his family for the present and the future. Thus the novel tries to trace the
development of the Sartoris family through the various stages by which it
has become the family we know in *Flags in the Dust*. By no means, of
course, have all of the stages in that development been described. *Flags in
the Dust* and *The Unvanquished* share many of the same characters and
scenes, but they are not unified by a single plan or structure, and *The
Unvanquished* is not, in any strict sense, a sequel—or even a retroactive
prelude—to the earlier novel. Indeed in chapter 7 I will argue that Faulkner
had no preconceived chronological or genealogical plan for his Yoknapatawpha series. It is essential, moreover, to see that in dealing with what is,
to a certain extent, a single body of fictional material—the story of the
Sartorises—Faulkner has created two very different novels which take two
very different approaches to an understanding of the past

In *Absalom, Absalom!* and *Go Down, Moses* Quentin Compson and Ike
McCaslin make comparable attempts to understand the workings of historical process, to comprehend the past and its relationship to the present,
but Bayard's position in *The Unvanquished* is fundamentally different
from theirs in one respect: Quentin and Ike confront family and regional

pasts which cannot simply be recollected but must be reinterpreted with the aid of eyewitness testimony, with the support of historical documents, and, most importantly, with the crucial stimulus of their own imaginations. They must draw inferences from the scanty evidence of the past, identify with dead people, and recreate what it must have been like to live in the past even as they try to understand themselves. Bayard, on the other hand, confronts a personal past that is the readily available subject of his own recollections; he does not have to struggle with or cling to other people's pasts.

3

The Recreation and Reinterpretation of the Past
in *Absalom, Absalom!*

The italicized scene in Chapter VIII (351–58), in which Thomas Sutpen tells his son Henry that Henry's brother Charles Bon has Negro blood, is clearly of crucial importance to the whole question of the recreation and reinterpretation of the past in *Absalom, Absalom!.* Is Quentin and Shreve's discovery intuitive? Did Henry Sutpen tell Quentin about Bon's blood? Is this "fact" arrived at through conjecture based on the scant evidence that Quentin and Shreve have at hand? Chapter VIII as a whole helps to answer these questions, but few critics have systematically studied its contribution to the interpretative progress of the novel. John Hagan has convincingly demonstrated how the chapter pulls the preceding parts of the novel into coherence,[1] but he has only briefly characterized Quentin and Shreve's development as historical interpreters.[2] It seems to me that Chapter VIII is the climax of the novel because it is the outgrowth of all previous interpretations of the Sutpen story, and because it is also, in some ways, Quentin and Shreve's unique creation, which could not have occurred at any other time than their present moment.[3]

In order to establish the context out of which Chapter VIII arises, it seems necessary to offer a brief review of the narrators and their accounts of Sutpen as they appear in Chapters I through V. In the opening chapter the scene is Miss Rosa Coldfield's house in Jefferson, Mississippi, on an afternoon in September 1909. The first fourteen pages are narrated in the third person. Descriptions are given of Miss Rosa, of Quentin, of Quentin's attitude toward Miss Rosa, and of what he already knows about Sutpen. Within this scene a short dialogue is reported (12–13) in which Mr. Compson suggests to Quentin that perhaps Miss Rosa wants to tell her version of the aborted engagement between herself and Sutpen because Quentin may have already heard another version of it from his father, who in turn had learned about Sutpen from his father, General Compson, Sutpen's only confidant. Mr. Compson then speculates on the purpose of

Miss Rosa and Quentin's forthcoming visit to Sutpen's Hundred and anticipates, in a figurative way, the scene in Chapter IX in which Quentin discovers the corpse-like Henry Sutpen: "'And so, in a sense, the affair, no matter what happens out there tonight, will still be in the family; the skeleton (if it be a skeleton) still in the closet'" (13). In Mr. Compson's view, Miss Rosa hopes that Quentin will help her to reveal the remaining mystery in the Sutpen story but at the same time prevent the apparently shameful facts from being publicly exposed; Quentin, on the other hand, gains from Miss Rosa the impression that "she wants it told" (10). Thus even before Miss Rosa begins to speak, we are aware of the conflicting accounts of the unresolved Sutpen story, and of Miss Rosa's possible motivations for inviting Quentin to her house.

The second half of the chapter (14–30) consists primarily of Miss Rosa's account of Sutpen's early years in Jefferson. To her he is a self-created demon who comes out of nowhere with no suggestion of a past and tears from the earth his house and plantation. Certain other events, such as Sutpen's forbidding Judith to marry Bon, and Bon's later death at the hands of Henry, are incomprehensible to her, and she pictures Sutpen as a man of brute, unthinking violence. Miss Rosa is interrupted twice by Quentin's "'No'me'" (20) and "'Yessum'" (21), and twice by the narrator, who focuses on Quentin's reaction to her story (21–22). Thus we are continually reminded that this chapter is as much about Quentin's reception of her story as it is about the story itself.

All of Chapter II takes place on the front gallery of the Compson house in Jefferson around twilight of the same day in September 1909. The first half of the chapter is the narrator's summary of a portion of what Mr. Compson tells Quentin while the latter is waiting to go out to Sutpen's Hundred with Miss Rosa later in the evening. The narrator puts Miss Rosa's historical data into chronological sequence (34–37, 40–41). He reports Sutpen's initial stay of two months in Jefferson (June to August 1833), his abrupt departure and return with the French architect, the two years it took to build his mansion (1833–35), and how the mansion stood for three years (1835–38) like a "Spartan shell." Mr. Compson then picks up the narrative and proceeds without interruption (43–58) with his version of Sutpen's second departure from Jefferson and his return with the materials to furnish his house, his involvement with Mr. Coldfield, Rosa's father, his plans for marrying Ellen, Rosa's sister, and his subsequent confrontation with the distrustful and outraged townspeople in April 1838. Most of this information, according to the narrator, Quentin "already knew" (31).

Chapter III is assigned no specific time or place, but it seems to be a continuation of Mr. Compson's conversation with Quentin which is partially given in Chapter I (12–13) and which apparently precedes Chapter II in point of strict chronology. In his study of "logical sequence and continuity" in *Absalom, Absalom!*, John A. Hodgson has suggested that "Chapter 3 in fact is not continuous and contemporaneous with chapters 2 and 4 but represents instead a conversation taking place at a later date, after Quentin has returned from Sutpen's Hundred."[4] He cites the combination of italicized speech attributions ("Quentin said," etc.) and unpunctuated quotations which to him "denote a significant temporal distinction."[5] But, as Professor Michael Millgate points out in a letter to me,

> the clue to the timing of Chapter III is found in the opening phrase of the second paragraph, p. 59: "Ah *Mr. Compson said again*," which clearly links back to the beginning of the bottom paragraph on p. 12: "'Ah,' Mr. Compson said." And Faulkner very specifically dates or rather times that passage as occurring after Quentin's return home after calling on Miss Rosa but before going out to Sutpen's Hundred. The reason therefore for the different typography of Chapter III is that Faulkner wants us to register that it is out of strict chronological sequence.

Thus Quentin's comment at the beginning of Chapter III ("if he [Sutpen] threw Miss Rosa over, I wouldn't think she would want to tell anybody about it" [59]) is a response to Mr. Compson's suggestion on page 12 about Miss Rosa's reasons for confiding in him (Quentin). Clearly Mr. Compson is preparing him for his visit to Sutpen's Hundred later that evening in the company of Miss Rosa. Mr. Compson states that Miss Rosa was brought up by her aunt to regard Sutpen as a demon. Having been raised by middle-aged parents as (probably) an unwanted child, and living in almost complete isolation and ignorance, unable even to count money in any consecutive fashion, in her portrayal of Sutpen Miss Rosa no doubt reflects a child's disregard of chronology and sequence. Because she does not know very much about the outside world, she cannot make the necessary connections between the different parts of Sutpen's career which would make his behavior intelligible, and therefore sees him only in fixed and extravagant terms, like a caricature.

From Miss Rosa's static picturing of character, Mr. Compson shifts to the "fluid cradle of events" (66). Life becomes a process. Rosa is failing to grow up and Judith is beginning to mature (67). Ellen withdraws from the world entirely, and so is permanently excluded from a genuine participation in her family's fate (69). Sutpen's career progresses smoothly until 1859 when Charles Bon, an apparent stranger, appears at the Hundred. "Then something happened. Nobody knew what," Mr. Compson says (79). The abruptness of the break, not between Sutpen and Bon, but between Sutpen and his son Henry (so the Sutpen Negroes report), is what troubles Mr. Compson.

His last observation is one of several clues to the solution of the Sutpen mystery which he leaves for Quentin and Shreve. Early in his account he mentions that Sutpen had named all of his children, "the one before Clytie and Henry and Judith even" (62). Professor Hodgson suggests that in this chapter Mr. Compson already knows that Bon is Sutpen's child and therefore is talking to Quentin after the latter has returned from Sutpen's Hundred. But the only concrete proof that Professor Hodgson cites is Mr. Compson's comment on page 62.[6] Nowhere does Mr. Compson connect Bon with his knowledge – gained from his own father, General Compson (265) – that Sutpen had another child. Most of what Mr. Compson is saying about Bon in this chapter is in reference to Miss Rosa's "image" of a man she never knew. But is it not too much to assume that Mr. Compson would withhold his knowledge of Bon's ancestry while discussing Miss Rosa's view of Bon? And if he has new information about Bon, it is very strange indeed that he would not use it to advance his own narrative. Mr. Compson clearly does not know yet that Sutpen's first child is Charles Bon, but his statement that another child existed by another marriage and his casually offered comments that some in the community had predicted Sutpen's downfall – believing that there might yet be a "nigger in the wood-pile somewhere" (72) – are, from a retrospective view of the whole Sutpen story, clues which may, with others, have led Quentin to the discovery of both Bon's kinship to Sutpen and his Negro blood.

Chapter IV begins with the narrator's rendering of Quentin's thoughts of Miss Rosa before their visit to Sutpen's Hundred, and thus is a continuation of Chapter II. Mr. Compson has a letter from Bon to Judith he intends to give to Quentin. The letter, which is one of the most important documents in the book and which will figure prominently in Mr. Compson's interpretation and later in Quentin's and Shreve's, is not quoted until the end of the chapter, when it becomes apparent that Quentin has been reading it while his father has been talking (129–32). In other words, Quentin establishes contact with the primary historical data even while Mr. Compson is trying to integrate it into his commentary.

Again Mr. Compson selects for special consideration those parts of Sutpen's career which have not been adequately explained. Why did a man like Bon, whose reputation as a Don Juan was well known, show no interest in ruining Judith, a seemingly easy prey (99)? Why did Bon four years later insist on their marriage (100)? Why did Henry, who loved Bon, according to Mr. Compson, oppose the marriage? Why did Sutpen take the trip to New Orleans, and why did he wait so long before revealing the information he had gathered there (99)? Mr. Compson tries to account for all of these disturbing questions by elaborately explaining that the Sutpens, especially Henry, objected to Bon's octoroon mistress. But Mr. Compson cannot understand why Henry should have waited so long before he killed Bon, and finally realizes that he has not made Henry's reasons for the murder credible (100). Hence Quentin, who conceives of the past somewhat differently from his father, begins his own search for the meaning of the murder. He engages in his first imaginative reenactment of the confrontation between Bon and Henry at the gates of Sutpen's Hundred and earnestly tries to relive what Mr. Compson has only talked about, substituting a dramatic scene for his father's discursive descriptions, which continue even after his "awareness of the story's fragmentary nature. He offers more detail than ever about what characters thought and said, perhaps as a result of his compulsion to understand."[7]

Printed almost wholly in italics, Chapter V represents Quentin's reception of Miss Rosa's narrative on the afternoon in September 1909: it retrieves, that is to say, a narrative that occurred before Mr. Compson's remarks on Miss Rosa in Chapters I, II, III, and IV.[8] Thus Miss Rosa's afternoon account of her desperate circumstances in the war and postwar years, her hatred of Sutpen, her shadowy image of Bon, at once anticipates (in terms of strict chronological time) and confirms (in terms of the novel's structure) Mr. Compson's commentary at twilight of the same day, and it is significant that Quentin, not burdened by memories of any personal contact with Sutpen, can rapidly absorb himself in one of the crucial but unexplored climaxes in the story. The confrontation between Judith and Henry that happened shortly after Bon's death is referred to very briefly by Miss Rosa (135), but Quentin recreates it with a striking immediacy (172). Chapter V, then, like Chapter IV, ends with Quentin's own work of imaginative recreation beginning to overtake Miss Rosa's and Mr. Compson's previous interpretations even before they have been fully presented.

Almost all commentators on the structure of *Absalom, Absalom!* have identified Chapter VI as its pivotal point. The place and time are shifted to Quentin and Shreve's Harvard dormitory room in January 1910. On the table before Quentin is his father's letter announcing the death of Rosa Coldfield, the last eyewitness of Sutpen's activities. This is a critical moment for Quentin. As John Middleton observes: "Now that Miss Rosa is dead, Quentin is heir to her narrative and sole surviving witness of what they both discovered."[9] Now his memory and Shreve's inquisitive intellect must between them render a plausible accounting of the past.

At first Quentin's "father's sloped fine hand" reminds him of "that dead dusty summer where he had prepared for Harvard" (173) and of that dead summer twilight, the wistaria, the cigar-smell, and the fireflies so richly evoked in Chapter II (31). On that day in September 1909 when Quentin was preparing to go out to Sutpen's Hundred he could breathe the same air and hear the same church bells of that Sunday morning in 1833 when Sutpen first entered Jefferson (31). And now, five months later, Quentin still cannot "pass" that scene between Henry and Judith that occurred shortly after Henry killed Bon.

Shreve has just entered the room from the cold outside with snow still on his overcoat sleeve, suggesting the immense distance there is between him and the Mississippi afternoon and evening Quentin is recalling. Quentin must explain to him who Miss Rosa was. His father's letter lying on the open textbook becomes, in a sense, Quentin's text, a document for him in much the way Bon's letter to Judith was for Mr. Compson. Both letters secure a small piece of the past in writing, so that Mr. Compson and Quentin are constantly reminded that the past had had a tangible reality. As Mr. Compson shared his letter with Quentin, so Quentin must now share his father's letter with Shreve. Just as Mr. Compson had answered Quentin's questions, so now Quentin must answer Shreve's; for by going to Harvard and by living in the Northern climate Quentin has not escaped from the Sutpen story or from his Southern background. But if Quentin feels the identity of time and place that links him to Sutpen in Chapter II, he also shares an identity of time and place with Shreve. Both young men will breathe the same air and hear (or fail to hear) the same chimes at Harvard which mark the time they must spend in recapturing the past.

Shreve's initial interest in the Sutpen story is aroused by the simple fact that his friend has played a part in it, has actually known some of the principals, like Rosa Coldfield, and accompanied her on a visit to the mystery hidden in the Sutpen house she vacated forty-three years earlier (176). Shreve wants Quentin to "wait," to slow down so that his friend's story will make more sense, but the story itself has no urgent claims upon him. His repeated failure to defer to Rosa as "Miss" shows his unfamiliarity with the social etiquette of Quentin's Southern background. But in calling Rosa an "Aunt," Shreve is also suggesting that somehow Quentin and Rosa *must be related.* Quentin's resistance to "Aunt" reveals not just his upbringing as a proper Southerner, but also his attempt to reject the intolerable bond between himself and Rosa Coldfield which has been created by his family's role in helping to establish Sutpen in Jefferson. Shreve's constant interrogation forces Quentin out of his passivity, makes him actively confront the story's anguish and pain. Quentin can no longer simply listen to Miss Rosa or to his father tell the story; he must himself retell it under Shreve's probing cross-examination.

At the same time, Shreve already seems to have reached the stage where he must offer his own version of the Sutpen story. Evidently he has heard a great deal, for his first summary of the story adds certain details about Sutpen's death the reader has not before encountered (176).[10] Since he is outside of the tradition in which the story has been handed down, he feels free to play the role of debunking historian. Thus he measures Miss Rosa's evidence against her idleness, her vindictiveness (hating her father, aunt, and sister's husband) and her need for proving "she had been right" about Sutpen (176). Shreve's references to Sutpen as "this Faustus, this demon, this Beelzebub" (178) and as "an ancient stiff-jointed Pyramus to [Miss Rosa's] eager though untried Thisbe" (177) ridicule Miss Rosa and Mr. Compson's tendency to distort the Sutpen story into Gothic legend or Greek myth. At the same time, however, Shreve offers no alternative to their interpretations. They still stand, and thus his initial account remains simply an extension of what they have said — to such an extent that Quentin is again and again reminded of his father (181), and finds it difficult to listen to Shreve because he has heard all of this version before (207, 212-13). Even so, Shreve's summary of Sutpen's return from war does penetrate Quentin's thoughts. (Compare the phrasing on 182 with 178, 180.) It is easy to see how Miss Rosa's demon and Mr. Compson's doom still pervade the narratives of these two young men.

Nevertheless, Chapter VI does mark a great advance in the interpretation of the Sutpen story. While Shreve is talking, Quentin visualizes Sutpen's life and death in the postwar period (181-87) and proceeds to his memory of his visit with his father to the Sutpen graves (187-210). Within Quentin's passage of recollection is Mr. Compson's direct, continuous conversation with Quentin (192-210), in which he cites General Compson as an authority for his relation of Judith and Clytie's struggle to bring up Etienne Bon and of the latter's subsequent life in Jefferson. Quentin interrupts (in italics) his own memory of his father's account (at 207-8) with his present thoughts (i.e., January 1910) on both what his father was saying and what Shreve is now narrating:

> (*Because there was love* Mr. Compson said *There was that letter she brought and gave it to your grandmother to keep.* He (Quentin) could see it, as plainly as he saw the one open upon the open text book on the table before him, white in his father's dark hand against his linen leg in the September twilight where the cigar-smell, the wistaria-smell, the fireflies drifted, thinking *Yes. I have heard too much, I have been told too much; I have had to listen to too much, too long* thinking *Yes, Shreve sounds almost exactly like father: that letter....*)

Bon's letter and Mr. Compson's letter, Mr. Compson's voice and Shreve's voice, all merge in Quentin's "thinking." As Quentin will later say: *"Maybe we are both father"* (261).

The distinctions between past and present seem to be dissolving in Quentin's stream of consciousness. Several layers of time follow each other in rapid succession. On pages 207-8 he imagines what Judith's relationship with Etienne Bon must have been like. By page 209 we are getting more of Mr. Compson's direct narrative of Judith's nursing of Etienne and the eventual deaths of both of them, while on page 210 the controlling narrator conveys Quentin's thoughts about the next twelve years (1884–96) during which Clytie raised Jim Bond. Then we have two pages (211–12) of Quentin's present thoughts (again in italics) on Rosa Coldfield's burial of Judith, and on Judge Benbow's role as executor of Goodhue Coldfield's estate.

All of these time shifts, it is important to remember, occur within the context of Quentin's memory of his visit with his father to the Sutpen graves, which seems to have provoked in him a profound awareness of his lifelong connection with the Sutpen family. In particular, it causes him to recall a childhood encounter with Jim Bond at Sutpen's Hundred when he had become

> *large enough to go out there one day with four or five other boys of your size and age and dare one another to evoke the ghost* [Sutpen], *since it would have to be haunted, could not but be haunted although it had stood there empty and unthreatening for twenty-six years.* (213)

Sutpen died in 1869, thus making him eligible for ghosthood. Evidently Quentin visited Sutpen's Hundred twenty-six years later, in 1896, when Jim Bond was still a boy: "*the hulking slack-mouthed saddle-colored boy a few years older and bigger than you* [Quentin] *were*" (214). Although we do not know how much time passes between Quentin's visits to Sutpen's Hundred, we do know that what his father said "*struck, word by word, the resonant strings of remembering*" (213). As Quentin hears Jim Bond's name, he realizes that he "hadn't even thought that he must have a name that day when you saw him in the vegetable patch" (215).

This childhood visit to the Hundred haunts Quentin's memory as an epitome of the mystery which pervades the Sutpen story. He recalls that there was no report of any ghost until a "wagon full of strangers fled the house in panic—at what is not known (213). Did a dying and ghostly looking Henry shut up in a small room terrify them, or did they simply encounter Jim Bond, or Clytie? We do know that along with four other boys Quentin saw Clytie on his childhood visit to Sutpen's Hundred, and that she asked the boys what they wanted. One of them answered "'*Nothing*'" (214), and they all ran away. Quentin says nothing to Clytie, but his vivid impression of her foreshadows their contact on his last visit with Miss Rosa to the Hundred. Clearly something in the house, or about the house, troubles Quentin's memories from the very earliest days of his childhood, memories stimulated by Shreve's growing mastery of the sequence of events leading to Quentin's last visit to Sutpen's Hundred.

By the end of the chapter Shreve is speaking of Quentin's visit (with his father) to the Sutpen graves, and both he and Quentin seem about to reveal the secret that Quentin discovered at Sutpen's Hundred, but Shreve, recapitulating what he has learned so far, begs his partner to "wait" (216). To truly know the meaning of the Sutpen story Shreve feels he must discover it for himself: he has mocked and questioned the previous versions, and soon he must offer his own interpretation of the past.

In Chapter VII we learn that Quentin and Shreve have been talking for about an hour (217). Shreve tries to resume his casual banter, and he still refers to Quentin's story as an outlandish spectacle: "'Jesus, the South is fine, isn't it. It's better than theatre, isn't it. It's better than Ben Hur, isn't it'" (217). But he is intently watching Quentin (218, 256), and his frequent interjections point to his increasing dedication to reconstructing the Sutpen story. As Quentin tells of Sutpen's boyhood years, the long trip out of the mountains, his humiliating rebuff at the planter's front door, his decision to go to the West Indies, and his determination to complete his design, Shreve keeps changing Quentin's references to Sutpen as "he" to "the demon" (218, 223, 246, 265, 267, 270, 274), as if to keep alive the dichotomy between Miss Rosa's outraged depiction of him as an evil being and Quentin's sensitive portrayal of Sutpen as a fallible human being who found himself faced with certain difficult choices in circumstances not of his own making. As Terrence Doody remarks, Quentin's is the most compassionate portrayal of Sutpen in the novel—particularly noteworthy for its "sympathy and justice."[11] Much of Chapter VII, however, is really Sutpen's autobiography, sometimes given in his own words (239–43, 248, 254, 263–65, 273–74). True, the story has changed hands several times, from Sutpen to General Compson to Mr. Compson and thence to Quentin who is now telling it again to Shreve. Nevertheless, Sutpen's deliberateness, directness, and laconic nature suggest he chooses his words very carefully, so that his account of himself has an especially vivid, unadulterated impact on General Compson. Donald M. Kartiganer points out:

> Free not only from the particular biases of Miss Rosa and Mr. Compson, Sutpen's version is free of distortion itself, and this makes it unique in the novel. Unlike other narrators, he is trying to probe objectively his own past. Since symbolic consolations are meaningless to him, it never occurs to him to try to distort his story in order to persuade General Compson or anyone else of his own justification. The correctness or incorrectness of action, Sutpen will always believe, is part of that action, not a shifting abstraction to be colored and reversed by anyone with sufficient imagination to add a bias. It is the *facts* of the past, not its meaning or value, its why or worthiness, that dominate Sutpen's version of his life.[12]

Doody observes that Sutpen "is frequently heard within the quotation marks of direct address" and "the authority of these quotations is never questioned."[13] Sutpen deliberately suppresses "the possibility he might invent, explore, or reconstitute himself through narrative," Matthews concludes.[14] Thus, as Quentin understands it, Sutpen was not bragging (247); he simply "'told Grandfather — told him, mind; not excusing, asking for no pity; not explaining, asking for no exculpation'" (240). The verisimilitude of Sutpen's autobiography is also enhanced by Quentin's reserved tone, which usually permits Sutpen's narrative to remain in the foreground. Thus Sutpen's speech, like Bon's letter, is a genuine piece of historical evidence which contributes, as I will show later, to Quentin and Shreve's reconstruction of the past in Chapter VIII. After we have listened so long to Miss Rosa's and Mr. Compson's versions of what Bon and Sutpen were like, Bon's and Sutpen's actual words give their stories a sense of immediacy and urgency breaking through the barrier of time separating them from Quentin and Shreve.

Quentin offers no insight into his own reaction to the story he is telling, but the narrator supplies us with one. Quentin has become quite still, "brooding, almost sullen" (218). He continues speaking, "his voice level, curious, a little dreamy yet still with that overtone of sullen bemusement, of smoldering outrage" (218). His "curious repressed calm voice" betrays his effort to control himself, perhaps to prevent an open expression of outrage which would liken him to Miss Rosa, whom he will indeed resemble by the end of the novel. He is still looking at his father's letter, "now open, three quarters open, whose bulk had raised half itself by the leverage of the old crease in weightless and paradoxical levitation" (217). The letter, as we know from Chapter VI, reminds Quentin not just of his father, but of the whole Sutpen story, and here it becomes, in a way, a symbol for the past itself, which is "weightless" and, through Quentin's recitation of Sutpen's own words, has raised itself in "paradoxical levitation." Instead of being dead and buried, Sutpen and his story continue to confront Quentin, to rise up in his mind, so that he is impelled to tell Shreve everything he knows. The "levitation" is paradoxical because the narrator has referred to the past as a "dead time," and Mr. Compson has referred to the contents of the letter as "just the words, the symbols, the shapes themselves, shadowy inscrutable and serene" (101). Yet Shreve, who has had no contact at all with Miss Rosa and who comes from a background that is alien to the South Quentin describes, is also able to make the past levitate — even to the point of anticipating what Quentin is going to say:

> "Grandfather said there was the first mention — a shadow that almost emerged for a moment and then faded again but not completely away — of the — " ("It's a girl," Shreve said. "Dont tell me. Just go on.") " — woman whom he was to tell Grandfather thirty years afterward he had found unsuitable to his purpose." (247)

The first mention of Sutpen's wife occurs seven pages earlier in Quentin's narrative (240), but Quentin does not tell Shreve how Sutpen met her.

Nevertheless Shreve easily makes the connection, which is not at all obvious, between the earlier information and what Quentin is *about* to tell him concerning the young woman who helped Sutpen load the muskets in the Haitian room.

When Shreve is observed again, several pages later, he has become totally absorbed in the story: "he would not perform his deep-breathing in the open window tonight at all" (255). Instead he watches Quentin "from behind his (Shreve's) expression of cherubic and erudite amazement which the spectacles intensified or perhaps actually created" (256). As in the earlier description of the "lamp-glared moons of his spectacles" (217), the narrator seems to endow Shreve with a very special kind of imagination, unique to him as a person. Magdalene Redekop observes that Shreve "is not so innocent as his pink chubbiness might suggest." Like all of us, he sees not "out of some mystic centre of revelation" but out of glasses, "the codes of [a] particular culture." And he is educating himself to "look for and recognize the recurring structures" in the culture Quentin has supplied for him.[15] On the one hand, Shreve's "cherubic" youth suggests that he has been unscarred by history and is therefore not afraid to delve into the secrets of the past. On the other hand, his amazement is "erudite," reminding us of Mr. Compson's detached, almost scholarly attitude toward the past, and foreshadowing Shreve's own "erudite" presentation of many new details in Bon's biography in Chapter VIII.

Just as in earlier chapters Miss Rosa and Mr. Compson explain the past *to* Quentin, so now the narrator concentrates on the fact that Quentin and Shreve have been talking *to* each other as well as *about* the past:

> both born within the same year: the one in Alberta, the other in Mississippi; born half a continent apart yet joined, connected after a fashion in a sort of geographical transubstantiation by that Continental Trough, that River which runs not only through the physical land of which it is the geologic umbilical, not only runs through the spiritual lives of the beings within its scope, but is very Environment itself which laughs at degrees of latitude and temperature, though some of these beings, like Shreve, have never seen it — the two of them who four months ago had never laid eyes on one another yet who since had slept in the same room and eaten side by side of the same food and used the same books from which to prepare to recite in the same freshman courses, facing one another across the lamplit table on which lay the fragile pandora's box of scrawled paper which had filled with violent and unratiocinative djinns and demons this snug monastic coign, this dreamy and heatless alcove of what we call the best of thought. (258)

In terms of age, spiritual life, "Environment itself," and the four months experience of having lived together, Quentin and Shreve are indissolubly connected. In terms of the present setting, where they face one another across the lamplit Harvard table, they stand in the same relation to Mr. Compson's letter and the Sutpen story. And while the "snug monastic coign" affords Quentin and Shreve a facility for the observation of the past which the other narrators have not enjoyed, it also removes them from the passion the historical figures actually experienced. Quentin and Shreve are like Miss Rosa and Mr. Compson in that they are rationalizing what they *think* went on in the minds of the historical figures who rarely revealed their own purposes and motivations.[16] Calling the letter a "pandora's box" makes their recreation of the past a very problematical exercise indeed. Pandora's box, the gift of Jupiter to Pandora, enclosed

> the whole multitude of human ills, which flew forth when the box was foolishly opened by Epimetheus; according to a later version, the box contained all the blessings of the gods, which, on its opening, escaped and were lost, with the exception of hope, which was at the bottom of the box.[17]

The narrator is perhaps implying that Quentin and Shreve's attempt to recapture the past is dangerous because they expose themselves to the "whole multitude of human ills" in the Sutpen story—though he perhaps perceives some unspecified residual hope in their attempt.

Quentin's own attitude toward what he and Shreve are doing reinforces the narrator's ambiguous mixture of skepticism and faith:

> *Maybe we are both Father. Maybe nothing ever happens once and is finished. Maybe happen is never once but like ripples maybe on water after the pebble sinks, the ripples moving on, spreading, the pool attached by a narrow umbilical watercord to the next pool which the first pool feeds, has fed, did feed, let this second pool contain a different temperature of water, a different molecularity of having seen, felt, remembered, reflect in a different tone the infinite unchanging sky, it doesn't matter: that pebble's watery echo whose fall it did not even see moves across its surface too at the original ripple-space, to the old ineradicable rhythm* thinking *Yes, we are both Father. Or maybe Father and I are both Shreve, maybe it took Father and me both to make Shreve or Shreve and me both to make Father or maybe Thomas Sutpen to make all of us.* (261–62)

Quentin converts the narrator's image of the Mississippi as a "geologic umbilical" stretching across the continent into an "umbilical watercord" meant to express his insight into the continuity of time itself. In immersing themselves so profoundly in Mr. Compson's accounting of events, perhaps Quentin and Shreve do in a sense become *"both Father."* The series of pools can be thought of as the series of narrators, all containing a different molecularity (a unique individual makeup), but all connected to each other as the several reflections of the same "infinite unchanging sky" (the universal and abiding truth, that is, inherent in the Sutpen story).[18] Thus it is possible for Quentin to think that *"Father and I are both Shreve"* in the sense that Shreve is able to follow the pattern of Sutpen's career without having seen him, and Shreve is able to merge himself into the "old ineradicable rhythm" of all the interpreters who have been swept up in the wake of Sutpen's downfall. As Edmond Volpe has said of the passage: "Physically, the human being exists in fragmented time, but when he thinks, he is in the realm of indivisible time."[19] Events separated by many years can be perceived by the mind as a continuum. Such "thinking" no doubt prepares Quentin and Shreve for the later experience of identification with Henry and Charles in which the distinction between thinking about and reliving the past seems temporarily to be abolished.

But we must also remember that this passage represents the nature of thought, and not what is necessarily true. "Thinking" stands out conspicuously in the otherwise italicized passage just quoted (see also p. 207), as does the continual repetition of "*maybe.*" Quentin is not sure that what he is thinking is true; rather, these are the tentative thoughts which come to him at this point in the reconstruction of the past, evidence of the struggle he and Shreve are carrying on, not simply to understand the past, but in some sense also to go beyond it, to become independent of it by absorbing it into the living bloodstream of the present as they do in Chapter VIII. Here in Chapter VII, however, they are still striving for a proper perspective. Shreve, for example, tends to treat his retelling of the story too abstractly, as though it were a game rather than an account of the tragedy of human life.[20] He cuts Quentin off at one point and says: "'Let me play a while now'" (280). The cold room in which this game is played could conceivably encourage Shreve's tendency to rationalize, to detach himself ruthlessly from the story. But this does not happen.[21] Instead he hugs himself and tries to create some warmth (275) just as he tries to endow the historical figures with life. The narrator, moreover, sees in Shreve "that protective coloring of levity behind which the youthful shame of being moved hid itself" (280).

It is, ultimately, because they do, willingly or unwillingly, take the risk of opening Pandora's box and exposing themselves to the dangers of involvement, of "being moved," that Quentin and Shreve progress to new discoveries and fuller understandings. Unlike the other narrators, they are working together in a cooperative effort. When Quentin refers to Mr. Compson's belief that Sutpen named his son Charles Bon, Shreve immediately questions what is to him new information:

"Your father... He seems to have got an awful lot of delayed information awful quick, after having waited forty-five years. If he knew all this, what was his reason for telling you that the trouble between Henry and Bon was the octoroon woman?"

"He didn't know it then. Grandfather didn't tell him all of it either, like Sutpen never told Grandfather quite all of it."

"Then who did tell him?"
"I did." Quentin did not move, did not look up while Shreve watched him. "The day after we—after that night when we——"
"Oh," Shreve said. "After you and the old aunt. I see. Go on. And father said——"
(266)

Shreve even preserves Quentin's "father said" as part of the ongoing narrative line. He interrupts only at those points where clarification is needed, thus establishing just those parts of the story which are uniquely Quentin's and which Quentin's grandfather and father did not know. In speaking to General Compson thirty years after their first conversation, Thomas Sutpen referred to

"'the one very factor which would destroy the entire plan and design which I had been working toward, concealed it so well that it was not until after the child was born that I discovered that this factor existed'——" (274)

Sutpen was of course alluding to Charles Bon. But the General did not realize that Bon was Sutpen's son, nor that Bon's Negro blood was the "factor" to which Sutpen referred. Shreve nails down once and for all that Quentin is the source of this new information:

"And when your old man told it to you, you wouldn't have known what anybody was talking about if you hadn't been out there and seen Clytie. Is that right?"
"Yes," Quentin said. (274)

With the knowledge that Bon is Henry's brother, Shreve sets out on a major revision of the Sutpen story in Chapter VIII. As Cleanth Brooks observes, "it is clearly Shreve who is speaking from p. 303 to p. 333, from p. 336 to p. 345, from p. 350 to p. 351, and from p. 358 to p. 359. Moreover, save for a dozen or so words, nothing in section 7 [sic] is specifically assigned to Quentin."[22] Although the narrator repeatedly notes that Shreve is speaking for Quentin as well as for himself, it is just as apparent that he is in the process of discovering new layers of significance in what Quentin learned on his visit to Sutpen's Hundred with Miss Rosa, and that without Shreve Sutpen's story would not be nearly as coherent as it eventually becomes. Shreve is "a solvent to keep it real...otherwise it would have vanished into smoke and fury."[23] On another occasion, Faulkner noted that "McCannon had a much truer picture of Sutpen from what Quentin told him than Quentin himself did."[24] Shreve is palpably present for Quentin in a way that is not quite true of Miss Rosa or Mr. Compson. Shreve is "the actual other who is realized down to the individual hairs on his red arm," Redekop observes.[25] Quentin's only significant piece of sustained narration—his rendering of Sutpen's autobiography—constitutes, in Doody's view, a confession of his need "to talk out" and realize "an identity of his own":

> Alienated even before he listens to Rosa (p. 9), he has nothing to say to anyone in Jefferson. Rosa would not listen to him, since she has no room for any interpretation of Sutpen but her own; and his father does not share Quentin's emotional dislocation. At Harvard, though, Quentin needs an audience like Shreve precisely because another outsider gives him the necessary freedom. Quentin does not want the social confirmation Sutpen seeks from General Compson, nor the intensely personal affirmation Rosa seeks from him. He has, in effect, heard both their confessions, and for himself he wants something "purer."[26]

The "something purer" would be a sense of himself and the Sutpen story that could transcend the complex memories and loyalties tearing him apart.

Shreve's role as historian, while not entirely separable from Quentin's, is nonetheless a significantly individual one. He does not need to side with any of his sources, and can ruthlessly reject them when they do not accord with his own idea of the story. His attention to Bon, for example, reveals not only his empathy for someone of roughly his own age, but also his interest in imagining a shadowy figure who spends most of his life outside of the "Southern context" of the Sutpen story. Beyond that, his need to understand Bon is inseparable from his overall quest to understand what Quentin discovered at Sutpen's Hundred.

Once Shreve knows that it was the incest, not the octoroon, which caused conflict between two brothers, not two friends, he is ready to rework Mr. Compson's version of the story, saving as much of it as is compatible with the new information. That Bon was Henry's brother, for example, is a fact potentially discoverable within the context of Mr. Compson's explanation of Bon: "'He is the curious one to me. He came into that isolated puritan country household almost like Sutpen himself came into Jefferson: apparently complete, without background or past or childhood'" (93). Mr. Compson's tendency to treat Henry and Charles more as brothers than friends (96) is consciously developed by Quentin and Shreve in their recreation of Henry and Charles's college years (316). Similarly, the contrasts Mr. Compson establishes between the provincial Henry and the cosmopolitan Bon obtain also in the college scenes created by Quentin and Shreve (compare 95–96 with 315–16).

Even Mr. Compson's creation of the scene in which Sutpen informs Henry that Bon has an octoroon mistress (90) is still recognizable when Shreve uses it to show Henry's reaction to the fact that Bon is his brother (293). Sutpen's abruptness and Henry's reaction, the percussion and repercussion of both scenes, are identical. But there are major differences too. Mr. Compson's account is more abstract. He says he can "imagine" what happened, but he cannot do more than refer to a "statement" whereas

Shreve speculates on precisely what was said. In Shreve's scene we can observe Henry and Sutpen looking at each other, and even reacting to each other's facial expressions. Neither Mr. Compson nor Shreve claims to be giving a verbatim report of the occasion, but because Shreve's more dramatic version is more richly developed, more lifelike, it impresses us as a closer approximation to what "actually" happened.

Of course, Mr. Compson could have done better with his account had he known that Bon was Henry's brother and Sutpen's son. In a sense Shreve is just filling in the gaps, providing the "statement" to which Mr. Compson could only allude. Nevertheless, Mr. Compson would not have been able to identify with Henry in the way that Shreve and Quentin do. As the narrator puts it, Quentin and Shreve share with Henry and Charles "the heart and blood of youth" (294). While Mr. Compson can talk about Henry's obsession with virginity, Quentin and Shreve can act out and experience that obsession. This does not ensure an authentic reconstruction of the past, for we cannot be entirely satisfied that Mr. Compson's introduction of the theme of "virginity" is historically justified. It is, rather, a "fact" he deduces from the provincial conditions in which Henry lived, from Henry's youth, and from his unusually close ties with both his sister and Bon. As for Quentin and Shreve, their first portrayal of Henry watching Charles and Judith in the garden after Sutpen has told him Charles is his brother is plainly erroneous. The narrator notes that, contrary to what they imagine, "the time had been winter in that garden...[and] judged by the subsequent events, it had been night in the garden also" (295). Their thoughts are not on the historical setting, but on Henry and Charles themselves. The mistake in the season "would not matter here in Cambridge... it had been so long ago" (295). Unlike the historian, they are not interested in making the "tedious transition from hearth and garden to saddle" (295). Instead they are riding away from Sutpen's Hundred along with Henry and Charles, and Shreve is already explaining what Charles knew about Henry's meeting with Sutpen.

Shreve's eagerness to explain what Henry and Charles were thinking is countered by the narrator's repeated references to the cold, "tomblike" room, which seems to symbolize the deadness of the past, and hence its irretrievability, yet these two young men are able to withstand the deathlike atmosphere of the room and to convert their account of the past into the terms of their own process of maturation. Miss Rosa's outrage at what Sutpen did to her and Mr. Compson's rather complacent view of the past, of its "simple passion and simple violence, impervious to time and inexplicable" (101), are replaced by Quentin and Shreve's obsession with the fluidity of time (299), in which the fragments of Miss Rosa's and Mr. Compson's narrative can at least be put in motion, and the historical figures made into extensions of Quentin and Shreve's "vaporizing breath" (303).

In the course of this self-projection into the past a more meaningful and authentic historical knowledge is acquired. All the events leading up to the first meeting between Henry and Charles at college are discussed and sifted, with the false parts of the recreation discarded in favor of what seems true or appropriate to the preconceived patterns of Miss Rosa and Mr. Compson. In this way Quentin and Shreve "overpass" what has already been said by others and see the Sutpen story from another perspective, which has not been produced through the "talking alone" but through a mutually supportive process: "some happy marriage of speaking and hearing" (316).

The few significant facts about Bon are aptly summarized by Mr. Compson: so out of place is Bon, "a young man of worldly elegance and assurance beyond his years, handsome, apparently wealthy," and "some few years older than Henry...a little old to be still in college...a small new college in the Mississippi hinterland and even wilderness, three hundred miles from that worldly and even foreign city which was his home," that it is curious that he has turned up to figure so decisively in the Sutpen story. Bon appears to Mr. Compson "phoenix-like, fullsprung from no childhood" (74). Presumably Mr. Compson is thinking of the self-progenitive "mythical bird of gorgeous plumage, fabled to be the only one of its kind."[27] But the allusion also carries with it the idea of the bird's rebirth from its own ashes, which is appropriate to what we learn from Chapter VIII—that Bon is Sutpen's son and is repeating, in some respects, his father's life.

Although Quentin and Shreve do not know anything about Bon's childhood, his lack of a family and his probable solitariness must remind them of the other childhoods they have learned about in the course of hearing the Sutpen story. And although they never seem aware of it, they use Miss Rosa's, Sutpen's, and Etienne Bon's childhoods as historical models of thwarted development for their reconstruction of Bon's past. Quentin has had to listen to Miss Rosa tell how her childhood was spent in an isolation which greatly retarded her development as an adult. As she herself says: "*I...had learned nothing of love, not even parents' love*" (146). Shreve imagines that Charles Bon also learned nothing of parents' love, and that instead he was "created between a lawyer and a woman" (306). The lawyer joins the woman in standing in a parental role vis-à-vis Bon, just as Judith and Clytie were to become substitute parents for his son Etienne. Clytie's "fierce ruthless constant guardianship" (197), the way she thrusts food at Etienne with "restrained savageness" (195), can be compared with Eulalia Bon's similar treatment of her son (297). Just as Clytie acts as Judith's agent by going to New Orleans to fetch Etienne and by keeping fierce watch over him thereafter, so, in Shreve's narrative, Eulalia Bon's lawyer acts as her agent by planning every aspect of Charles Bon's life, by sending him to the University of Mississippi.

As a child Rosa stares "across the table [at Sutpen] with still and curious and profound intensity" (66), but receives no recognition. Shreve presents Bon as gazing yearningly at his father's face years later only to find "no sign, no more sign at parting than when he had seen it first" (321).[28] Shreve imagines that Bon was led to Sutpen's Hundred just to see the man who might be his father, and who might therefore acknowledge him; when, however, Bon realizes that the acknowledgment will never be given, he exclaims over and over again: "I am young, young!" (321, 333, 347). Unlike Mr. Compson's passive and resigned Bon, Shreve's agonized and tormented Bon resembles Miss Rosa in his vulnerability.

One might also compare the ways in which Etienne and his father Charles are snatched away from their native environments and isolated from their pasts in New Orleans and Haiti, pasts of which they have only a vague recollection (199, 298). The refrain of what Bon can and cannot remember also occurs throughout Sutpen's dim memories in Chapter VII of his childhood in West Virginia.

It is fascinating to see in Chapter VIII just how skillfully Quentin and Shreve are able to recreate Bon's career in terms of the historical pattern already outlined in the lives of his son Etienne in Chapter VI and his father Sutpen in Chapter VII. All three are devoid of any real sense of the past, and without a past their lives can have no sense of continuity. Shreve's comment that Charles Bon had to begin each stage of his life anew would seem equally true of Sutpen who began his design with nothing at the age of fourteen, abruptly gained a fortune at twenty-one in Haiti, and then had to start all over again at the age of twenty-five in Mississippi. The disjointed quality of Bon's life, as imagined by Shreve, is also apparent in Etienne Bon, who repeats his grandfather's mysterious appearance in Jefferson, his abrupt departure, and his subsequent return to a community he does not understand and which does not understand him.

Quentin and Shreve's approach to understanding Bon's past is, then, largely learned from the earlier parts of the Sutpen story. Given the fact that so much about Rosa and Sutpen is revealed in their own accounts of their childhoods, it is not difficult to see why Shreve should describe Bon's childhood in order to explain Bon's attitude toward Sutpen, Henry, and Judith. As Olga Vickery says, in order for Miss Rosa to explain how Clytie can touch the "central I am" and how the "eggshell shibboleth of caste and color can fall," she must "reiterate her entire history, her childhood, her dreams, and her disappointments."[29] So Bon's entire history, his childhood, his dreams about a past he can never know, and his disappointment that Sutpen will not acknowledge him all must be related, however scarce the evidence may be, if Bon is to be understood.

But, as with Sutpen, Bon's own words give Shreve and Quentin some clues concerning his character. In one instance Shreve conflates Miss Rosa's notion of Bon with what the latter says in his letter to Judith in order to present what may have been Bon's attitude toward Judith and the Sutpen family. In describing her knowledge of Bon, Miss Rosa says:

> *One day he was not. Then he was. Then he was not.* (152)

> *He was absent, and he was; he returned, and he was not; three women put something into the earth and covered it, and he had never been.* (153)

In his letter to Judith Bon speaks of the war and says:

> *I cannot say when to expect me. Because what WAS is one thing, and now it is not because it is dead, it died in 1861, and therefore what IS...is something else again because it was not even alive then.* (131)

Judith later repeats part of Bon's thoughts on time when she gives Bon's letter to Mrs. Compson in the hope that at least something of Bon will survive through time, a possibility which Miss Rosa denied:

> At least it would be something just because it would have happened, be remembered even if only from passing from one hand to another, one mind to another, and it would be at least a scratch, something, something that might make a mark on something that *was* once for the reason that it can die someday, while the block of stone cant be *is* because it never can become *was* because it cant ever die or perish. (127–28)

Rosa's, Bon's, and Judith's thoughts on time all seem to coalesce in Shreve's speculation that Bon wished to marry Judith so that "if there were sin too maybe you (Bon) would not be permitted to escape, uncouple, return." Thus Bon's concern with the *"was-not: is: was:"* cycle Shreve describes (324) would be transcended. As Shreve explains it, Bon's relations with women up until this time had been ephemeral and transient, but to commit the sin of incest would damn him, and would at least signify the permanence of his relationship with Judith through eternity.

This theme of not having really lived, of the fear that one may leave no impression or mark upon the world, be deprived of the opportunities for making such a mark, runs throughout Shreve's accounts of the other people involved in Sutpen's tragedy. He likens Eulalia Bon's situation to Miss Rosa's. Both women had suffered indignity at Sutpen's hands, but Miss Rosa was unable to make Sutpen pay for his insult. Eulalia Bon, on the contrary, had to expect that moment of revenge on Sutpen (even if she could not foresee its exact timing) or relinquish her right to live as Miss Rosa had relinquished hers. But in pursuing her revenge, Eulalia Bon sacrificed her humanity, just as Sutpen, in pursuing his design, sacrificed his.[30]

The chart of Eulalia Bon's lawyer and his financial accounting of Sutpen's career remind us of Sutpen's own material calculations. Like Sutpen too, the lawyer (as presented by Shreve) has no sense of time. He does not know the correct moment at which to take Sutpen for all he has, and as with Sutpen, procrastination contributes to his major miscalculation. When Bon arrives at the Hundred, Sutpen bides his time, trying to figure out the mistake he had made in his design. Beside his own neat ledger-like calculation, the lawyer had written many years before "*daughter? daughter? daughter?*" (309) — waiting and hoping to see how this new "factor," the birth of Judith, would fit into his scheme. His fatal error is to misread the profundity of Bon's feelings for the Sutpens; the shift from the threat of incest to its actual possibility is what wrecks his plan for making a profit from his long years of service as Bon's guardian and Eulalia Bon's counsel. Just as Sutpen had no moral understanding of the great outrage his wife had suffered when he put her aside, so the lawyer has no moral sensitivity to the way he has insulted Bon by implying that Bon's only motives for proposing to marry Judith are blackmail or revenge, after which he will put her aside. Ultimately, the lawyer's craving to extort money from Sutpen, like the itch for revenge felt by Rosa Coldfield and Eulalia Bon, eventually deprives him of any meaningful life. He spends his time contriving plots which never materialize and finds, like the two women, that he cannot oppose Sutpen without transforming himself into an image of his adversary.

Most critics have spoken of the lawyer as an "invention" or "fabrication" of Shreve's, and so in one sense he is. But in another sense he represents an extension of the Sutpen story that is absolutely necessary and provides an example of what Joseph Reed calls Quentin and Shreve's

> central regard for historical, biographical, and emotional consistency. For instance, they try out the idea that Bon knew that his father was Sutpen, that he had been told by his mother at some time— —then that he must have been told before he was old enough to take it in. Neither of these produces enough fullness or depth, so they invent the lawyer who invents the boy as instrument of revenge. Their drive is to supply the fitness of the perfect accidental conclusion with fit intentional causes in individuals' actions, and to combine both harmoniously in a single design.[31]

The invention of the lawyer also seems necessary because Quentin had earlier told Shreve how Sutpen came to General Compson after he had perceived

> that mistake which he could not discover himself and which he came to Grandfather, not to excuse but just to review the facts for an impartial (and Grandfather said he

believed, *a legally trained*) mind to examine and find and point out to him. (267, my emphasis)

[He hoped that] *the legal mind* might perceive and clarify that initial mistake which he still insisted on, which he himself had not been able to find. (273, my emphasis)

The lawyer Shreve creates does indeed discover Sutpen's error, and he uses the fact that Sutpen puts his first wife aside to track him down, as perhaps only a certain type of legal mind could do. In other words, the lawyer is true to the dimensions of the world which Shreve and Quentin have reconstituted out of the meager evidence that has been left to them, and true also to the maniacal world Sutpen has engendered through his design.

The invention of the lawyer has a certain historiographical sanction. John Hunt, relying on W. B. Gallie's *Philosophy and the Historical Understanding,* remarks that

the historian must make inferences about necessary and prior conditions, venture hypotheses about the interconnectedness of evidence and the genetic relationship of events by analogy to general human experience, ascribe states of feeling and motive on the basis of type, relate actions and attitudes to cultural role, make contingencies acceptable, establish sequences. Even the device of a "dummy variable," a species of inference of necessary and prior condition, must at times be used.[32]

Shreve's "greatest historiographical stroke," Hunt contends, is the creation of the New Orleans lawyer, the "dummy variable,"[33] which is, in Gallie's words, a device employed by the historian as a way "of asserting that someone was doing something highly relevant to his narrative but unfortunately he knows neither who nor what."[34]

The kind of historical vision behind Shreve's invention of the lawyer[35] can be illuminated by Cleanth Brooks's astute remarks on the role that Bon and Sutpen play in the novel:

Sutpen is the secularized Puritan; Bon is the lapsed Roman Catholic. Whereas Sutpen is filled with a fresh and powerful energy, Bon is world-weary and tired. Bon is a fatalist, but Sutpen believes in sheer will: "anyone could look at him and say, '*Given the occasion and the need, this man can and will do anything*'"(p. 46). Bon possesses too much knowledge; Sutpen on the other hand is "innocent." The one has gone beyond the distinction between good and evil; the other has scarcely arrived at that distinction. The father and the son define the extremes of the human world: one aberration corresponds to—and eventually destroys—the other.[36]

Perhaps Brooks's last point should be expanded to suggest that Shreve and Quentin are defining the limits of good and evil in the human world, and hence in history, in all of their recasting of the Sutpen story in Chapter VIII. Thus Quentin's earlier memory of Judge Benbow's benevolent role as executor of Goodhue Coldfield's estate is given its reverse image in the cold material calculation of Eulalia Bon's lawyer (compare 212 with 300–301). Each lawyer works in secrecy for many, many years, but Judge Benbow labors for Miss Rosa's welfare while Eulalia Bon's lawyer plots Sutpen's ruin. Each lawyer designs a very precise ledger-like record and carefully tabulates the profit and the loss of his actions, but Judge Benbow does not expect to collect from Miss Rosa the expenses he has incurred in attending to her father's estate. Eulalia Bon's lawyer is betting, like Judge Benbow, but not on horses; his game is human lives. There is something terribly ironic in his futile efforts to compute *"intrinsic val."* Human beings for him have no intrinsic value. They can be tabulated on a chart. Judge Benbow's account is merely "mythical" whereas that of Eulalia Bon's lawyer is an historical record in which Sutpen's every move is followed in the belief that he will be caught in some error which can be used to destroy him. Both ledgers are revelatory of the "legal mind," but they show the legal mind being put to quite antithetical purposes.

In speaking of Quentin and Shreve as defining the extremes of the human world, I do not wish to make their interpretation seem too schematic. Its power derives not from some thesis or theory, but from its accurate appraisal of the dimensions of human life. Their portrait of Bon, for example, is not just a composite of what they already know about Etienne's and Sutpen's childhoods. Neither morally insensitive like Sutpen nor violently alienated like Etienne, Shreve's Bon is invested with his own unique tragic sense of life: "so if he just didn't make the mistake of believing that he could beat all of it [all of his mother's and the lawyer's lifelong designs for him], if he just remembered to be quiet and be alert he could beat some of it" (310). His fatalism is tempered by a hope that perhaps he can effect some change in his life, exercise some modicum of free will. He does, moreover, grope for self-knowledge, and for the love his father was incapable of feeling.

In the same way, Shreve uses but does not simply repeat Judith and Clytie's treatment of Etienne Bon in his reenactment of the lawyer and Eulalia Bon's treatment of Charles. Unlike Judith, Eulalia Bon makes no effort to redeem the past. Judith can be faulted for isolating Etienne Bon from the community, for depriving him of what little past he may have remembered, but she nurses him in sickness and seems to suffer for the pain she has caused him. Eulalia Bon never thinks of her child's welfare at all. When she learns of the grief she has caused Henry and Charles, she, in the narrator's words, sits "laughing harshly and steadily at Henry" (335).

Shreve himself provides the criterion upon which he has based his recounting of events:

> "What was it the old dame, the Aunt Rosa, told you about how there are some things that just have to be whether they are or not, have to be a damn sight more than some

other things that maybe are and it dont matter a damn whether they are or not?" (322, see also 325)

Where the evidence is lost Shreve must supply it by relying on his understanding of human beings, however flawed that may be, and however much his own emotions and attitudes may color and distort those of the historical figures he is trying to understand. What little Shreve does know about Bon, what he can surmise from Bon's letter, what he can deduce from the fact that Bon was Sutpen's son, and finally, what he thinks was unique in Bon as an individual human being—all these elements go into this complex reconstruction of the past.

I have emphasized the process by which Shreve integrates Bon, his mother and the lawyer into the total pattern of the Sutpen story because it is this integration which provides the impetus for the rest of his and Quentin's joint interpretation in the chapter. Having fully explored the background of Bon's motivation, Shreve and Quentin return to the scene in which Henry repudiated his birthright and then rode away from Sutpen's Hundred with Bon. Shreve no longer contends that Bon did not know that Sutpen had told Henry that they were brothers. When they had begun an explanation of this scene, Quentin and Shreve were not interested in providing the "tedious transition from hearth and garden to saddle" (295). Now Shreve is able to offer a tentative account of the time between Sutpen's meeting with Henry and Bon's waiting for some word from his father (333), and then Shreve ceases speaking, since a certain evolutionary stage has been reached in his and Quentin's rethinking of the story (334).
     After the narrator brings together the various versions of the story, sometimes paraphrasing one of the character-narrators, occasionally adding his own details, in order to summarize what has been achieved in the course of interpretation (335–36),[37] Shreve becomes so excited at the prospect of the past which he has recreated that he begins to pant as he describes Henry's panting at Shiloh—where, Shreve insists, it was Henry, not Bon, who was wounded. The narrator offers no judgment on Shreve's speculation, but it is clear that he and Quentin are nearing but have not yet achieved union with Henry and Charles. There is still something of that subjective arbitrariness in their reconstruction which the narrator noted earlier in this chapter: "[Shreve] supply[ing] *his* shade not only with a cue but with breath to obey it in" (344, my emphasis). Nevertheless, the rigor and discipline which he and Quentin have practiced in order to identify with their shades, Henry and Charles, bring them closer to what seems to be that past itself, for they endure the cold, that barrier which symbolizes the past's deadness, its seemingly irretrievable nature, "as though in delib-

erate flagellant exaltation of physical misery transmogrified into the spirits' travail of the two young men during that time fifty years ago" (345).

Now oblivious to their present surroundings, Shreve and Quentin seem immersed in an actual past, designated by italics (346–50). The circumstantiality of this passage is remarkable. Bon is thinking of "*how that Jefferson regiment of which his father was now colonel was in Longstreet's corps*" (347). He is imagined as being still obsessed with the hope of obtaining some sort of recognition from his father, but his obsession is rendered dramatically, rather than as part of a discursive explanation: "'*I will just touch flesh with him and I will say it myself: You will not need to worry; she shall never see me again*'" (348). Honor and pride, Bon tells Henry, are empty words. Henry seems to accept Bon's nihilism, and he gives up his opposition to the marriage by allowing Bon to write the letter to Judith which she eventually gives to Mrs. Compson.

In spite of the immediacy of this italicized scene it is clear that Quentin and Shreve are attributing statements to Henry and Bon which are based upon conjecture: "*so it must have seemed to him...maybe he thought for just a second.*" Their conjectures are, however, based on Bon's letter, as can be seen by comparing pages 349 and 129. The italicized passage as a whole reflects Quentin and Shreve's state of mind at this point in the interpretative process, for it ends with the announcement that Sutpen wishes to see Henry in his tent (350), which suggests that they are not yet ready to discover (or project) what the father and the son said to each other. Immediately after the announcement, Shreve reverts to Quentin's trip to Sutpen's Hundred with Miss Rosa and tries to establish just how Quentin came to know that Bon had Negro blood. We cannot understand from Shreve's words alone just how this secret was obtained, and indeed words alone, ratiocination, never do seem able to explain Quentin's insight. But we cannot come to any ultimate conclusions about Quentin's knowledge until we encounter his own version of the Sutpen's Hundred visit in Chapter IX and witness his brief interview with Henry. The fact that the interview is not given until page 373, at the very end of the novel, suggests that Faulkner deliberately intends to provoke us into thinking back over the previous episodes of the novel in order to determine just how Quentin arrived at this "fact."

Shreve himself gives up explanations and moves with Quentin toward the crucial meeting between Sutpen and Henry, a meeting Mr. Compson mentioned (276) but knew nothing about. All distinctions between past and present appear to be wiped out, so that Quentin and Shreve "were both in Carolina and the time was forty-six years ago, and it was not even four now but compounded still further, since now both of them were Henry Sutpen and both of them were Bon, compounded each of both yet either neither" (351). Instead of a descriptive overview of the war scene, as in the introduction to the previous italicized passage (345–50), we shift immediately into the unfolding of the war scene itself: "...smelling the very smoke which had blown and faded away forty-six years ago from the *bivouac fires burning in a pine grove.*" We are meant to see and hear and smell the past for ourselves, without mediation (351–58). The only past we see is the immediate past of four years of war: Henry "*gaunt and ragged and unshaven; because of the last four years and because he had not quite got his height when the four years began.*" (352). Time does not extend forward beyond the unfolding of this scene: "...*he is not as tall by two inches as he gave promise of being, and not as heavy by thirty pounds as he probably will be a few years after he has outlived the four years, if he do outlive them*" (352).

Like the previous italicized episode, however, the scene is a synthesis of much of what Quentin and Shreve have already imagined or speculated upon. For example, Shreve's guess that it was Henry, not Bon, who was wounded is incorporated into this scene as though it were an incontrovertible fact: "*— You were hit at Shiloh, Colonel Willow tells me, Sutpen says*" (353). Also, a flashback occurring within Henry's meeting with Sutpen retrieves an encounter between the two men at Sutpen's Hundred four years previously (354), but this retrieval is neither Henry's nor Sutpen's but Quentin and Shreve's remembrance of the scene *as they had recreated it* earlier on the evening in January 1910 (294). Even Henry's moving "*Brother or not, I have decided. I will. I will* (354), is borrowed from Mr. Compson's imaginative portrayal of Henry's determination to accept the values which legitimize Bon's right to the octoroon mistress: "*I will believe; I will. I will*" (90, see also 111–12). Indeed, the basic setting of the scene on pages 351–58 has been derived from Mr. Compson's passing mention of "the defiance and the ultimatum delivered beside a bivouac fire" (132). And Sutpen's crucial admission of the secret that Bon has Negro blood (354–55) is hinted at by Sutpen himself in conversation with General Compson (264). That General Compson and the narrator both mention that Sutpen's father-in-law had told him that his wife was the daughter of a Spaniard (252, 335) might also be taken as a clue to Bon's mixed racial composition.

Nevertheless, this italicized passage seems authentic as an actual rendering of what happened in the past because it seems to be through Henry's point of view, as if to suggest that Henry did give Quentin the information that would make this recreation so believable. Note especially the remarkable circumstantiality of this scene, the subtle shifting of tenses, and what seems to be the particularity of personal memory in the passage devoted to Henry on page 355.[38] In truth, this passage is essentially an extension and heightening of what Quentin and Shreve have already been imagining as Henry's viewpoint (294, 334). All of these passages, then, demonstrate Quentin's and Shreve's attempts to subvert time, to crash through the barrier separating past and present, and to know reality as Henry must have known it. Such a portrayal of the past is compelling because of the way it incorporates what Richard P. Adams calls the "energy of motion... through time, which is life."[39]

The improvement that Quentin and Shreve as an interpretative team have made in the dramatic coherence and human credibility of the confrontation between Charles Bon and Henry Sutpen is apparent when the end of the italicized passage on page 358 is compared with Quentin's earlier visualization on page 133. The last version of the confrontation is a more compelling, because more fully and concretely imagined, rendering of the past.[40] On the other hand, Shreve's conjecture following the later scene, that Bon left his picture of the octoroon mistress and child in order to say that he was no good and that Judith should not grieve for him (359), is perhaps rightly rejected by critics as a romantic formula, a fanciful fabrication that Shreve, to quote Mr. Compson, would "like to believe."[41] We do not know what Bon's ultimate motivations were at the very end of his life; we can only assume that he was fully determined to make Henry stop him. In this sense he was as ruthlessly determined as Sutpen to accomplish a design.[42] As Sutpen seems to have goaded Wash into killing him so Shreve sees Bon as forcing Henry into killing him. Both despaired; one because he had lost his son (292), and the other because he had lost his father.

In Chapter IX Shreve has adjusted again to his casual, conversational tone. In opening a window, releasing the tension, he once again puts a distance between himself and the past he has been trying to understand. Nevertheless he finally confesses his genuine absorption in Southern history:

> "Wait. Listen. I'm not trying to be funny, smart. I just want to understand it if I can and I dont know how to say it better. Because it's something my people haven't got. Or if we have got it, it all happened long ago across the water and so now there aint anything to look at every day to remind us of it. We dont live among defeated grandfathers and freed slaves (or have I got it backward and was it your folks that are free and the niggers that lost?) and bullets in the dining room table and such, to be always reminding us to never forget." (361)

His question—"'What is it? something you live and breathe in like air?'"—captures just what Quentin has been feeling all along, that he himself has been not so much listening to the various accounts of Sutpen as he has been just naturally taking them into his being as one takes in air.

Shreve's question may also have been prompted by the fact that for a time he too has emitted the shades from his vaporizing breath in the cold room, been "ghost-dominated," and taken the story of Sutpen "in stride," as the narrator says on page 336.

Quentin replies that Shreve would have to be born in the South in order to understand its history. Shreve retorts:

> "Would I then?" Quentin did not answer. "Do you understand it?"
> "I dont know," Quentin said. "Yes, of course I understand it." They breathed in the darkness. After a moment Quentin said: "I dont know."
> "Yes. You dont know. You dont even know about the old dame, the Aunt Rosa."
> "Miss Rosa," Quentin said.
> "All right. You dont even know about her. Except that she refused at the last to be a ghost." (362)

This dialogue, reminiscent of their first exchange in Chapter VI (176), reveals how unwilling Quentin has been to confront his own tradition head-on—something, Shreve suggests, which even Miss Rosa was finally willing to do.

For Quentin there is only the ghost-filled remembering, the mental paralysis keeping him fixated on the past. Even though "the chill pure weight of the snow-breathed New England air" is on his face, he can "taste and feel" the dust on that September evening in 1909 when he and Miss Rosa made their visit to Sutpen's Hundred. He can "even smell the old woman in the buggy beside him, smell the fusty camphorreeking shawl and even the airless black cotton umbrella.... He could smell the horse; he could hear the dry plaint of the light wheels" (362). His strange jerking in bed is clearly not due to the coldness of the room (360–62). He begins to breathe hard as he remembers Miss Rosa's panting on that night (364). His obsession with his visit to the Hundred begins to recall Miss Rosa's obsession with Sutpen, and each in this chapter is associated with images of rigidity (365–67, 373).

The few details of Quentin's meeting with Clytie, and then with Henry, are finally presented. What we have here accords with Shreve's version in Chapter VIII. Quentin thinks: "'Yes. She [Clytie] is the one who owns the terror'" (369–70). Shreve has tried several times to say exactly what Quentin did learn, but his testimony, though suggestive, has remained fragmentary, singling out Clytie, who "did not tell Quentin in so many words" (350–51). In fact, words just seem to fail Shreve when he attempts to explain what I take to be Quentin's intuition of Bon's Negro blood *before* he goes up to see Henry. Yet we are told something about the context in which this intuition occurs. Clytie seems to know more than the fact that Henry is hiding in the house. The "secret" is "*about* whatever it was that was upstairs" (351, my emphasis). Clytie is not protecting Henry alone, but the Sutpen family, "for the sake of the man who had been her father" (350). Miss Rosa seems to think Clytie knew more than she told anyone (137–38). If Clytie had known nothing more, then why should Shreve allude to her appearance in the room "that day when they brought Bon's body in" (350)? Mr. Compson has referred to Clytie as a "Cassandra" (62) and mentions, without explanation, that "no one but your grandfather and perhaps Clytie was ever to know that Sutpen had gone to New Orleans too" (70). Did Sutpen confide in Clytie? Does this explain her rather savage upbringing of Etienne Bon? At any rate, Quentin's contact with her seems to have generated the "fact" of Bon's Negro blood.[43] Quentin is not aware of Henry's presence at Sutpen's Hundred before he sees Clytie, for he is reluctant to enter the house and he tries to play down the importance of Miss Rosa's visit (364). He is, however, thinking of Henry and wishing he were there "to stop Miss Coldfield and turn them back" (364). Just after he encounters Clytie but before he encounters Henry, Quentin is recorded as thinking of Jim Bond as "'the scion, the heir, the apparent (though not obvious)'" (370) — a clear indication that he already knows, or has just grasped, what the Sutpen relationships actually are.[44]

The scene with Clytie proves to be the culmination of Quentin's search for the "secret" explaining the mystery surrounding Henry's killing of Bon. Quentin has known for some time that Sutpen had discovered "a fact which I did not learn until after my son was born" (264). It caused him to set both wife and child aside. Sutpen uses the word "fact" or "factor" no less than six times (264, 273–74) in his second conversation with General Compson, a conversation which took place thirty years after the first. It is also significant that all references to the child come in this second conversation: in the days before Bon arrived to plague him, that is to say, Sutpen had seen no reason for telling General Compson about his first child. Quentin has also heard his father mention the child much earlier as "the one before Clytie and Judith and Henry even" (62), so that the child has already been mentioned in the novel four times, including three times by Sutpen himself (264, 274); moreover, Sutpen has directly referred to the child as a "son" (264). Without Sutpen ever telling quite all of the story, it is possible, at least in retrospect, to perceive the context in which Quentin could intuit the "fact" that the child had come back to trouble Sutpen.

David Levin has also found in Sutpen's own words the clue that eventually leads us to Quentin and Shreve's final interpretation of the Sutpen story:

From the time Sutpen admits to Grandfather Compson that he "put aside" his first wife, we wonder why he deserted her. There is a hint that he had a trump card to play against Charles Bon and the proposed marriage; but we never know Bon is part Negro until Shreve and Quentin reconstruct the scene in which Thomas Sutpen plays the trump card by telling Henry. That moment, it seems to me, is the climax of the novel because it also represents the triumph of Quentin's and Shreve's patient yet passionate search for historical understanding. At that moment both of them stop talking and the dramatic scene we read represents the understanding at which both of them have arrived. All of us see here that the Negro ancestry is the only fact that is adequate to explain the actions of the father and the two sons.[45]

Bon's Negro blood is the "factor" which Sutpen could not privately accept, even though, as he says to General Compson, in the eyes of the public his design would have been complete once (we can infer) Bon had married Judith. Presumably it was Bon's blood, the *"inexplicable unseen,"* which Clytie was aware of, and which Quentin also intuited.

When Quentin finally sees Henry, he faces the shocking reality of the past which heretofore has haunted him through Miss Rosa's and Mr. Compson's stories, and through his childhood visit to Sutpen's Hundred. But the scene itself is an anticlimax, in the sense that Quentin already knows all there is to know about Henry Sutpen and Charles Bon:

> *And you are— —?*
> *Henry Sutpen.*
> *And you have been here— —?*
> *Four years.*
> *And you came home— —?*
> *To die. Yes.*
> *To die?*
> *Yes. To die.*
> *And you have been here— —?*
> *Four years.*
> *And you are— —?*
> *Henry Sutpen.* (373)

Many critics have assumed that this scene is "the shock that motivates the search for understanding."[46] Perhaps it is, but by the time it occurs Quentin already possesses the key fact of Bon's Negro blood; what he and Shreve do in their Harvard room is expand this intuited fact into a credible story.

In referring to the short interview between Henry and Quentin, Hyatt Waggoner has suggested that "in giving us the incident only in the barest outline, Faulkner is following the Jamesian formula of making the reader imagine."[47] But is there any warrant for thinking that anything more transpires in this scene than what we are given? I think it is important to read this scene from Quentin's point of view. For Henry's answers are really the completion of Quentin's questions, which is to say that Henry simply confirms what Quentin already knows. In fact, the whole passage could be rearranged to show how Quentin creates and controls its meaning:

And you are Henry Sutpen?
And you have been here four years?
And you came home to die?
Yes.
To die?
Yes. To die.
And you have been here four years?
And you are Henry Sutpen?

The exchange registers Quentin's shock at having actually encountered the ghost that has largely been the product of his imagination. Suddenly the imaginative and the real worlds collide. Such a collision is bizarre, unreal, as fantastic as the whole Sutpen story, and yet Quentin knows that the collision has actually taken place, and that the past, however much a product of the imagination it may be, is also, indeed, a reality. To ask anything more of Henry is futile, and probably impossible for Quentin anyway. The whole weight of the narrator's comments in Chapter VIII bears on the fact that the present must always reconstruct the past in its own terms. The past can never exist, ever be understood, in quite its own terms. In one sense, Henry does indeed remain an enigma, the past unreal, even in a scene which we positively know to have happened.

James Guetti reads the interview as showing Quentin's inability to know the past. While I interpret the interview quite differently, Guetti is right, I think, in contending that Quentin learns nothing from the interview in the sense that Henry tells him nothing. Guetti suggests that Quentin's repeated questions show the futile circularity of his imagination. To me the circularity merely reinforces the fact that they are Quentin's questions, and that at the end of his search he finds Henry, who was really his beginning. Guetti seems right too in saying that Quentin's knowledge that Bon has Negro blood springs from "nothing."[48] No one ever tells Quentin in so many words about this "fact," so that in a sense it is based on nothing but Quentin's intuition.

Cleanth Brooks offers an elaborate argument to support the contention that Quentin could have learned about the Negro blood from Henry. Even though he is forced to admit that "it is not easy to find explicit indications showing that there was any lengthy talk between Quentin and Henry Sutpen,"[49] he suggests that

Quentin probably had ten minutes to talk with Henry—although their conversation *may* have been much longer. The fragment of it that keeps running through Quentin's head does not pretend to give more than the awesome confrontation. There is no warrant for concluding that it represents all that was said.[50]

But there is absolutely no evidence in the text of the novel that the scene with Henry and Quentin is just a fragment. It ends quite decisively, is shaped into a whole by its circularity, and the narrator next refers to the cold room at Harvard in which Quentin has remembered the meeting. Think also of the context in which the meeting takes place: "the bed, the yellow sheets and pillow, the wasted yellow face with closed, almost transparent eyelids on the pillow, the wasted hands crossed on the breast as if he were already a corpse" (373). Could Henry have been capable even physically of saying much more than he is represented as saying? Brooks himself observes:

> As for Quentin's conversation with Henry, what would Henry have told—if anything—to a young man whom he had never seen before? And would Quentin have dared to put to the pallid man on the bed any other questions than those which we know he did put?[51]

Quentin certainly has shown no ability to interrogate anyone in this novel, and it seems doubtful whether he would have questioned this terrifying vision further. Both he and Miss Rosa return from Henry's room as though they were sleepwalking out of some terrible dream.

Hershel Parker has rejected both Brooks's timing of Quentin's talk with Henry and the notion that we are given only a fragment of it:

> Miss Rosa and Jim Bond have left the house before Quentin enters Henry's room, but when he leaves the house himself he is soon within earshot of their voices, though it is too dark to go fast. Also, there is reason for thinking that the italicized twelve lines on page 373 are indeed meant to represent the whole of the conversation between Quentin and Henry. The symmetry of the sets of questions and answers is hard to account for unless one takes it as marking Quentin's physical and psychological approach toward the man who is in a state of living death, then his retreat away from him.[52]

Parker goes on to suggest that there is a clearly identifiable "Sutpen face" which is mentioned at various points in the novel and which Quentin, after scrutinizing Clytie's face on two separate occasions, eventually associates with Jim Bond.[53] Parker does not consider it strange that Miss Rosa, who surely knows the "Sutpen face" better than Quentin, sees no resemblance between Bond and the Sutpens. Parker admits the weakness of his argument by noting that "no contemporary witness cites Bon himself as having, much less transmitting, a Sutpen face."[54] Yet he insists that Shreve's imaginative conjecture (which Quentin does not contradict) that Bon had Sutpen features, and Faulkner's own language ("which stresses not what Quentin heard at Sutpen's but 'what he had seen out there'" [372]), prove that Quentin had finally put together the Sutpen story by observing the resemblances between different generations of the family.[55] It seems more likely, however, that what Quentin sees is simply Henry Sutpen, who represents the reality of the past which Quentin has tried to evade throughout the novel.[56]

If Henry had to *tell* Quentin that Bon had Negro blood, or if the Sutpen story had to be resolved by Quentin's detection of a "Sutpen face," then some of the power of the past to impinge on Quentin's consciousness is diminished, and his obsession with the past becomes not entirely convincing. It is clear, however — indeed, it is part of Quentin's problem — that he does not have to be told about the past, or to see it in physical terms but can imagine it all too well: *"No. If I had been there I could not have seen it this plain"* (190).

Quentin's tragedy lies precisely in this fact that his vision of the past has usurped all of his emotional and intellectual faculties. He now can see life only in terms of the past; for him Miss Rosa's last visit to Sutpen's Hundred, when she went to fetch Henry to the hospital, and his father's letter announcing her death (which he is reading at the end of the novel) are not just the end of a story (as they are for Shreve) but events which overtake and dominate his consciousness, even though he has not witnessed them. The circularity of Quentin's experience — his beginning with (in Chapter VI) and returning to (in Chapter IX) his father's letter — suggests an inability to live an independent life, for his very being seems permeated with a sense of age and death: "'I am older at twenty than a lot of people who have died'" (377).

At the end of *Absalom, Absalom!* Quentin and Shreve dissolve their partnership. Quentin retreats into the world of the past and into his ambiguous attitude toward the South, while Shreve reverts to the cocky and flippant summarizing of the Sutpen story that had marked his attitude at the beginning of their discussion. Sutpen's family line has finally degenerated into the idiot Jim Bond, who has no consciousness of the past. The "Genealogy" at the end of the novel informs us that Quentin will die in 1910, the very year in which he and Shreve have reclaimed and reinterpreted the Sutpen story. And Shreve adds to Quentin's burden by suggesting that Jim Bond stands for the unresolved part of the Sutpen story:

> "You've got one nigger left. One nigger Sutpen left. Of course you can't catch him and you don't even always see him and you never will be able to use him. But you've got him there still. You still hear him at night sometimes. Don't you?"
>
> "Yes," Quentin said. (378)

As the novel has frequently shown, Quentin would like to avoid the Sutpen story, but it keeps welling up in his consciousness; now Shreve suggests:

> "In time the Jim Bonds are going to conquer the western hemisphere. Of course it won't quite be in our time and of course as they spread toward the poles they will bleach out

again like the rabbits and the birds do, so they won't show up so sharp against the snow. But it will still be Jim Bond; and so in a few thousand years, I who regard you will also have sprung from the loins of African kings. Now I want you to tell me just one thing more. Why do you hate the South?" (378)

Shreve makes no explicit connection between his last question and his forecast of the future, but their juxtaposition implies that the blending of black and white that Sutpen felt was inimical to his design, and the blending which his son Henry seems to have abhorred in and of itself is part of an historical process in the western hemisphere that will eventually affect Shreve himself. Thus it seems that Shreve is ultimately asking Quentin why he hates the South when what he hates is really the future of the western world, a grim future in which the Jim Bonds "will bleach out again" — become uniformly white and lose their black identity — but "will still be Jim Bond," that symbol of an alienated and degenerate family line.

Although Shreve is speculating in a rather grandiose and sophomoric fashion, his interpretation of the Sutpen story has revealed that the human conflicts of the past are still part of the present and probably part of the future too. Quentin cannot bear to think that what he and Shreve have uncovered is part of an endless continuum, but thinking, consciousness itself, brings Quentin to the conclusion that he will have "'Nevermore of peace. Nevermore of peace. Nevermore Nevermore Nevermore'" (373). Thus the ending of *Absalom, Absalom!* reinforces the novel's sense of history as an ambiguous and unceasing product of the human predicament — a predicament which Quentin and Shreve have brilliantly explored and explained but which they have not resolved. Quentin's hysterical rejection of Shreve's suggestion that he hates the South is, in sum, his quarrel with himself; he is still pursuing that argument described at the beginning of the novel between the two Quentins, one too young to be a ghost (9) and the other "a barracks filled with stubborn back-looking ghosts" (12).

Quentin's excruciating dual consciousness and the powerfully unresolved ending of *Absalom, Absalom!* are precisely what set the novel apart from historical fiction of the nineteenth century, especially as it was established by Scott in his depiction of the traditional hero who "has completely internalized the social values he represents; when he falls on evil days, he remains utterly secure in his identity as founded on those values."[57] There may be "divided and equally valid claims (from birth, upbringing, affection, or principle) upon his loyalty," but his historical fate as an embodiment of his society is never in doubt — indeed it is shaped, usually, by a sagacious narrator and by "older and at least partially wiser men."[58] The hero may be a "battleground" upon which the forces shaping his era contend,[59] yet, like Quentin Durward, he will never have to confront, as Quentin Compson does, his own self-alienation.[60] No part of Durward is split off when he leaves home for the France of Louis XI; he departs a whole man.

Where there are parallels between Faulkner and Scott, they serve only to show how far away from his childhood reading the former progressed.[61] Certainly Faulkner continued to see resemblances between his region and Scotland,[62] and it may be that *Absalom, Absalom!* evokes strongly the strategy of Scott's least conventional historical novel, *Redgauntlet*, in order to demonstrate that Faulkner could only come near the nineteenth-century novel of history by utterly transforming it, by making it new according to the modernist writer's credo.[63]

Unlike Scott's other Jacobite novels, *Waverley* and *Rob Roy*, *Redgauntlet* is not set in the midst of the rebellions of 1745 or 1715 but in 1765, twenty years after the last major attempt to restore the Stuarts to the throne of Great Britain. The plans of the feeble Jacobite party in 1765 do not—as does the action of *Waverley* and *Rob Roy*—come at a crucial turning point in an historical crisis, and the stirring events of 1745 are portrayed in this novel only as a still remembered but rapidly retreating past, a dead time that is evoked in a number of anecdotes and tales.

Darsie Latimer, like Quentin Compson, is the descendant of a family and a society which have fought for a lost cause, but he has not himself participated in historical events, and only knows these events through the memories and speculations of participants and observers. Scott protects his hero by having him grow up in the Fairford household, which has always been staunchly Hanoverian—on the winning side, so to speak, of the historical forces which have made Darsie's present what it is. Thus, unlike Quentin, he is not superannuated to begin with—although his quixotic youth and romantic disposition are checked by his friend, Alan Fairford, who, like Shreve, brings a broader perspective to what otherwise would be a fanciful picture of the past.[64] Magdalene Redekop notes in passing Shreve's "obviously Scottish name—McCannon—and his repeated use of European analogies suggest[ing] a larger historical context which puts the Southern sense of 'the past' into perspective."[65] She might have added a remark on Quentin's own Scottish ancestry, chronicled in the *Compson Appendix*, as a way of signifying the appropriateness of these two young men giving birth to an historical narrative, which is also an inquiry into origins. Darsie and Alan in an exchange of letters and in the former's journal also engage in a story of their own making—furthered along and contextualized by a narrator who is somewhat more sure of himself than the one in *Absalom, Absalom!*.

"Wandering Willie's Tale" in *Redgauntlet* and the story of the French architect in *Absalom, Absalom!* are comparable attempts by Scott and

Faulkner to elaborate fables or paradigms of the hero's efforts to come to terms with the presence of the past. In both fables, told to Darsie and Quentin, powerful ancestral figures, Sir Robert Redgauntlet and Thomas Sutpen, attempt to impose their will on events and thoroughly determine their outcome. Yet they are restrained—even thwarted—by Steenie, an itinerant musician whose family has been beholden to the Redgauntlets and by the seemingly "captive architect" (8). Steenie refuses to give up his "ain"[66], a rent receipt that represents his independence maintained through subtle perseverance and patient policy. The architect, in Mr. Compson's words, bore Sutpen's ruthlessness and hurry and still managed "to curb the dream of grim and castle-like magnificence at which Sutpen obviously aimed" (38). Both Steenie—no more than a lowly family retainer—and the frail and effete architect seem entirely unlikely figures to check the designs of their masters, but that, of course, is exactly the point Scott and Faulkner wish to assert against all probabilities to the contrary. Although the architect fails to elude Sutpen's pursuit, they meet more as equals (both are "grim" and "indomitable" [38, 254, 257]) than as hunter and hunted when the architect is recaptured.

Like "Wandering Willie's Tale", the story of the French architect is, in the final analysis, a fable about humanity itself, applicable to all men, great or small, who are capable of enduring catastrophe with courage and fortitude. Darsie and Quentin, who pass on these fables to their friends Alan and Shreve, suggest the limitations of these seemingly self-progenitive and indestructible figures; they also remove some of the mystery and obscurity in which Redgauntlet's and Sutpen's motivations are enveloped.

Faulkner, however, finds ironies and mysteries in his fable that are absent in Scott's. For example, while the architect has stood and even, to a degree, prevailed against Sutpen's outrageous plans for his mansion, Mr. Compson—always the fatalist—points out that in vanquishing "Sutpen's fierce and overweening vanity or desire for magnificence or for vindication or whatever it was...[the architect] so created of Sutpen's very defeat the victory which, in conquering, Sutpen himself would have failed to gain" (38–39). In other words, the architect actually brings a kind of order and achievement to the chaos of Sutpen's motives, thus furthering his employer's plans. But what were Sutpen's motives? Mr. Compson offers us three choices that simultaneously enrich our awareness of a complex past and cause us to wonder how knowable the historical figure's intentions actually are. There is no question that Mr. Compson has a sound source (General Compson) for his account, but the interpretation of characters and events is problematic. We have a feel for past incidents, a strong grasp of the setting, but there is much we do not understand, so that Mr. Compson's "history" becomes, in part, a parable about historical knowledge, about our way of learning—but not ever learning quite enough—about the past, "whatever it was."

History is never handled quite this way by Scott, Thackeray, or by their successors in the nineteenth century. As Albert Guerard points out:

> the historical novelist is also engaged in conjecture. But traditionally he hides this fact and pretends to omniscience or, at least, to the authority of an eyewitness. Scott and Hawthorne, among others, may talk about the problems of penetrating the past before proceeding to a nominal omniscience.[67]

As Richard Waswo reminds us, fact and fiction tend to complement each other in Scott's historical novels, but the author has his sly way of asserting the primacy of fiction by employing sham prefaces and "presentational personae to undermine the status of fact to which other parts of his apparatus [footnotes and historical documentation] lay constant claim."[68] Nevertheless, Scott does not go nearly so far as Faulkner in boldly fashioning and probing history as a fiction, a construct of man akin to the twentieth-century idealist historian's emphasis on the practice of history as a reenactment in the present of the thoughts of the past.[69]

We can locate the difference between Scott and Faulkner by noticing how they use language to convey the past. John T. Matthews fastens on the narrator's comment in *Absalom, Absalom!* that "the characters conjured up by Quentin and Shreve may never have existed and yet are 'true enough' (335). Correspondingly, the tellers of the tales seem to have no life or consciousness—no selfhood—exterior to their speech; Quentin and Shreve do not merely 'discuss' the shade of Sutpen, they 'rather, exist' in it, as the passage above suggests."[70] This way of characterizing Quentin and Shreve is to doubt but not dismiss their recreation of the past, to make it curiously self-authorizing even though it is unverifiable. Or as Guerard puts it, "a difference from Conrad [to whom Faulkner is often closest in his recreation of the past] lies in Faulkner's ultimate refusal, on occasion, to define his cognitive authority or lack of it. All conjecture, even the most biased, can be credible."[71] Speculation has special sanction in Faulkner because out of it arises, as in the fable of the French architect, a gestalt, a way of seeing things plain, even when—like Quentin—the historian has not witnessed the past and can only approximate its reality.

Not that the rudiments of Faulkner's uses of the past cannot be glimpsed in Scott, especially in *Redgauntlet*, even though language functions more reliably—like a container of the past and a medium of exchange between Darsie and Alan. They do not approach the past through language itself or transcend words to transport themselves backward in time, but in opposition to the Redgauntlets (of whom Darsie's uncle, Sir Hugh, is the latest avatar) they reconstruct a family drama, which in its very making empowers Darsie and Alan with an historical vision the Redgauntlets have denied.

As the fables of Steenie and the French architect suggest, the Redgauntlets and Sutpen have their own internal clocks which seemingly negate the normal functioning of time. Because they deride time, they appear to be superhuman, becoming the subjects of ghost stories. The Redgauntlets are portrayed as still communicating with the living even though they are in hell, and even after his death Sutpen is still said to haunt the Hundred. Sir Hugh Redgauntlet shrugs off the momentous defeat of 1745, and persists in believing that the Stuarts can be restored to the throne. After the holocaust of the Civil War Sutpen resumes an unflagging pursuit of his design, as if he has encountered only a momentary stoppage of his plans. Their view of time is essentially static, but their heroic efforts to recover from defeat make them seem dynamic.

Redgauntlet and Sutpen try to preserve the continuity of their plans through the family, but in fact destroy the family by rejecting the individual beliefs and feelings of its members. Sir Hugh Redgauntlet would rather kill his nephew Darsie than see him support the Hanoverian monarchy, just as Sir Alberick Redgauntlet, the first of his house, killed his own son because of a difference in political opinions between them. Sutpen is willing to risk his second son Henry's repudiation of the family rather than acknowledge his first son, because Charles Bon, whose mother was part Negro, is perceived as the "factor" which would destroy the design. Because both men are striving against the processes of time in which their families and societies have been undergoing radical changes, both men live long enough to become anachronisms—Redgauntlet desperately failing to shore up the "sinking cause" of Jacobitism, and Sutpen just as desperately failing in a third effort to rebuild his design.

By linking Darsie to Alan in the intimate bonds of friendship, and Quentin to Shreve in the intense and ever growing intimacy of the interpretative process, Scott and Faulkner are able to highlight the narrowness and provinciality of Redgauntlet and Sutpen against the broader and to that extent more sophisticated synthesis of the four youths. Alan and Shreve demand the explanations from Darsie and Quentin which make the latter two accountable to other points of view, in contradistinction to Redgauntlet and Sutpen who deem themselves answerable to no one. Alan, the fledgling lawyer, and Shreve, the future doctor, are soberminded but lively and imaginative young men who correct, but also sympathize with, their more dreamy, impractical friends. Initially they are skeptical and sometimes intolerant of Darsie's and Quentin's stories. Alan, for example, ignores the ominous implications of Darsie's first letter, attributing them solely to his friend's romantic imagination. Shreve parodies parts of the Sutpen legend and implies that its bizarre quality has more to do with Quentin's Southern-ness than with the meaning of the legend itself. But Alan must abandon his position as the objective critic of Darsie's activities and place himself directly within the unravelling pattern of action that reveals Darsie's true ancestry. On his journey to find his friend and to release him from captiv-ity, Alan also hears an account of Darsie's Redgauntlet forebears. He too suffers from illness and is caught within the net of conspiracy spread by Sir Hugh Redgauntlet, who plans to use his nephew to persuade other noble families to revolt against George III. Like Darsie, Alan is "overawed" by the audacity of a "demon" who would by force of will bend an entire kingdom to *his* reality. Similarly, Shreve feels compelled to recapitulate the events of the Sutpen story in his own fashion, but at the same time he takes up Miss Rosa's fascination with the "demon." Then he begins to reinterpret the Sutpen story, laying special emphasis on the relationship between Henry Sutpen and Charles Bon which so fascinates Quentin, and finally, cooperates with Quentin in actually recasting the whole story so that it accords with their joint analysis of what actually happened, and with the meaning both young men now attach to *their* story. Thus both Alan and Shreve find that they must project themselves emotionally and intellec-tually in their friends' problems, and it is this growing sense of identifica-tion between Darsie and Alan, Quentin and Shreve, that provides the impetus for the reassessment of the past in the two books.

In *Redgauntlet* Darsie and Alan successfully oppose the Redgauntlet tendency to isolate the family from reality and from the movement of his-tory, for throughout the novel these two young men see their destinies as complementary but not identical, requiring that they try to reconcile their differences but not restrict their independent courses of action. The Red-gauntlets, on the contrary, have nearly destroyed their family line by insist-ing on the undeviating uniformity of the family's actions and point of view. In *Redgauntlet,* therefore, a family line is retraced, the causes of its degen-eration are discovered, and the past is redeemed—in the sense that it is refashioned into a coherent constituent of the present, rather than remain-ing as simply a mysterious and fearful force.

As several of Scott's critics have suggested, his heroes (particularly Quentin Durward, Edward Waverley, Darsie Latimer, Francis Osbaldi-stone, and Henry Morton) are survivors. Their allegiance to an outmoded, romantic past is always carefully qualified by personality traits and circum-stances which guarantee their eventual accommodation with a rapidly changing present. Usually it is the urbane, sophisticated, and tolerant nar-rator of the novels who offers an overview of history and an insight into the development of historical consciousness. The resolutions of the plots in Scott's novels are worked out conveniently as resolutions of historical conflicts. In *Absalom, Absalom!* Faulkner eschews easy resolutions of plot and history. Indeed, he avoids the use of a well-made plot and views historical consciousness from within the development of the characters' inner and outer lives, so that there is no third-person narrator who can confidently summarize the meaning of the narratives as totalities. For Faulkner, historical consciousness is itself the problem; whereas for Scott, historical consciousness is the solution to the ignorance of his characters.

Faulkner indicates in the *Compson Appendix* the way in which historical consciousness and self-consciousness have become equated in the most self-defeating manner. Benjy's pasture has been sold to provide for Quentin's year at Harvard, and Quentin regards the sale as a futile gesture that only deprives Benjy of one of his few pleasures and reminds Quentin of the extremity of his plight. The dissolution of the Compson land is the end of the family's pretensions, not the beginning of Quentin's triumphs, not the start of a quest for self-sufficiency that a Quentin Durward is able to equate with a stable sense of history.

4

The Past as the Product of Historiography
in *Absalom, Absalom!*

In his book *William Faulkner: From Jefferson to the World* (1959), Hyatt Waggoner was the first critic to suggest that *Absalom, Absalom!* "has much in common with the best historiography of the thirties and of our own time." He believed that Faulkner's idea of history was consonant with Herbert Butterfield's essays on the philosophy of history, and with some of the writing of historical relativists like Becker and Beard. Even the form of the novel, Waggoner argued, with its presentation of the "clash of conflicting views of history" and Quentin and Shreve's "creative search" for meaning in history, was comparable to the method of historical works like Oscar Handlin's *Chance or Destiny: Turning Points in American History.*[1]

Cleanth Brooks also suggested, a few years later, that the story of Thomas Sutpen was a product of historical thinking, but as Waggoner himself noted in a subsequent article, "Cleanth Brooks had developed much the same line of thought—but without, apparently, being aware of how much this discussion overlapped with mine."[2] David Levin does not seem to have realized, at the time he wrote his essay on the problem of recreating history in *Absalom,*[3] that his central thesis—that history has a cumulative meaning enabling Quentin and Shreve to discover more about the Sutpens than any of the other narrators[4]—had already been adumbrated by Waggoner.[5] Indeed Levin placed so much stress on the reconstruction of the past that he failed to deal with Waggoner's and Brooks's contention that the analogy between the novel's method and historiography should not be pushed too far, that Quentin and Shreve were sometimes more like novelists than historians.

Waggoner suggested that "*Absalom* is the novel not denying its status as fiction but positively enlarging and capitalizing upon it." The book showed that "fiction is neither lie nor document but a kind of knowledge which has no substitute and to which there is no unimaginative shortcut." But his conclusion that "fiction is not unique in its dependence upon imagination and the necessary deviousness of its strategy"[6] was not in fact tested against the strategies modern historians employ to obtain their knowledge of the past. Brooks, for his part, said on the one hand that

> *Absalom, Absalom!* is a persuasive commentary upon the thesis that much of "history" is really a kind of imaginative construction. The past always remains at some level a mystery, but if we are to hope to understand it in any wise, we must enter into it and project ourselves imaginatively into the attitudes and emotions of the historical figures.[7]

On the other hand, he acknowledged that both Quentin and Shreve "show a good deal of the insights of the novelist and his imaginative capacity for constructing plausible motivations around a few given facts."[8]

Brooks does not make clear whether or not he sees Quentin's and Shreve's activities as novelists as compatible with the historian's reconstruction of the past. His first statement assumes that there is indeed a past to be reconstructed. To say that we must "project ourselves imaginatively into the attitudes and emotions of the historical figures" is to equate the ontological status of characters in fiction with that of historical figures in a work of history. We do indeed learn about characters in *Absalom, Absalom!* in much the same way as historians learn about historical figures, through letters, hearsay, conjecture, interviews, and eyewitness accounts, and the novel as a whole does partially satisfy one of R. G. Collingwood's "rules of method, from which the novelist or artist in general is free.... The historian's picture stands in peculiar relation to something called evidence."[9] But Brooks's second statement regarding the paucity of historical data in *Absalom, Absalom!* undermines its status as an historical narrative. Furthermore, he cautions:

> If the reader reminds himself how little hard fact there is to go on — how much of the most important information about the motivation of the central characters comes late and is, at best, vague and ambiguous — he will appreciate how much of the story of Sutpen and especially of Sutpen's children has been spun out of the imaginations of Quentin and Shreve.[10]

Brooks finds their interpretation plausible, but apparently there is not enough evidence in the novel to support their interpretation as an historical narrative. He makes no attempt to distinguish between what he calls "hard fact" and the abundance of circumstantial evidence of the kind noted on pp. 49–50 above, nor does he consider the general question of the importance of circumstantial evidence in historical narratives. Rather he is here siding with the skepticism of critics like Olga Vickery and Ilse Lind,[11] who doubt that Quentin and Shreve, or indeed any of the narrators, are recapturing anything more than a legend made up of the projections of their own minds.

Vickery and Lind concentrate on the "psychic bias"[12] of each narrator in order to show that each generation distorted history in its own image.[13] Yet, like Brooks, they recognize that the whole story is what provides them with a criterion for judging the faults of the individual narrators. Joshua McClennen clarifies this problem of the psychology of the narrators and the reliability of their stories by suggesting that each narrator's sense of history can be used by us as part of our criterion for judging what a true historical account of Sutpen must be.[14] As Faulkner himself once said, each narrator does see a part of the truth,[15] but each one's attempt to tell the story is also another attempt to explain his own biography.[16]

In support of Waggoner and McClennen's thesis that the novel presents the "clash of conflicting views of history," I observe that the narrators frequently direct attention to their method of retelling past events. As James Guetti remarks,

the narrative problem appears to be a defined psychological problem. But also like Mr. Compson, Rosa Coldfield's supposed psychological difficulties are questioned by her own awareness of the way in which they work; she insists, in fact, upon the fallibility of her perspective: *"there is no such thing as memory: the brain recalls just what the muscles grope for: no more, no less: and its resultant sum is usually incorrect and false and worthy only of the name of dream"* (143). If we say that she sees what she wants to see, we must also admit that she knows that she is doing so.[17]

Margaret Uroff notes, however, that after this passage Miss Rosa "returns to her brief against Sutpen [and] shows no indication that she considers her memory inaccurate or false; in fact she claims she remembers what she could not quite believe, and she goes on to provide a meticulous record of the whole process of Bon's burial and the long wait for Sutpen's return."[18] Uroff shows that still later Miss Rosa

evokes quite without intending to a much more sympathetic image of Sutpen, who is a man *"clinging, trying to cling with vain unsubstantial hands to what he hoped would hold him, save him, arrest him . . .* (p. 171). Sutpen's story gets away from Miss Rosa as she tells it and assumes a shape of its own even when she is trying to shape it to her own purposes. The realization dawns on Miss Rosa who, shocked by what she has done, draws back from this sympathetic image to attack it with the final comment: *"Dead? I cried. Dead? You? You lie; you're not dead; heaven cannot, and hell dare not, have you!"* (p. 172)[19]

There is, then, within her view of Sutpen as demon a suggestion of its opposite that no "psychic bias" can dispel. She can shy away from her contradictions, but she will unwittingly help other interpreters to get more out of her narrative than she intends.

Mr. Compson (100–101) and Quentin and Shreve (324) all recognize that the past they create may not have existed at all. But this very awareness suggests a critical attitude toward historical knowledge which stimulates the search for an adequate explanation of past events. As R. G. Collingwood said in his rebuttal of Descartes's skeptical attitude toward history:

> To say that historical narratives relate events that cannot have happened is to say that we have some criterion, other than the narratives which reach us, by which to judge what could have happened. Descartes is here adumbrating a genuinely critical attitude in history which if fully developed would be the answer to his own objection.[20]

In this connection Ilse Lind has noted that as the Sutpen story grows in significance, we also progress in our ability to detect the distortions in the various versions of the story.[21] The skill is acquired not just through a comparison of the various narratives but through our sense of the Sutpen story—a sense which is larger than the sum of the narratives combined. The ultimate criterion for judging the narratives which reach us is our own stimulated sense of the past's reality. The sources we rely upon do not in themselves add up to a coherent history. As Herbert Butterfield suggests:

> It is when the reader can feel...that the man about whom the stories are being told really lived although the stories about him may not all be true; it is when the thread of incident in the novel, as well as what might be called the texture of the book, can in some way be called "historical," that the work is most effective in its grip on actuality.[22]

It is precisely in its "texture" that *Absalom, Absalom!* resembles a work of historical interpretation, for the narrators are engaged in what historiographers call the "history of history"—a description of which is given in Butterfield's historiographical study, *George III and the Historians*:

> Perhaps the ideal kind of history is the kind in which a story is given and events are presented in motion, but the story is re-told so to speak "in depth", so that it acquires a new dimension; it is both structure and narrative combined. This has been achieved on occasion by scholars and writers; and here, where history is both a story and a study, one may gain a profounder insight into both the ways of men and the processes of time.[23]

As the four narrators retell the Sutpen story, the story itself acquires a new dimension. In particular, the story changes as Quentin and Shreve gain experience in interpreting past events, and as they learn to put the results of previous interpretation into a coherent structure. It is in this way that the novel is both the story of Sutpen and the study of that story combined.

Patricia Tobin has questioned the validity of this interpretation of the "novel as history."[24] She suggests that only after several readings of the book, and after a "plot summary" has been constructed, is "the critic" able to perceive *Absalom, Absalom!* as a novel which focuses on change and development in the manner of an historical work: "The reader in the process of confronting the book knows only its impediments. Historical realism has been best served by an omniscient and trustworthy narrator."[25] It does not seem valid, however, to make such absolute distinctions between "the critic" and "the reader" in dealing with a novel which forces all of its readers to make so many "critical" choices between conflicting versions of past events. *Absalom, Absalom!* seems to invite repeated readings precisely because there are these "impediments" to be overcome. "Historical realism" is not dependent on an "omniscient and trustworthy narrator" but on the testimony of many narrators or "authorities" whom the reader and the historian subject to rigorous criticism. "Historical realism" is not something given to us by a reliable narrator; on the contrary, it is earned through our insight and analysis.

Professor Tobin points out that for Miss Rosa and Mr. Compson "Sutpen belongs to a time which they cannot enter, retrieve, or comprehend — a mythical time that is absolutely discontinuous with the historical time in which they live."[26] But I suggest that within Miss Rosa's and Mr. Compson's mythic readings there are elements which Quentin and Shreve seize upon in order to construct an historical account of the Sutpen story. For the two young men are uncovering the historical foundations of a myth. And certainly Sutpen's own words and the biography of his life given in Chapter VII must contradict Professor Tobin's assertion that Sutpen's "presence is so overwhelming and inscrutable that it seems to forbid his inclusion in a plot that is comprised of realistic elements."[27] Only Miss Rosa approaches such a totally mythic view of the man.

Professor Tobin completely ignores Mr. Compson's contribution to Quentin and Shreve's "construction of a plausible narrative about" Sutpen's "descendants," and she therefore exaggerates Quentin and Shreve's shift from subject matter of "a mythical character to an historical plot."[28] She tends to break the novel's structure in two and to juxtapose mythical and historical interpretations, whereas Quentin and Shreve's "plausible narrative" actually grows out of the novel as a whole. She also seems to suggest that Quentin and Shreve depart from their "historical plot" when "they place themselves in a mythic mode of thought, when their whole being rejects the search for objective logic which dominates their minds."[29] But if most historians would not go as far as Quentin and Shreve do in identifying with historical figures, historians like R. G. Collingwood, Herbert Butterfield, and Martin Duberman suggest that much more than "objective logic" is needed to understand historical figures, and that empathy and the ability to recreate and to follow the mental processes of historical figures are absolutely crucial to a convincing reconstruction of the past.[30]

Indeed Martin Duberman forthrightly acknowledges the need for Faulkner's type of historiography, in which the personality of the historian (narrator) enters into the process of turning the historical events into an historical narrative:

> Every historian knows that he manipulates the evidence to some extent simply because of who he is (or is not), of what he selects (or omits), of how well (or badly) he empathizes and communicates. Those "fallibilities" have been frequently confessed in the abstract. Yet the *process* by which a particular personality intersects with a particular subject matter has rarely been shown, and the intersection itself almost never regarded as containing materials of potential worth. Because "objectivity" has been the ideal, the personal components that go into historical reconstruction have not been candidly revealed, made accessible to scrutiny.
>
> This book [*Black Mountain: An Exploration in Community*] is an effort. . .to let the reader see who the historian is and the process by which he interacts with the data—the actual process, not the smoothed-over end result, the third person voice, or no voice at all. My conviction is that when a historian allows more of himself to show—his feelings, fantasies and needs, not merely his skills at information-retrieval, organization and analysis—he is *less* likely to contaminate the data, simply because there is less pretense that he and it are one.[31]

Duberman is insisting that the historian show the process by which he develops as an historian. Only by demonstrating that all historical thinking and writing is a fusion on several levels of the historian and the history he interprets will history's existence as a contemporary event, which vibrates "in the historian's mind," be revealed.[32]

F. Garvin Davenport Jr., Harry B. Henderson III, and John W. Hunt all follow Hyatt Waggoner in suggesting that *Absalom, Absalom!* is complementary to works of twentieth-century historiography. Davenport observes that ten years before the writing of the novel "Carl Becker had noted that the historian cannot deal with the event of the past itself since the past has disappeared. What he can deal with is the 'statement about the event,' an affirmation of the event. 'In truth,' Becker goes on, 'the actual past is gone; and the world of history is an intangible world, recreated imaginatively, and *present in our minds*'" (my emphasis).[33] Duberman and Faulkner go beyond Becker in exploring the personal content of the imaginative recreation of history. Behind Duberman's dissatisfaction with history as it is presently written is an attack on the assumption that emotion and intellect are antithetical, and that the historian must therefore rid his narrative of the personal motivations which might color and perhaps harm his reconstruction of the evidence. As in *Absalom, Absalom!*, the "feelings, fantasies and needs" of the historian do not necessarily distort the past which he must recreate—on the contrary, precisely out of the interaction between the historian and the past there may come materials of the greatest potential worth. Duberman's historian and Faulkner's narrators, by virtue of their personalities as well as of their intellects, bring a great measure of understanding to otherwise impenetrable past events.

A strong trend in recent criticism of *Absalom, Absalom!* has denied or subordinated interest in the novel's historicity. John Irwin's book, in particular, has weighted nearly all of the critical concern on Quentin's side in order to show how *Absalom, Absalom!* continues "the struggle between the father and son in the incest complex"[34] begun in *The Sound and the Fury*. Governing Quentin's obsession with the Sutpens (Thomas, Henry, Charles, and Judith) is his compulsion to repeat the story of his incestuous feelings for Caddy. His tormented dialogue with a father who will not validate the son's conflicting feelings, and his futile effort to defend his sister's virtue in front of her lover, Dalton Ames, who refuses to fight Quentin or to even acknowledge there is a moral principle worth fighting for, are essential to Irwin's reading of *Absalom, Absalom!*.

Much more sophisticated than Estella Schoenberg's book, which holds *Absalom, Absalom!* hostage to *The Sound and the Fury*, Irwin's study argues for "that imaginative space that the novels create *in between* themselves by their interaction."[35] In her discussion of *Collected Stories,* Lisa Paddock has cogently demonstrated that Faulkner clearly designed his fiction to be "at once reflexive and continuous" and in accord with his esthetic theory that "the truths of a literary work lie in its interstices, its silences."[36] Thus Irwin must be right in supposing that Faulkner expected readers of *The Sound and the Fury* to carry with them a background that would enrich their reading of *Absalom, Absalom!*.

The ambiguous issue, of course, is how that background can be applied to a subsequent novel. Schoenberg is surely wrong to say that *Absalom, Absalom!* is incomplete for readers who do not know *The Sound and the Fury.*[37] Rather, the former is a different novel when taken by itself, more a novel of history that is about Sutpen and his heirs—his children and his interpreters—and about Quentin, who "is less a person than a severely disoriented state of consciousness evoked by relatives and neighbors who constantly impose upon him, willy-nilly, haunting images of the past."[38] Knowing Quentin from *The Sound and the Fury* intensifies the reality of the Sutpen story in the present time of *Absalom, Absalom!*. As Faulkner put it, "he is the protaganist so that it is not complete apocrypha."[39] The "full foreground action," as Hunt calls it, gives "historical credibility" to Sutpen's story:

In this way, each of the two stories turns upon the other, so that the question at the base of Faulkner's own search for ["more out of the story itself than a historical novel would be"] — how does the past become the historical past? — is answered in a plot of the narrative present in which Faulkner creates the conditions for individuals of diverse interests and temperaments to create a specific history.[40]

Hunt's last phrases are telling, for as Irwin presses his analysis of *Absalom, Absalom!* in the light of *The Sound and the Fury* he forgets the later novel's specificity and diversity. It is as if *Absalom, Absalom!* were collapsed into the earlier novel's second section.

To say that Faulkner's fiction is "reflexive and continuous" is to suggest a turning backward in order to modify as well as extend what has gone before. As I will argue in Chapter 7, Faulkner did not feel bound by the precedent of earlier work. No novel was simply an extension of its predecessor; on the contrary, as Gary Lee Stonum has recently held, each new work grew out of and reacted against past fictions.[41]

Schoenberg is mistaken in her claim that "*The Sound and the Fury* and *Absalom, Absalom!* constitute a 'multi-novel or dual-novel.'"[42] True, the Quentins of both works seem entirely consistent, and one can usefully elaborate on Quentin's attitudes in the earlier novel to amplify his stance in the later one — as both Irwin and Schoenberg do — but Guerard's admonition stands: "our feelings for one Quentin should not *control* our feelings for the other."[43] As I argued in Chapter 2, Faulkner's Sartoris novels are not unified by a single plan or structure, and *The Unvanquished* is not, in any strict sense, a sequel — or even a retroactive prelude — to *Flags in the Dust.* I see no reason to regard *The Sound and the Fury* and *Absalom, Absalom!* as a much closer pair.

In the text of *Absalom, Absalom!* Faulkner scrupulously avoids reference to Quentin's suicide, to Caddy, to Benjy — to all the Compson relationships, preferring instead to focus on the discourse between father and son. Naturally, the discourse would skirt the edges of *The Sound and the Fury* and generate the imaginative space between the novels to which Irwin refers, but Faulkner deliberately avoided shaping *Absalom, Absalom!* as simply a projection of Quentin's mind.

Quentin, no matter how far his mind wanders from the dialogue with others, is placed in a social and historical reality rather than being sectioned off to pursue wholly private fantasies. Beginning with Miss Rosa, he is forced to attend to the ramifications of his heritage — as others seem to define those ramifications. History — the past as fact and fiction — cannot be evaded by tracing a single character's pathology, or even by positing the existence of a psychological structure "created by means of an interplay between texts."[44] Irwin claims to be oscillating between "two or more texts at once," as in the "solving of a simultaneous equation,"[45] yet it is the Quentin of *The Sound and the Fury* who is used as the basis of comparison. In a sense, by putting *The Sound and the Fury* first, Irwin imagines the work Faulkner refused to write in *Absalom, Absalom!* when he deleted in manuscript a single reference to Quentin's death[46] that might have led to a convergence of the two novels and to the deprivation of the latter's integrity. A considerable gap opens up, therefore, between Irwin's aims and practices.

There is, however, an interplay between characters within *Absalom, Absalom!*: "The novel forces the reader constantly to oscillate from son to father, from the dreamed to the dreamer, from the created to the creator, from the narrated to the narrators."[47] For all the emphasis on distortion, bias and so on, this dialectical method insures an objectivity and a historiography that subsumes the peculiarities of individual accounts. It is historical consciousness and never personal consciousness alone that is the subject of *Absalom, Absalom!*.

Sutpen's tragedy, indeed, is his lack of historical consciousness, his inability to adjust his sense of the past to the present, as Faulkner did in viewing the design of his career from the vantage point of each new creation. Sutpen's tragedy can be explained in terms of this need to make the past a part of one's own contemporary experience. He could not see the past as part of the continuum of time and of his own life. He wanted a son. He valued man's efforts to extend himself in time through his offspring but destroyed the possibility of such an extension in his own case. In a sense his actions imply a denial of the historical knowledge of life, because they were part of an abstract pattern or "design" which isolated him from others and thus from the interaction between the self and the world upon which a sense of history is founded. As the narrators scrutinize his career, and as they interact with each other, we begin to see the ramifications of his denial. Consequently the novel also becomes the story of the four narrators' attempts to acquire a sense of history that is great enough to measure the dimensions of Sutpen's own ignorance of history.

Sutpen grows up in the West Virginia mountains where caste and color problems and land ownership are virtually unknown. Family attachments are only thought of in terms of everyday life, and there is no sense of genealogy, of pride in family line. When his family moves away from the mountain community, Sutpen does not know whether his father is leaving home or returning to it, nor even whether his father is moving in the direction of the future (to new land) or the past (where he was born). In not knowing whether his father "wanted to remember" Sutpen cannot even tell what his father's feelings about the past may have been, or even whether his father was conscious of the past (223). It is as though Sutpen were suffering from amnesia. If his father had some definite reason for moving,

Sutpen has long ago forgotten what it was. In leaving the mountain community Sutpen abandons what little background and tradition he may have possessed. In starting out on a journey with no purpose in mind his family destroys any possible sense of continuity between the generations.

What limited sense of time the young Sutpen may have had is eroded by the long journey "not progressing parallel in time but descending perpendicularly through temperature and climate" (224), and led by an "insensible" father. Sutpen loses track of his age; members of his family vanish (226) without much notice being taken of their disappearance. The sense of moving, but going in no linear direction, of family members dropping off into nothing, makes time seem static. Taking an individual or two from the scene seems to make no difference in the general scheme of things. Time, in short, impresses no mark upon the child Sutpen's life: "So he knew neither where he had come from nor where he was nor why" (227).

Sutpen's most impressive experience takes place when, at the age of fourteen, he is sent to the planter's mansion with a message from his father. He approaches the front door expecting to obtain some acknowledgement of his message, but is turned away before he can announce his intentions. He is profoundly shocked and considers the rebuff a direct attack on his integrity and individual worth. After this episode, all that he has vaguely observed—his father beating a Negro for no apparent reason, his sister's refusal to move aside before the planter's carriage, the very idea of owning land, of basing individual worth on one's position in a caste or class, or on one's color—comes rushing into his consciousness and coalesces into a picture of a world that deprives him of his dignity. But he is perplexed about what he should do in such an intolerable world: "He was seeking among what little he had to call experience for something to measure it by, and he couldn't find anything" (233). To Sutpen society is a static entity with no historical dimension. His only solution is to imitate the wealthy planter who had denied him a respected place in the community.

The rest of Sutpen's career and even the way he tells his story show that he never did find any criterion by which to judge whether his imitation of the planter was the right course to pursue. His autobiography takes the form of specific scenes and episodes usually presented without any sense of continuity (239, 240, 244, 246).

A good example of precisely how Sutpen thinks occurs as he is hunting down the French architect. After describing to General Compson his resolution to go to the West Indies, he immediately shifts to his account of himself in the "besieged Haitian room" trying to put down the slave insurrection:

> This anecdote was no deliberate continuation of the other one but was merely called to his mind by the *picture* of the niggers and torches in front of them [himself and General

Compson]; he not telling how he got there, what had happened during the six years between that day when he had decided to go to the West Indies and become rich, and this night when, overseer or foreman or something to a French sugar planter, he was barricade[d] in the house with the planter's family. (246, my emphasis)

The reason for Sutpen's memory of the next "anecdote" is that his running down of the French architect is obviously similar to his own desperate circumstances during the slave revolt when it appeared that he would be overrun and captured.[48] One spectacle or "picture" stimulates in him the memory of another without his being able to compare the two situations or even link them chronologically. Thus his mind works in a way that is similar to Benjy's in *The Sound and the Fury*. As Quentin says, commenting on Sutpen's narrative method, he was "getting himself and Grandfather both into that besieged Haitian room as simply as he got himself to the West Indies" (246).

Sutpen provides the material for historical inquiry precisely because he is so "innocent," so naive, so unconscious of the parts of his story that do not make sense to General Compson. In particular, he seems unaware that his brief references to his wife and child must excite curiosity (240, 249, 252, 264, 274). General Compson must ask Sutpen to "wait," just as Shreve asks Quentin, so that some transition can be established between the different parts of the story. But unlike Quentin, Sutpen cannot improve his story very much. The best he is able to do is to "stop and back up and start over again with at least some regard for cause and effect even if none for logical sequence and continuity" (247). Richard Poirier remarks:

Such an inability to tell his own story is indicative of Sutpen's refusal to believe that anyone could have any interest in his past activity. He can ignore the details of his past because, as far as he is concerned, they hold no portent of his future. In terms of his "design," he has achieved a self-identification beyond anything that has been done or can be done to him.[49]

In the Haitian dark Sutpen seems unaware of the significance of the rebellion. Perhaps this is why he is able to break its spirit so firmly: his actions deny the workings of history; his indomitability cancels out what is surely General Compson's understanding, not Sutpen's, of the "thousand secret dark years" (249), "the two-hundred years of oppression."[50] Sutpen "believed (Grandfather said) that earth was kind and gentle and that darkness was merely something you saw, or could not see in; overseeing what he oversaw and not knowing that he was overseeing it" (251–52). Sutpen does not for a moment consider that the darkness he sees might actually be inside himself: he is in the heart of darkness, but unlike Kurtz, he fails to see the horror. He entirely lacks Quentin's consciousness of the burdens that history places upon the present: to him the uprising is a "spectacle" (250) but not a stage in a developing history which includes himself. Sutpen cannot even identify with some parts of his own past:

> He was telling a story. He was not bragging about something he had done; he was just telling a story about something a man named Thomas Sutpen had experienced, which would still have been the same story if the man had had no name at all, if it had been told about any man or no man over whiskey at night. (247)

Perhaps this is why Sutpen fails to see the similarity between his childhood memory of the man in the hammock being served by the Negro (228) and the service of his own Wash Jones. In demeaning Jones he does not see that he is, in a way, demeaning himself, since Jones comes from the same poor white background as Sutpen himself. Past and present never intersect each other in Sutpen's point of view, and in reading R. G. Collingwood's criticism of Arnold Toynbee's view of history, one can begin to see why Sutpen's way of perceiving past experience is inimical to historical knowledge:

> He never reaches the conception of historical knowledge as the re-enactment of the past in the historian's mind. He regards history as a mere *spectacle*, something consisting of facts observed and recorded by the historian, phenomena presented externally to his gaze, not experiences into which he must enter and which he must make his own.[51] (my emphasis)

Each of the narrators of Sutpen's career must face just this problem: how to reenact the past so that it becomes "experiences into which he must enter and which he must make his own."

Although she expresses no sympathy for Sutpen himself, Miss Rosa, the first narrator of Sutpen's career, gives us an extremely insightful portrayal of how he appeared to his contemporaries. Her family was deeply implicated in Sutpen's search for respectability and in his success in settling down in the hostile environment of Jefferson. Her sister Ellen married Sutpen and willingly supported his grand plan to establish a family of wealth and prestige. Goodhue Coldfield, her father, was corrupted into abetting Sutpen in one of his shady schemes for material profit. Furthermore, Coldfield's miserliness, his calculation of profit and loss, were as abstract and mechanical as Sutpen's impotent logic and morality.[52] Although respected by the community, Coldfield was an alien figure who shut himself up in an attic during the Civil War rather than cooperate in what he saw as the waste of material wealth.[53] After the war, Sutpen is reduced to a parody of Coldfield, the miserly shopkeeper, as he isolates himself from the community and bargains with Indians and Negroes over the few trinkets he sells in a small store set up on his once prosperous land.

Like her father, Miss Rosa at first collaborates with Sutpen, and then is shocked by the consequences of her collaboration. Sutpen proposes that they try an experimental coupling in order to see whether she can produce a male heir for him. Like her father, she eventually exiles herself from the community, thus intensifying her resemblance to the outcast Sutpen, the man whom she professes to hate. Her voluntary isolation may also remind us of how consonant her adult behavior is with her childhood, which, like Sutpen's, was one of "spartan solitude" (140). She has very little background with which to measure her experiences in the world, her outrage at Sutpen's insult, just as Sutpen had no standard by which he could evaluate his rejection at the planter's front door. As a result, Miss Rosa has very little sense of time as a continuum. For her, as for Sutpen, all change is abrupt and without transition, without explanation. Quentin's impression of her narrative reminds us very much of Sutpen's pictorial imagination:

> Out of quiet thunderclap he would abrupt (man-horse-demon) upon a scene peaceful and decorous as a *schoolprize water color,* faint sulphur-reek still in hair clothes and beard, with grouped behind him his band of wild niggers like beasts half tamed to walk upright like men, in attitudes wild and reposed, and manacled among them the French architect with his air grim, haggard, and tatter-ran. (8, my emphasis)

She paints a childlike picture with no lifelike dimension to it; or rather, the picture is of a conventional type until Sutpen crashes through with a dynamism that baffles and astounds Miss Rosa. In Miss Rosa's telling, events separated by long intervals of time, such as Sutpen's first entrance into Jefferson and the architect's later escape, are telescoped into a single image, just as Sutpen himself condenses into two "anecdotes" the Haitian room and his original trip to Haiti six years earlier.

From the very beginning of the novel the narrator himself associates Miss Rosa with Sutpen. Sutpen's mansion, for example, is "unpainted and a little shabby, yet with an air, a quality of grim endurance as though like her it had been created to fit into and complement a world in all ways a little smaller than the one in which it found itself" (10). Miss Rosa's narrative, like Sutpen's design, is too simple, insufficiently commensurate with the complexity of the world she seeks to explain. Sutpen conceives of a design which rejects anything that is not incremental to it. He must keep faith only with himself in order to succeed. Rosa Coldfield's story also has a narrow design which insists on treating Sutpen exclusively as a demon. The way she bases her whole story solely on her attitude toward Sutpen is very similar to Sutpen's own obsession with his rejection at the planter's front door.

But where Sutpen is simply ignorant of the fact that the past has any special relevance to the present, Miss Rosa positively denies the possibility of historical knowledge. Her concept of mind is as mechanical as Sutpen's, relying on the trigger of "sense, sight, smell," but it is consciously expressed as a rejection of history. Where Sutpen claims he cannot remember his past, Miss Rosa claims that there is very little of the past which can ever be accurately remembered (143)—although, as Uroff has shown, she recalls more than she realizes. In seeing the French architect chased by his wild Negroes, he is stimulated to recall a similar "sense, sight, smell" experience in the past. Miss Rosa and Sutpen are automatons in this respect: as John Hagan puts it, "each compulsively continues to respond to a single peculiar stimulus with which his past history is crucially assorted—the smell of wistaria in Rosa's case and the smell and taste of sugar in Sutpen's."[54] For Sutpen, the smell and taste of sugar recall the burning of the cane in Haiti during the slave revolt. For Rosa, the smell of wistaria recalls the summer of her barren youth. But both the smell and the taste do no more than summon up the past which itself remains in stasis, blocking their consciousness of time as a process in which past experience is reinterpreted as well as recalled.

Perhaps the most limiting aspect of Miss Rosa as a narrator is also what makes her most like Sutpen. She cannot generalize from her own experiences; she disregards or is incapable of discovering in them the universal element which could be used to understand Sutpen. While describing her adult experiences in Chapter V Miss Rosa assigns to herself some measure of blame for her attempt to cooperate with Sutpen. Yet she constantly brings up the mitigating circumstances of the war years as if to prevent censure of her behavior. She never concedes that another set of extenuating circumstances in Sutpen's life might equally help to account for his seemingly bizarre career.

At times, however, Miss Rosa may be vaguely aware that there are some contradictions in her account of character and circumstances. At one point she declares that Sutpen impulsively proposed intercourse without marriage; at another she conjectures that he must have thought of such a proposal for "*a day, a week, even a month maybe*" (171).[55] Her second conjecture implies a degree of ratiocination in Sutpen which she usually will not admit. Perhaps in order to protect herself from such speculation, she takes refuge in an absolute standard that will not countenance any excuses for herself or Sutpen. Perhaps this is why she obsessively repeats that she holds "*no brief, no pity*" for herself (164, see also 159, 163, 165).

Our later knowledge of Sutpen's childhood enables us to see him somewhat differently from Miss Rosa, but her eyewitness descriptions of the adult Sutpen prevent us from losing sight of the monstrous being into which he transformed himself. Thus Miss Rosa's initial interpretation, however biased, sets up the context in which we must perceive Sutpen, just as many initial interpretations of historical figures and events establish the terms by which historians then pursue their interpretations of the past. As Herbert Butterfield points out:

> The starting-point for historical interpretation must lie in the ideas of the people who were living while the events in question were taking place. Their way of envisaging their struggles and formulating the issues of the time provides the historian with his initial framework. This version may continue to be reproduced for a long period; yet it may actually have been devised to serve as a weapon in the conflict which the historian is trying to narrate.[56]

Miss Rosa, then, is the only narrator who can supply the authenticity of a contemporary's attitude toward Sutpen. At the same time, we know that her account is used as a weapon against the man who corrupted her family and even seduced Miss Rosa herself into abetting his design.

Just how much of the past's actual impact is felt through Miss Rosa's narration is measured by Mr. Compson's commentary on what is to him the shadowy remoteness of the past. Immense changes that have occurred in a relatively short period of time seem to make the life of the past look incredibly simple, devoid of the complexity and ambiguity of modern life. Thus, for different reasons, Mr. Compson agrees with Miss Rosa that historical knowledge may not be possible. To him the fact of change itself suggests that all knowledge of the past is tenuous and insecure, and the growing instability of contemporary consciousness makes it appear still more doubtful that past and present can be integrated in a single narrative. He reinforces Miss Rosa's reading of Sutpen in the sense that he maintains that the characters are "not dwarfed and involved but distinct, uncomplex" (89).

But perhaps because of his bafflement, his suspicion that the present is estranged from the past, he feels a greater need to explain that Sutpen was, in some ways, a rational human being who confronted and, to some extent, succeeded in mastering a difficult situation (37). His view is much more objective than Miss Rosa's, but it is considerably less passionate, less attuned than hers to pick up any sense of what it was like to live with Sutpen. At a greater distance from the events he describes, Mr. Compson takes note of all the evidence he can scrape together and tries to reconcile the divergent and contradictory reports of Sutpen's career. Yet he acknowledges his failure to make sense of the evidence (100–101). Mr. Compson errs, I think, in believing that reconstructing the past is like a "chemical formula." His materialism is not so crass or unsophisticated as Miss Rosa's or Sutpen's, but he still tends to discount, as they do, the interpretative processes of the mind. It is not the relics of a bygone age, the meager indications of what was once a fully experienced life, that explain the past; rather the past is made imaginable by the intricate connections such as Mr. Compson himself is able to make between the human thoughts and activities suggested by this evidence. As R. G. Collingwood observes in his discussion of Hegel, history consists of "empirical events" which are the "outward expressions of thought, and the thoughts behind the events — not the events themselves" — make possible a "chain of logically connected concepts. When you only look at the events and not at the thoughts behind them you see no necessary connexion at all."⁵⁷ Mr. Compson has failed to make enough connections and, in his disappointment, he supposes that the very notion of reconstructing the past has been discredited.

Mr. Compson is at his best when he is trying to make sense of a part of the Sutpen story which obviously interests him, and where he must make the "connexions." He is fascinated with Charles Bon, perhaps because Bon is a good deal like himself. Compare, for example, Mr. Compson's letter to Quentin with Bon's letter to Judith.⁵⁸ Bon's letter reveals his concern with the subject of time, with the war that is just ending, and thus with a part of life which, to borrow Mr. Compson's phrase, is now "dead." Mr. Compson's letter describes Miss Rosa's funeral, and notes that now that she has passed away the Sutpen story too may reach its ultimate conclusion in her death. In a way both Bon and Mr. Compson are wrong about the disappearance of the past: Bon's letter lives on in Judith's thoughts and eventually finds its way into the Compson family's hands; Mr. Compson's letter continues to reverberate in Quentin's mind at Harvard and is eventually conveyed to Shreve. As I pointed out earlier, Quentin also seems fascinated by the resemblance of the letters to each other, and keeps juxtaposing the two of them in his memories of his trips to Sutpen's Hundred in Chapter VI. Some passages in the letters even seem to echo each other in style and content. Compare Bon's tentative thoughts on peace after four years of war with Mr. Compson's qualified hope that Miss Rosa's forty years of outrage have somehow been resolved by her own death:

[Bon:] *So that means that it is dawn again and that I must stop. Stop what? You will say. Why, thinking, remembering — remark that I do not say, hoping — —*(131)

[Mr. Compson:] *It will do no harm to hope — You see I have written hope, not think. So let it be hope.* (377)

In a curious way there is a continuity between these two letters, between past and present, which both men have tried to deny. Bon's letter is inscribed on seventy-year-old French stationery, *"the best of the old South which is dead,"* but the words themselves *"were written upon it with the best* [stove polish]...*of the new North*" (131–32). Mr. Compson's letter comes written in his "sloped whimsical ironic hand out of Mississippi attenuated, into the iron snow" (377) of New England, to be read by his son Quentin, now attending college in the North among those whose ancestors conquered his land.

In suggesting that there is this curious continuity between the two letters, and between the two men, I am not forgetting that Mr. Compson's portrayal is also a projection of himself into an historical figure. The contrast of the older, cosmopolitan, rather fatalistic Bon to the adolescent, provincial, and idealistic Henry is similar to the relationship between Mr. Compson and his own son Quentin. Mr. Compson imagines that Bon attempted to persuade Henry that his objections to the octoroon mistress were not in accord with the values generally held by sophisticated and mature men: the world must be accepted for what it is; it cannot be rejected because it does not measure up to what the protestor had supposed it to be. Bon's argument reminds us of Mr. Compson's counsel to Quentin in *The Sound and the Fury* that his chivalric emotions and attitudes will gradually disappear as he gains more experience in the actual ways of the world.

Once we know that the real trouble between Henry and Bon was not the octoroon mistress but incest and miscegenation, then we can no longer credit Mr. Compson's all too static version of Bon's character (93). As with Miss Rosa, Mr. Compson reverts to a mechanical explanation of human behavior when he does not understand what in fact were the motivations of the historical figures. The description of Bon as observing the situation as though he were "watching the muscles in an anesthetized frog" (93) seems more appropriate to Mr. Compson's own attitude of scientific detached speculation than to Bon.

Even from the passage just quoted, however, Quentin and Shreve retain Mr. Compson's belief that Bon withdrew into a mysterious passivity after Henry had repudiated Sutpen (335), although they account for his seeming indifference by reconstructing a whole new set of motivations for him. He was, they believe, in despair over his father's refusal to acknowledge him (333). Similarly, Mr. Compson's suggestion that Henry chose Bon as his "brother-in-law" so that he could commit "the pure and perfect incest" (96) must appeal to Quentin, who has—if we accept *The Sound and the Fury* as relevant evidence—a similar obsession with his sister Caddy. Mr. Compson's description of Bon as the outsider in the Southern community who comes from another culture and brings a different set of values into the Sutpen world may in turn appeal to Shreve, who also stands outside of the tradition in which the Sutpen story is retold.[59] In other words, even though Mr. Compson may emphasize the closeness of Henry and

Charles as a quasi-father-son relationship rather than a brother-to-brother or friend-to-friend relationship, these other possibilities are clearly inherent in his own narrative.

However much in error he may be, then, Mr. Compson's choice of episodes and his attempt to place human action into understandable contexts mark his narrative as a major advance toward Quentin and Shreve's interpretation.[60] As W. B. Gallie says of historical explanations,

> not only do they enable the historian to classify and clarify and endorse facts which at first seem puzzling or improbable, they help him to enlarge his vision of the context and potential relevance of particular actions and episodes. In fact, the quest for explanations is a main cause of the "outward drive" of historical interests—away from contemporary and parochial happenings to a larger, more complete and more complex presentation of the surrounding whole.[61]

Mr. Compson's emphasis on Bon's role in the Sutpen story helpfully shifts attention from Miss Rosa's parochial obsession with Sutpen and leads to the discovery that Sutpen's story is linked to events that occurred far away from the immediate locality of Jefferson, Mississippi, from the South which Miss Rosa sees as doomed. Mr. Compson's explanations inevitably enlarge the facts, making more of them than he himself is aware of, very much in line with Collingwood's emphasis upon history as "a kind of knowledge in which questions about ideas and questions about facts are not distinguishable,"[62] and with David Levin's view that interpretation itself becomes part of the historical evidence.[63] Once again, Mr. Compson is clearly wrong to suppose that one is ever confronted with only "initials," "letters," "nicknames."[64]

Confronted with this fusion and confusion of fact and interpretation, Quentin and Shreve bring to the Sutpen story a deeper understanding of human interaction than Sutpen, Miss Rosa, or Mr. Compson have displayed. By boldly using their own sympathetic friendship as a guide to reenacting the emotions and attitudes of the historical figures, they transcend the block of time that is separating them from the past. That they are talking to each other throughout their reconstruction of the past is of the utmost importance in explaining how they go beyond the other versions of the Sutpen story, and how they exceed the historian's normal reach and control over his subject matter. There is something inherently dramatic and life-giving in their portrayal of the relationship between Charles and Henry. We seem not only to gain knowledge about the past, but also to regain some of its actual experience. As Martin Duberman suggests, the historian cannot rival the verisimilitude of "the spoken word, which benefits from the direct confrontation of personality.... If we [as historians] could bring the spoken word's immediacy and emotion to the presentation of history, a new richness of response, a new measure of involvement with the past, would be possible."⁶⁵ All of *Absalom, Absalom!* enlivens history through the spoken words of its narrators, but the "direct confrontation of personality" between Quentin and Shreve brings to the story of Sutpen's career "a new richness of response, a new measure of involvement with the past."

But because the spoken word is so much the peculiar product of a particular speaker, it is often imprecise, unrefined, sometimes unreflective, and therefore especially dangerous to invoke in attempted reconstructions of the past. In *Absalom, Absalom!*, however, the narrator clearly identifies those moments in which Quentin and Shreve do no more than project their own feelings into the historical figures. Similarly, Duberman recognizes that a call for immediacy and emotion in the presentation of the past often subverts the historian's traditional task of presenting facts rather than moral truths or philosophical statements or even past experience as such. Nevertheless, a more conventional historian like Herbert Butterfield agrees that in order to make sense of the "facts" the historian must take some risks. He should reach beyond the written documents and evidence of the historical figure's conscious intentions and drive below to the motivations underlying human actions in the past:

> The historian may need to have a *feeling* — a sort of *sympathetic sense* — for areas of life and history where he knows that the evidence must be lacking. We may suspect that historical personages are like icebergs and though certain protruding parts of them are visible to posterity, the greater proportion of them is always submerged. The written evidence is inadequate, and if we take each piece of testimony, and draw a line from one point to another, we may produce a system or a *picture*, but the result is liable to be a caricature. (my emphasis)⁶⁶

But Butterfield cautions that the historian must often settle for a kind of knowledge different from that which Quentin and Shreve eventually obtain:

> All of us will be able to realize on the one hand how easy it is for a man to cheat his biographer, and, on the other hand, how little the people around us at the present day can know or understand of our profounder internal life. A man like Martin Luther must have taken some of his fondest secrets with him to the grave; and certainly the historian must often be defeated — must expect to be defeated — on those issues of private feeling and ultimate motive which are a mystery even to intimate contemporary friends, and which so often lie between a man and his Maker.⁶⁷

Shreve and Quentin, nonetheless, do attempt to penetrate Bon's fondest secrets, to determine his profoundest motives, whatever we may think of their ultimate success. In this way they resemble the novelist or historical novelist. Butterfield would call their history romantic history, in the sense that they desire "to touch the pulsing heart of men who toyed with the world as we do, and left it long ago." This kind of history, Butterfield observes, is only found in novels, and it represents the "quest for the most elusive thing in the world."[68] He does not argue that this "quest" is any less valuable than the historians', but insists that it is a different "'form' of history."[69] History as the historian writes it "cannot come so near to human hearts and human passions as a good novel can; its very fidelity to facts makes it not perhaps less true to life, but farther away from the heart of things."[70]

Russel Nye, summarizing an example of the historical imagination given by the Italian historian Gaetano Salvimini, has furnished us with a useful insight into the limitations the historian imposes upon himself in reconstructing the past:

> Suppose, [Salvimini] said, that we excavate a Roman statue with a missing head. The archaeologist and the historian agree that the head must have worn a helmet, perhaps even of a particular design, and demonstrate proof of this in various ways—by reference to other statues of the period, from contemporary sculptors' styles, from detailed knowledge of Roman military accoutrements. But at this point the historical imagination must stop, while the artistic imagination may continue. The sculptor who recreates the missing head has much greater freedom in visualizing and executing it; he must respect the style of the historical period in which it existed, of course, but the face of the statue he may see as he wishes. Two sculptors, in fact, might provide two quite different faces for it without violating the rules of credibility. Thus the historical and the artistic imagination, whose functions may be much the same, must operate under different conditions.[71]

With Bon also, many vital facts are missing: if they are to be established it cannot be by evidence but by an act of the artistic imagination. Like the historian looking at the Roman statue, Quentin and Shreve can follow the documentable outlines of Bon's life, but these outlines would no more produce for them the "fact" of Bon's Negro blood, or his feelings toward that "fact," than a reconstruction of the helmet of the statue would give the historian an image of the statue's head or face, or of the expression on that face.

In *Absalom, Absalom!*, therefore, Faulkner is implying that there is a meaning in history which eludes a logical, analytical approach. After all of the talking, Quentin and Shreve's abrupt submergence into the experience of Henry and Charles appears to achieve a direct knowledge of the past which resembles Bergson's "intuition," in that it is not simply an emotion but a peculiar act of knowledge or, rather, "a series of acts, of direct participation in the immediacy of experience."[72] I have, of course, argued previously that their direct knowledge is, in part, based on antecedent speculations and discoveries, but the total of this earlier interpretative activity does not of itself yield the actual experience of hearing and seeing Sutpen, Henry, and Bon speak to each other: there is an achieved imaginative whole which is discernibly if indefinably greater than the sum of the factual parts. The italicized scene in Chapter VIII (351–58) is designed to compel our belief—better perhaps, our suspended disbelief—in what Quentin and Shreve are presently doing, and it is surely our impression that they have acquired something more than relative knowledge. As Bergson says, "description, history, and analysis leave me here in the relative. Coincidence with the person himself would alone give me the absolute."[73]

My point is not simply that Faulkner as a novelist is free to have his characters imagine the past in ways the historian may not attempt. Faulkner formulates a specifically historical problem: what caused Henry to kill Charles Bon? The ultimate clue to the killing is not so much a motivation as it is a "fact," Bon's Negro blood. But this "fact" was partially arrived at in ways contrary to the normal methods of historical investigation. It was discovered through the emotional as well as the intellectual transactions of Quentin and Shreve. I take it that this is one of the things that Waggoner means when he says that *Absalom, Absalom!* "upsets our received notions of...'history' as an academic discipline":[74]

> Considered as an integral symbol the form of *Absalom* says that reality is unknowable in Sutpen's way, by weighing, measuring, and calculating. It says that without an "unscientific" act of imagination and even of faith—like Shreve's and Quentin's faith in Bon—we cannot know the things which are most worth knowing.[75]

Not only do Quentin and Shreve correct Sutpen's materialistic ordering of reality, they also provide a comment on Mr. Compson's way of understanding the past by "weighing, measuring, and calculating" the evidence. They may have learned to distrust the logical, empirical emphasis on fact from Miss Rosa, who speaks of "the sickness somewhere at the prime foundation of this factual scheme"[76] To the extent that the historian relies solely on his documents, he too is guilty of Mr. Compson's abstract conception of the past. What is needed, as Martin Duberman points out, is the particularity of feeling demonstrated when the historian openly involves himself in the past he is interpreting.

In taking a purely documentary approach to history in his play *In White America,* Martin Duberman discovered that

> the past does not speak for itself, and the ordering intelligence that renders it, necessarily injects some degree of idiosyncrasy. The advantage of the documentary approach (if one is primarily interested in historical accuracy) is that it does at least minimize subjectivity and restrict invention. Its disadvantage (if one is primarily interested in making

statements about experience) is that it circumscribes reflection and generalization. Instead of confining myself, for example, to the actual words John Brown spoke at his trial, I might have invented words to represent what I guessed to be his thoughts and feelings during his speech. In not doing so, I suspect that what I gained in accuracy I lost in insight. Truth of fact has less durable relevance than truth of feeling, for a fact is rooted in a particular context, whereas a feeling, being universal, can cross time.[77]

Duberman's dissatisfaction with facts rooted in a particular context stems from his belief that the past must somehow live now and be refocused in terms of the present moment; it must be a statement about current human experience. Of course this is just what Quentin and Shreve are doing with the past in their Harvard room. Duberman's dissatisfaction with facts is expressed even more radically by Faulkner as a positive distrust: "Fact is not too important and can be altered by law, by circumstance, by too many qualities, economics, temperature, but truth is the constant thing."[78] Presentation of fact, moreover, is not, as Duberman discovered, durable, because it depends not on insight and understanding, but on accuracy. A fact, said Faulkner, has no depth: "you cant stand a fact up, you've got to prop it up, and when you move to one side a little and look at it from that angle, it's not thick enough to cast a shadow in that direction."[79] Moving to another angle of vision is the essence of Faulkner's method in this novel; it provides the corrective to the stasis into which Duberman felt he had trapped himself by remaining loyal to the facts.

This constant circling around the so-called facts and events, looking perhaps for a point of vantage but never settling for the exclusivity of one's own vision, ensures that interpretation is an unending process. This is perhaps emphasized in *Absalom, Absalom!* more than in Faulkner's other works because the points of vantage are located not only in individuals of varying temperaments and intellects, but also in different places and periods of time. Sutpen, General Compson, Miss Rosa, Quentin and Shreve encompass over a hundred years of experience. Different cultures and different climates—the West Virginia mountains, Haiti, New Orleans, Mississippi, Canada and Cambridge, Massachusetts—all figure in the backgrounds of the characters and narrators.

The remarkable coherence of the Sutpen story (really quite remarkable in spite of the considerable residuum of ambiguity) is the product of a long historical process which relates past and present, not through an agreement on all of the facts which are the ephemeral surface of a particular moment in time, but through the human imagination (historical and artistic) which constantly turns over the facts to see what significance they now possess, whenever that "now" happens to be. The form of *Absalom, Absalom!* remains true to the process of historical interpretation, even though the place it accords to the artistic imagination is out of keeping with traditional concepts of the historian's reconstruction of the past.

Thus it is possible to compare Herbert Butterfield's description of the peculiar problems incurred in his study of the historiographical literature on George III with Olga Vickery's analysis of the form of *Absalom, Absalom!*:

> As a student of the history of historiography, I have long been interested not merely in the kaleidoscope of changing views on the subject of George III, but also in the causes of the changes, and, indeed, in the whole curve of development which scholarship has taken. I have tried to discover now the man responsible for the initiation of a new idea or attitude, now the location of the source of a myth or an error, now the forces and factors which helped to determine the next turn that would be given to the study of George III.[80]

> The perspectives [of the various narrators] are no longer self-contained and self-illuminating [as they were in *The Sound and the Fury*]; as a result, we have a kaleidoscope instead of a juxtaposition of views. Each successive account of Sutpen is constantly being merged with its predecessors. At every moment, there falls into place yet another pattern which disavows some parts of the earlier interpretations but never discards them.[81]

Both Mr. Butterfield and Mrs. Vickery employ the image of the kaleidoscope to describe the dynamic fusion of points of view which constitutes our perceptions of George III and Thomas Sutpen as historical figures. So the historian is careful to refer to the "subject" of George III, while the literary critic envisages Sutpen as the "dynamic...center" around which the various interpretations are successively organized.[82]

But if no absolute knowledge of the historical figure emerges from historical interpretation, an enlarging "curve" or "pattern" seems to be its compensating product. Historical interpretation has a form which exercises some control over diverging views of George III and of Thomas Sutpen. In particular, Professor Vickery's account of the dynamics of interpretation can be significantly compared with Hegel's historical dialectic.[83]

> The power of the method lies in its inner dynamic and universal applicability. One thought, in an almost literal sense, "gives" the next—thesis leading to antithesis, and both to synthesis, the latter serving as a new thesis for another train of thought encompassing the first, and so on *ad infinitum*—until the whole world and all things in it are caught in the chain of dialectic. This is possible, on the one hand, through the complete formalism of the method, that is, its independence from any concrete fact; and, on the other hand, its complete immersion in the concrete factuality of the world.[84]

Miss Rosa's thesis might be said to give way to Mr. Compson's antithesis, for Miss Rosa's interpretation is interrupted by Mr. Compson's remarks in

Chapter I. Then in Chapters II, III, and IV Mr. Compson confronts and sometimes contradicts Miss Rosa until she again explains and defends herself in Chapter V. Finally both thesis and antithesis are absorbed by and subsumed in the higher synthesis of Quentin and Shreve in Chapters VI–IX. As Herbert Butterfield argues,

> the day may come. . .when the historian, embracing both of the parties, or comprehending the issue at a higher altitude, will resurrect the forgotten aspects of the case, or see that all men were somewhat the victims of events—all of them struggling amid currents which they could not quite measure or understand. In such cases the history may have to be restratified and the narrative thoroughly recast.[85]

Quentin and Shreve, from the "higher altitude" of Cambridge, Massachusetts (and, in a way, of Canada), survey and resurrect every aspect of Sutpen's career and find that it is much more complex than either Miss Rosa or Mr. Compson imagined. Yet their joint account very much depends upon the insights of their predecessors.

This unique synthesis means that the truth inherent in the Sutpen story had to be present right from the very beginning of the story; that is, it had to exist within Miss Rosa's first recital of events to Quentin, even though she did not realize the full implications of her recital. In the compassionate rendering of Henry's agonizing struggles over the taboos of incest and miscegenation, Bon's moving but desperate hope for an acknowledgment from his father, and Judith's repudiation of Sutpen's design by accepting and caring for Etienne Bon, Quentin and Shreve expose the truth that, in trying to live in accordance with his design, Sutpen refined away any awareness of life as an entity demanding from the individual sacrifices contradicting his self-image or threatening to harm his self-interests. Sutpen, demythologized, becomes something like the demon Miss Rosa originally described. Appropriately enough, Butterfield concludes:

> But, whatever new structure the story may require, the ideas of the men who were living at the time will be somehow comprised in the final version of the narrative. The ideas that men have about the events in which their life is involved are to be regarded as a dimension of the events themselves. The things that men think they are fighting about are an ingredient in the very conflict in which they are engaged.[86]

Put quite simply, the reason for the continuing influence of Miss Rosa's demonizing and perhaps for the reason why the whole novel has so often been described as Gothic when in fact only Miss Rosa's narrative can be properly termed so is that the ideas she projects about Sutpen as a man with whom she had become so deeply involved prove indeed to define one of his main dimensions. Although she exaggerates the demonic in his character, it remains to the end one of the essential ingredients in the conflict in which she and the readers of *Absalom, Absalom!* have been engaged for so long.[87]

Our involvement as readers in Miss Rosa's problem needs emphasizing because, like Hegel's historical dialectic, the dialectic of *Absalom, Absalom!* might go on ad infinitum. It is "independent from concrete fact" —that is, the "chain of dialectic" is held together by something more than a linkage of facts—yet we are immersed in superbly realized scenes. A palpably specific and substantial world seems to grow out of the process of interpretation;[88] as a result, we seem to participate in as well as observe the making of history.[89] As Hegel himself affirmed: "We must hold that the narration of history and historical deeds and events appear at the same time; a common inner principle brings them forth together."[90] Eventually we see that man is both a product and an extension of what he studies; no logical way can be found either to enter into or exit from the historical world.[91]

This is true for both Butterfield's historical study of George III and Faulkner's fictional history of Thomas Sutpen. That the meaning of history and the direction of scholarship are subtly changing, in response to each other, even as he writes, is indicated by Butterfield's repeated use of "now" to make clear that he has arbitrarily stopped the "curve of development" which has led him to the "now," or the present moment of his study. In *Absalom, Absalom!* we are often plunged into the midst of interpretation, as if to imply that we, no less than the characters in the novel, are historical beings, who must respond to history with provisional judgments: so Professor Vickery, in the passage already quoted, attends to "every moment" in which our view of Sutpen's career is slightly modified.

Not only do Quentin and Shreve succeed as narrators because they have learned to think historically, but also our awareness of history gradually expands as we learn to assess their use of historical method and their attempts to go beyond it. In other words, our final reading of the novel is largely a product of the historiographical experience which the novel itself has given us. Although this claim could no doubt be made for other novels, a special case has been made for *Absalom, Absalom!*'s unique insistence that we do more than our normal share of historical thinking, that we perpetually reexamine what we take to be a "fact." And by forcing us to put together so much of the Sutpen story, Faulkner demonstrates the difficulty of separating *what* we know about history from *how* we know it. For "we seldom reflect on the activities which we perform quite easily. It is only the difficulties which we encounter that force upon us a consciousness of our own efforts to overcome them."[92]

5

The Dramatization of the Past and of Historical Process in *Go Down, Moses*

As in my first chapter on *Absalom, Absalom!*, an examination of the shape and proportions of *Go Down, Moses*, and of the precise temporal relationships of the various chapters to each other, is necessary as a way into showing how Part Four of "The Bear," like Chapter VIII of *Absalom, Absalom!*, is both a study of the history which the novel itself enacts, and a portrayal of the historical evidence and ideas that grow out of the novel as a whole.

In Part One of "Was" we are introduced to "Isaac McCaslin, 'Uncle Ike', past seventy and nearer eighty than he ever corroborated any more, a widower now and uncle to half a county and father to no one."[1] His cousin McCaslin Edmonds, from whom Ike derives the past events which are about to be narrated in Part Two of "Was," is "descended by the distaff" but inherits the plantation, even though Ike belongs to the male line of McCaslins who originally held the title to the land granted from the Indian patent. Ike finishes his life, however, in a "cheap frame bungalow in Jefferson" (3), the gift of his wife's father.

Although Ike will become a major figure in the novel, we have no way of knowing this. It is true that he is dealt with at the beginning of the book before the events described in "Was," but we do not yet see the relevance that those events have for him, and we are given more information about him than we can at this point understand or appreciate. The significance of this peculiar juxtaposition of present and past cannot be clearly understood or fully discussed until Part Four of "The Bear," from which we surmise that the present time of the novel is established in Part One of "Was" as 1941, which is the latest point in Ike's life, while the past events so vividly reenacted in the rest of the chapter occur in 1859, about eight years before Ike was born.

Although the story in "Was" is itself quite simple to follow, the relationship between Uncle Buck and his slave, Tomey's Turl, whom he is attempting to hunt down, is complex, because we are told that the black has some white McCaslin blood in him, and because Buck too is the object of a hunt by Miss Sophonsiba, who hopes to trap him into marriage. When the fox horn blows, indicating that Buck and Cass are near the Beauchamp plantation, where they will "den" (18) Tomey's Turl, we also realize that Buck is approaching the bear's "den" (22) of Miss Sophonsiba. Once Buck is caught in Sophonsiba's room, he must gamble for his freedom and for the "niggers," according to Hubert Beauchamp's wager. Beauchamp would like to pursue a simple, rather crude way of life, but he is forced to accommodate himself to his sister's claims of aristocratic descent and adherence to a chivalric code. The extent of Miss Sophonsiba's interference in her brother's life is not fully appreciated until we see her evict his Negro mistress from "Warwick" in Part Four of "The Bear."

After having "won" Sophonsiba through losing the card game, Buck must send for his brother Buddy to help him escape from the threatened marriage. In the meantime Buck is reduced to acting like a "nigger," telling Cass that "if they pushed him too close...he would climb down the gutter too and hide in the woods until Uncle Buddy arrived" (25). Although his brother does regain his freedom for him, the ending of "Was" suggests that eventually Buck will be caught in Miss Sophonsiba's trap. For when they return home, the old dog "Old Moses" is found with the fox's crate around his neck — surely a symbolic forecast of the foxy Miss Sophonsiba's placing the yoke of marriage around the neck of that other old dog, "old Buck," as Tomey's Turl calls him (19).

"The Fire and the Hearth," like the first part of "Was," is set in the present time of the novel, and centers on Lucas Beauchamp, a black descendant of old Carothers McCaslin, nearly as old as Ike, and the oldest McCaslin Negro on the plantation. But here, in contrast to "Was," past and present are constantly interpenetrating each other. Lucas is planning to dispose of George Wilkins, his young competitor in the moonshine trade and his daughter Nat's fiancé, who is a "fool innocent of discretion" (35), an intruder who, while posing no real economic threat to Lucas, has not only moved on to the "section" where Lucas had

> lived for going on seventy years but onto the very place he had been born on and set up competition in a business which he had established and nursed carefully and discreetly for twenty of them, ever since he had fired up for his first fun not a mile from Zack Edmonds' kitchen door; — secretly indeed, for no man needed to tell him what Zack Edmonds or his son, Carothers (or old Cass Edmonds either, for that matter), would do about it if they ever found it out. (34-35)

Whereas in "Was" we had been forced to guess at the relationship between past events and Ike's current circumstances, here the past must be directly invoked to explain Lucas's attitude toward George.

Lucas's search for buried treasure, stimulated by his discovery of the gold coin in the Indian mound where he was burying his still as part of the plot against George Wilkins, is interrupted twice in the telling by long episodes from his past which help to explain both his present attitudes and the present state of the McCaslin family and its plantation. Forty-three years earlier (1898) Lucas had risked his life to save the life of Roth Edmonds's mother, but she died, and Lucas's wife Molly took her place in Zack Edmonds's household. Believing that Zack had taken Molly as his mistress, Lucas demanded that the white man return her. Molly had come back, but with Zack's child as well as her own. Thinking that Zack had demeaned his manhood, Lucas felt compelled to confront him as an equal. Roth Edmonds is intensely aware in the present that somehow in the past Lucas had achieved an unusual degree of independence stemming from a confrontation with his father about a woman, and Roth is frustrated by that awareness because it inhibits his own authority on the plantation.

The second episode deals with an even earlier time (1895) when Lucas, turned twenty-one, came to Ike to ask for the legacy left him by old Carothers. Although he should have been in the inferior position of a Negro pleading for what was rightfully his, his proud demand for the legacy transformed it into a debt which was owed to him by the family and a responsibility which Ike had shirked. Living in a little bungalow in town, supported by fifty dollars a month from his cousin Cass, Ike realized that he was powerless to aid Lucas in any other way than by simply dispensing the legacy that had been in his trusteeship. Lucas's cold and distant response prompted Ike to think:

> *Fifty dollars a month. He knows that's all. That I reneged, cried calf-rope, sold my birthright, betrayed my blood, for what he too calls not peace but obliteration, and a little food.* (108-9)

At this point in the novel our only preparation for Ike's admission of his failure to cope with his family's heritage has been the prologue to "Was," to which we can return in order to piece together the consequences of Ike's refusal to accept his patrimony while still in his twenties. He is approximately six years older than Lucas, who demanded his birthright at twenty-one, the same age at which Ike debates with Cass in the commissary—a future event in terms of the narrative progression of the book but a past event in terms of the chronology of the McCaslin story.

As Lucas gives up the hunting days of his youth and young manhood (36), Ike dwells more and more on those very same experiences (106). Lucas accepts his McCaslin heritage in spite of the fact that he is denied the respect he deserves from the white community; Ike willingly gives up a position of respect and authority in his family and community which is his for the asking. Through the years Lucas seems to grow into a position of self-importance, his age being a considerable factor in his dealings with the much younger Roth, who is continually reminded of Lucas's claims as head of the family. As we shall see in "Delta Autumn," Roth rather easily rejects what should be Ike's similarly honorable position as an elderly man and as the oldest McCaslin descendant. One man grows in power whereas the other's power diminishes with age.

"Pantaloon in Black" might be seen as the third part of a trilogy of chapters which seek different ways of relating past and present to each other. Not only is the world of "Was" and "The Fire and the Hearth" shifted into the background of "Pantaloon in Black," that world seems *at first* to be only a tangential aspect of Rider's story. To complete the suspension of character development in the McCaslin story, so that the old times which Lucas remembers are not immediately juxtaposed to Isaac's memories of "The Old People," Faulkner further distances us from "The Fire and the Hearth" by referring rather formally to Roth Edmonds, a character we now know quite well, as "Carothers Edmonds, the local white landowner" (137). But Rider and his wife (whose name, Mannie, is similar to Molly, or Mollie as it is spelled in "Delta Autumn" and "Go Down, Moses") build a "fire on the hearth" on their wedding night "as the tale told how Uncle Lucas Beauchamp, Edmonds' oldest tenant, had done on his forty-five years ago and which had burned ever since" (138). As Cleanth Brooks observes, "the primitive world, to which Lucas reaches back in time, has, in this community, survived into the 1940s."[2]

Just as losing Molly to Zack Edmonds provoked a crisis in the twenty-four-year-old Lucas's life, a crisis which he tried to avoid but which brought him to the point where he believed he would have to die in order to assert his manhood, so now, forty-three years later, twenty-four-year-old Rider's loss of Mannie leaves him bereft of any reason to go on living, and convinced that he is "bound to die" (152). But Rider is also, like Lucas and Ike, set apart from both blacks and whites by the special integrity of his personality and his unusual bond with nature. All three are proud, solitary men, but Lucas and Rider curb the vanity of their own strength by cooperating with their wives in the union of marriage. Quite simply, "Pantaloon in Black" portrays Rider's despair when that union is destroyed. By implication, the chapter also defines the continuity which a fruitful marriage sustains and the sterility of those of the deputy and, as we shall see later, Ike, whose isolation from their wives is also an index of their inadequate sense of community.

Rather like Rider himself at the end of his life, the deputy is "spent now from lack of sleep and hurried food at hurried and curious hours and, sitting in a chair beside the stove, a little hysterical too" (154). The stove, the deputy's modern fire and hearth, reflects what should be the center of domestic harmony in his own life. Unfortunately he cannot imagine that Rider's acts were those of a man who had lost precisely what the deputy is now looking for from his wife: some comforting response which will allay the hysteria of the last several hours. It is a bitter irony that his spouse should be so inattentive to a story calling for sympathetic understanding of a man's loss of his wife. The deputy's unwillingness to grant Rider a sense of decency is the kind of attitude that had prompted Lucas to accuse Zack of taking Molly into his house because "'You thought that because I am a nigger I wouldn't even mind'" (53).

Yet the deputy, like Zack, is caught in a system of prejudice he did not create, no matter how much his own actions may perpetuate it. The very force of his concern with Rider's story suggests that he is genuinely troubled by his involvement in the life of this black man, and is searching for some way to explain it to himself. As Dirk Kuyk has recently put it, "the puzzlement in the deputy's voice reveals that Rider's fate, although beyond the deputy's comprehension, has entagled [sic] him."[3] Like Rider, the deputy cannot stop thinking, nor can he help looking for the meaning of what he has just witnessed. So he repeats Rider's last words and then adds a question of his own which unconsciously echoes Rider's own puzzlement:

> "'Hit look lack Ah just cant quit thinking. Look lack Ah just cant quit.' And what do you think of that?"
> "I think if you eat any supper in this house you'll do it in the next five minutes," his wife said from the dining room. "I'm going to clear this table then and I'm going to the picture show." (159)

By failing to understand her husband's desperate obsession with Rider's last desperate words, the white deputy's wife is as "lost" to her husband at this moment as Mannie was to Rider.

The very title of the next chapter of *Go Down, Moses*, "The Old People," suggests still another effort to delineate what was referred to in "Was" as "the old time, the old days" (4), and by Lucas in "The Fire and the Hearth" as "the old time" (37). But for Lucas, the old time goes back no further than the days when old Carothers got the land from the Indians; his affinity is clearly with the events described in "Was." Ike's sense of the past, on the other hand, extends far beyond these historical turning points to the prehistoric conditions of the wilderness before it began to recede under the "civilizing" advance of the white settlers.

Whereas old Carothers establishes the code which Lucas adopts as his own, Sam Fathers, the part-Negro descendant of an Indian chief, is Ike's spiritual guide. Though the chapter describes Ike's experiences from his eighth to his twelfth year, and makes references to the fact that he will still remember these experiences at eighty, the predominant time is 1879, when Sam marks Ike with the blood of the buck he has just slain, thus initiating the twelve-year-old boy into the order of nature, just as Cass, in a sense, was initiated into the life of the plantation at the age of nine in "Was."[4] Even though Cass has also been initiated by Sam Fathers into the life of the woods, he had as a child become an unwitting accomplice in Uncle Buck's hunting of Tomey's Turl. Just like the buck (178), Tomey's Turl "broke cover," as Uncle Buck puts it (14). The circular pattern of "Was," in which Tomey's Turl eventually returns to Tennie's cabin and Uncle Buck returns to the Beauchamp plantation and Sophonsiba's bed chamber (18, 20–21), conforms to Sam's reading of the buck's path in which "he will circle back in here about sundown to bed" (179). But there is no equivalent in "Was" to Ike's realization of "the buck moving in it [the wilderness] somewhere, not running yet since he had not been pursued, not frightened yet and never fearsome but just alert also as they were alert, perhaps already circling back, perhaps quite near, perhaps conscious also of the eye of the ancient immortal Umpire" (181). Despite the differences between the two hunts, however, the hunters and the hunted in both episodes share something like the same relationship. The young Cass, at one point, goes out and discusses with Tomey's Turl what Uncle Buck, proposes to do next in the hunt. Certainly Cass is expressing the simple ingenuousness of a child, but he is also revealing the underlying bond between himself and Tomey's Turl rather as Ike develops his awareness of the similarity between the hunters and the hunted animal in the wilderness.

In "The Bear" Ike first becomes aware of "Old Ben," not by sighting him or even hearing him, but through somehow participating in the sensation of the hounds: "a little different — an eagerness, passive; an abjectness, a sense of his own fragility and impotence against the timeless woods, yet without doubt or dread" (200). The primordial feelings Ike identifies in himself accord naturally with the wilderness itself, "which looked exactly as it must have looked when the first ancestor of Sam Fathers' Chickasaw predecessors crept into it and looked about him, club or stone axe or bone arrow drawn and ready" (202–3). Ike relinquishes his gun, compass and watch in order to get his first look at the bear, and to experience "a condition in which not only the bear's heretofore inviolable anonymity but all the ancient rules and balances of hunter and hunted had been abrogated" (207). But once he has done so, Ike is lost. To find his way back to where he has abandoned his watch and compass he makes, as Sam has "coached and drilled him," a "cast to cross his backtrack" (208). When he does not find the point at which he originally began, he makes the "next circle in the opposite direction and much larger, so that the pattern of the two of them would bisect his track somewhere" (208). He finds the watch and compass, and then he has his privileged vision of the "dimensionless" bear (209). There is no proper measurement for Old Ben because he is for Ike all-encompassing. The watch and the compass are time- and space-bound whereas the bear appears to move neither in time nor space. Where the watch and compass divide and separate time and space into units, the bear and the wilderness coalesce, soundless and solidified.

Ike's relinquishment of the watch and compass foreshadows his relinquishment of his white heritage.[5] To him his family line depends upon a relatively short chain of cause and effect, whereas the bear seems ancient and ubiquitous. For Ike, the bear does not vanish, is not lost; rather he simply recedes back into his element, always there, always present, in a changeless universe (209). Yet we are never in any doubt, even in the first pages of "The Bear," that the wilderness is doomed (198). In Part Two Ike is actively involved in the paradoxical situation of hunting Old Ben, who symbolizes for him the immortality of the wilderness. Ike's confusion is apparent in his failure to shoot the bear when the opportunity is given to him by the foolish little fyce who is able to make Old Ben turn toward him (211), thereby proving that besides being the "epitome and apotheosis of the old wild life," Old Ben is also just an aging bear. Ike is dimly aware that there is a fatality in the hunt, but he passively accepts its consequences as though he were just an observer of historical processes which he is, in fact, helping to bring about (226). Ike never squarely faces the fact that the hunt is the harbinger of the bear's and the wilderness's death, and that this death must also be part of his own initiation into the meaning of life.

The end of the hunt for Old Ben also marks an important turning point in the history of the McCaslins. Ike is sixteen. In two years he will set out on his attempt to locate Tennie's Jim, the same ubiquitous Tennie's Jim of this hunting story. After the fall of the bear, Ike and Tennie's Jim run forward and witness the death scene (241–42). Although we are more likely to concentrate on Boon's care for the dying Lion, and on Sam's sudden collapse, the repeated appearances of Tennie's Jim help to define the kind of world that dies along with the major figures in the story. We are never given any reason for Tennie's Jim's disappearance two years after this scene, but the scene itself argues that the world, and the place Tennie's Jim occupied in it, has been destroyed. All along Faulkner has carefully associated Tennie's Jim's whole life with these wilderness scenes, just as he grounded Lucas's life in his loyalty to the plantation.

Tennie's Jim is a part of many memorable scenes in "The Bear." He holds "the passive and still trembling bitch," who, in Sam's words, "would have to be brave once so she could keep on calling herself a dog" (199). Tennie's Jim pours the whiskey which is like a sacrament to the hunters (205). He holds the hounds on leash (237), saddles the mules (238), wakes

Ike up on the morning when he and Boon go into town for whiskey (227). Tennie's Jim is the Negro who pulls the towsack off of the horse that Boon and Ike purchased (232–33), and he is the one who is sent to the doctor for Boon, Lion, and Sam (243). He stays with Sam after the white men leave (246, 249).

Retrospection on the events related in "The Bear" has begun even before the events themselves can properly be said to have ended. Groups of men, very carefully chosen by Faulkner for the representativeness of their experiences in or beside the wilderness, gather around the old bear to remember the past, as though they instinctively understand that Old Ben's death is an historical event like the closing of the frontier, which can be preserved only through the imagination (248).

Part Four shows us that Ike's vision of history is seriously damaged, if not wholly discredited, by his inability to accept the change that is dramatized in the first three parts of "The Bear." Instead of starting from the fact that the wilderness had to perish, he expends most of his energy denouncing precisely that necessity. Instead of continuing the sixteen-year-old Ike's development from the killing of Old Ben to his last visit to Major de Spain's hunting camp when he is nearly eighteen (which is treated in Part Five), Part Four begins with Ike's rejection of his patrimony on his twenty-first birthday, and it then ranges from his sensitive reading of the commissary books at sixteen, to his attempts to "free" Fonsiba when he is eighteen, to Lucas's acceptance of his legacy when Ike is twenty-eight, to Hubert Beauchamp's bequest to Ike, and finally to Ike's refusal to share his McCaslin legacy with his wife by rejecting her plea that he assume the ownership of the plantation. What all these episodes have in common is Ike's obsession with the past and his constant attempt to atone for its evil. For the most part we see Ike as an isolated figure, retreating from family responsibilities and estranging himself from those like Cass and his wife who might have been his closest confidants.

In Part Five, as Ike sees the sidetracks and the loading platforms being prepared for the "new planing-mill," he looks about in "shocked and grieved amazement even though he had had forewarning and had believed himself prepared." Thus disturbed at the signs of "progress," he seeks to hide, "once more anyway," in the "wall of wilderness" (318). Ike is rather like the timid "half-grown bear" in the anecdote he remembers about the train's first trip into the wilderness (319). Like the bear, Ike is somewhat immature in not accepting the train's constant presence in the landscape; he would like to forget that it is there, and does forget, until he is once again shocked and grieved when he is forced to see it. One could almost say that Ike runs away and puts himself up a tree, like the bear, at the onset of change.

At the time of the episode of the half-grown bear, the train seemed nothing more than a "small dingy harmless snake"; the wooden ties of the railroad were to the bear "curious symmetrical squared barkless logs which had appeared apparently from nowhere in one endless mathematical line overnight" (319). But now Ike can see that the episode was a portent of how the wilderness itself would be squared (Sam's burial place is squared off from the rest of the land sold to the timber company), made symmetrical, and destroyed. Ike's vision of the slowly receding and disappearing wilderness is an instance of what Leo Marx calls "the machine in the garden," the unceasing encroachment of man upon nature.[6] Indeed, the shrieking little locomotive might be seen as a surrogate for man himself, who has been slowly but inexorably gnawing and scratching away at the wilderness. Throughout "The Old People," "The Bear," and "Delta Autumn," Faulkner constantly refers to the puny humans who swarm over the land to claw away at a seemingly invulnerable wilderness (177, 193, 195, 202, 254, 342). Against the wilderness man seems powerless, but throughout these three chapters we are made aware of the human persistence which radically changes the quality of life even while outwardly appearing as ineffective as the "little locomotive."

Ike ought to realize that the inevitable triumph of man over nature, or at least a part of nature, makes his own identification with nature temporary, or at best incomplete. As Cleanth Brooks puts it, "if man's veneration for nature is absolute, history becomes impossible. We have the unceasing round of the seasons, birth, copulation, and death, but no proper history."[7] Yet Ike seeks refuge precisely in the "unceasing round" of nature: "summer, and fall, and snow, and wet and saprife spring in their ordered immortal sequence" (326). Even though he sees that nature, like man, has its own measure of evil and death, which he acknowledges by addressing the snake as "'Chief...Grandfather,'" (330), he does not make the connection between this latter "dulled" snake and the train, which he had perceived as a "dingy" snake. Evil is a constant condition—not simply a product of human history. Man did not bring evil into the wilderness or into Eden; evil is immemorial, predating man, although man certainly is susceptible to evil and must be held responsible for the destruction of the wilderness. That Ike cannot accept the wilderness itself historically, as a dying phenomenon, is clear three years later when, in the commissary, he hinges his whole argument on the notion that man's violation of the wilderness is an irrevocable evil act future generations will have to expiate.

Ike's helplessness at the onset of change is further emphasized at the end of "The Bear" by the subtle link established between Ike and the inept Boon. As Ike is saluting the snake, another scene is taking place in another part of the wilderness. Led to the spot by "a sound as though someone were hammering a gun-barrel against a piece of railroad iron" (330), Ike discovers Boon sitting against a tree trunk with forty or fifty squirrels madly darting up and down the tree while he no less madly hammers away with the disjointed barrel against the gun breech. As Ike approaches, Boon cries, "'Get out of here! Dont touch them! Dont touch a one of them! They're mine!'" (331). Boon's beating of metal on metal and the frantic reaction of the squirrels are strikingly reminiscent of the shrieking, clattering, and frantic approach of the locomotive and the baby bear's frenzied attempt to take refuge in the tree. Like the locomotive, Boon and Ike have played a part in the invasion and destruction of the wilderness. Unlike Boon, Ike has imaginatively recaptured a sense of the prehistoric past and has reluctantly recognized the encroaching advance of modern civilization, but he reverts to the virtues and values of a lost world just as Boon retreats to an "old clearing" where he is assured of finding as many squirrels as he wants. Unlike Boon, Ike is aware of history as a process of change, but he cannot accept what his own consciousness encompasses, and is therefore as unfit for the present as Boon himself. Specifically, Ike thinks of himself as a part of nature, even though he hears the very sound of the railroad echoed in Boon's mad efforts to put his gun together. Ike can no more possess the wilderness, or relive his past in it, than Boon can hold on to the swarming squirrels. Like the squirrels, history is life in constant motion; it stops for no man.

In "Delta Autumn," which is very specifically set a year before America's entry into World War II (November 1940), Ike, now seventy-three, serenely rejects Roth's low opinion of mankind and his bitter tirade against the degeneration of the nation. Although Ike believes that man always has the potential to be just a little better than his circumstances allow him to be, he acknowledges his disappointment in man's failure to take advantage of his God-given opportunities. In particular, he deplores the destruction of the wilderness. But by speaking of the "chance" that God gave man (349), Ike is unwittingly offering a negative judgment of his own life, since Uncle Buck was willing to take his "chance" when he gambled with Hubert Beauchamp in order to escape from marriage to Sophonsiba (23), and Lucas took his "chance" in confronting Zack, so that he could assert his manhood (56). Both men accepted responsibility for their actions and grasped their opportunities as they occurred in time, whereas Ike fails to grasp his "chance" to redeem his heritage, to carry on for his forebears, as General Compson hoped Ike would during the hunting of Old Ben. "I had my chance last year and missed it," Compson says in handing over to Ike Katie, "the one-eyed mule which would not spook at wild blood" (237). Similarly, Sam counsels Ike in "The Old People" to "wait" for that moment when he can recoup his "missed opportunity" to sight the phantom buck (183).

Instead of following time as a series of onrushing "chances" one might be good enough to take, Ike overinterprets and overdetermines "certain selected moments"; he invests them with an "extraordinary [apocalyptic] meaning,"[8] and thus he destroys the continuum between past and present, the continuum of human actions that can alter (for better or worse) the historical process. This is partly Cass's point when he identifies Ike as "the direct male descendant" of Old Carothers, "who saw the opportunity and took it" to hold a land "worthy of bequeathment" (256).

Roth sees only tyranny, both in public and private life, and is disturbed by his own responsibility to the "does," the women who, according to Ike, make fighting for one's country a meaningful act of self-defense. All along Legate has been referring to Roth's Negro mistress as a "doe," and Roth is perhaps more irascible than usual, and takes a somewhat darker view of humanity than he would ordinarily take, judging by what we have already seen of him in "The Fire and the Hearth." In that chapter we saw his other side, his devotion to Molly, who taught him

> his manners, behavior — to be gentle with his inferiors, honorable with his equals, generous to the weak and considerate of the aged, courteous, truthful and brave to all — who had given him, the motherless, without stint or expectation of reward that constant and abiding devotion and love which existed nowhere else in this world for him. (117)

Ike believes that Roth is young, and terribly involved in the contradictions of everyday living. Looking back at his own life, Ike calmly reflects on Sam's marking of his face with the buck's blood, an event which occurred sixty-one years before, when Ike was twelve, and which he now interprets as Sam Fathers teaching him to understand: "*I slew you; my bearing must not shame your quitting life. My conduct forever onward must become your death*" (351). But Ike's long life has been no less fragmented than Roth's short one, his "conduct" no less contradictory. Ike had stood before his cousin Cass

> in repudiation and denial at least of the land and the wrong and shame even if he couldn't cure the wrong and eradicate the shame, who at fourteen when he learned of it had believed he could do both when he became competent and when at twenty-one he became competent he knew that he could do neither but at least he could repudiate the wrong and shame, at least in principle, and at least the land itself in fact, for his son at least: and did, thought he had: then (married then) in a rented cubicle in a back-street Stock-traders' boarding-house, the first and last time he ever saw her naked body, himself and his wife juxtaposed in their turn against that same land, that same wrong and

> shame from whose regret and grief he would at least save and free his son and, saving and freeing his son, lost him. (351)

Only the "principle" survived from Ike's earnest effort to redeem his heritage, and it is only the "principle" that we hear affirmed in Ike's debate with Roth, who serves, in a way, as a surrogate for Ike's nonexistent son.

The bond between Roth and Ike is strengthened by their solitariness. Although Ike believes in defending does and condemns Roth for failing to do so, he himself "had had a wife and lived with her and lost her, ay, lost her even though he had lost her in the rented cubicle before he and his old clever dipsomaniac partner had finished the house for them to move into it: but lost her, because she loved him" (352). He acts as Roth's agent in paying off his mistress and proves unable "for all his fine statements about love earlier in the chapter...to recognise it in the young Negress."[9] He assumes that her return to the hunting camp is motivated by feelings of revenge, but the girl's responses show how unfair Ike has been to both Roth and herself:

> "I would have made a man of him. He's not a man yet. You spoiled him. You, and Uncle Lucas and Aunt Mollie. But mostly you." (360)

> "Old man...have you lived so long and forgotten so much that you dont remember anything you ever knew or felt or even heard about love?" (363)

Earlier Roth had also suggested that somehow Ike is out of touch with reality, with the present: "'I suppose the question to ask you is, where have you been all the time you were dead?'" (345). Roth's question seemed vicious at the time, but when the Negress retells the main events of "Was," we see that in repudiating his claim to the plantation Ike also damaged his own sensitivity to the very human relationships which he condemned old Carothers for denying. By not becoming actively involved in his heritage, Ike not only deprived Roth of a chance to see Ike's principles in operation but left him to work out very complex problems for himself. As a result, he unwittingly abuses a black member of his own family, thus repeating in a new context the crimes of the McCaslin past.

Even after Ike is fully aware that the Negress is a descendant of Tennie's Jim, he evades the possibility that he himself might do something for her. He gives her cynical advice to go North and take revenge on "a black man" and surrenders in his own thoughts to a bitter condemnation of the present, making just such a depressing equation between the loss of the wilderness and the degradation of humanity as Roth had accused him of earlier (345) in their debate:

> *This land which man has deswamped and denuded and derivered in two generations so that white men can own plantations and commute every night to Memphis and black*

men own plantations and ride in jim crow cars to Chicago to live in millionaires' man-
sions on Lakeshore Drive, where white men rent farms and live like niggers and niggers
crop on shares and live like animals, where cotton is planted and grows man-tall in the
very cracks of the sidewalks, and usury and mortgage and bankruptcy and measureless
wealth, Chinese and African and Aryan and Jew, all breed and spawn together until no
man has time to say which one is which nor cares. (364)

Ike's tirade here seems to indicate that he has given up, that he despairs just as Roth had despaired at the beginning of the chapter, believing that principles are no longer relevant in a world where everyone is hopelessly confused about even the most basic values and the future seems to offer only dictatorship (338).

The first part of "Go Down, Moses" takes us North, the destination Ike had recommended to the girl in "Delta Autumn," and into the degenerate world Ike has just deplored. In stark contrast to Ike's values of free will and the attachment of the individual to a specific heritage is Butch Beauchamp, a convicted murderer awaiting execution in a Chicago jail. Beauchamp, born a McCaslin Negro, has been in the numbers racket, which depends on a mathematical ordering of chances, and he answers the census taker's questions in a "voice which was anything under the sun but a southern voice or even a Negro voice." He is imprisoned in a "steel cubicle" and lives in a denatured atmosphere, the antithesis of Ike's wilderness experience, in which all of the color, other than that of the steel fixtures, comes from the overdressed prisoner himself: "He wore one of those sports costumes called ensembles in the men's shop advertisements, shirt and trousers matching and cut from the same fawn-colored flannel, and they had cost too much and were draped too much, with too many pleats" (369).

The scene is a manifold contrast to the world presented in all the previous chapters of *Go Down, Moses.* We think of the integrity that Rider's Negro voice gives to his experience, of the natural beauty of the wilderness, and of the economy and frugality of Ike and the other hunters. Against Butch's "sports costume" we set Lucas's fifty-year-old hat, Miss Worsham's thirty-year-old hat, and Lucas's "small metal dispatch box which his white grandfather, Carothers McCaslin himself, had owned almost a hundred years ago," and in which Lucas kept the "knotted rag tight and solid with the coins, some of which dated back almost to Carothers McCaslin's time, which he had begun to save before he was ten years old" (51–52). In the second part of "Go Down, Moses" there are references to Stevens's "rumpled linen suit" (370) and the newspaper editor's "old fashioned boiled shirt" (373). On the other hand, Butch's "steel cubicle" may stir memories of Ike's "rented cubicle" in "Delta Autumn" (351–52). In Part One of "Was" Ike sleeps on an "iron cot" (see also 300, 343, 349, 355, 357, 361, 362, 369); in Part One of "Go Down, Moses" Butch lies on a "steel cot" in striking contrast to Rider, who tears his iron cot "clean out of the floor it was bolted to" (158).[10] The two chapters, indeed, give a brief outline of Ike's and Butch's pasts, and then explore the sources and background of each man's present life and state of mind. Although on opposite ends of a moral and historical and racial scale, both men are McCaslins who have, each in his own way, repudiated a heritage and tried to seal off the agony of loss that impels Rider's violence. In a sense Butch has also taken Ike's advice to the Negress in "Delta Autumn" and gone North.

Although the precise time of "Go Down, Moses" is never explicitly established, it evidently occurs in the month of July, probably of 1940,[11] since in the opening scene of the chapter Butch's name is being recorded in the U.S. census. July 1940 would fall just about a year before the midpoint of the time encompassed by "The Fire and the Hearth," between, that is, May and the fall harvest, and just a year and a month before Rider's death in August 1941 (137, 158). Both "The Fire and the Hearth" and "Delta Autumn" are obviously relevant to "Go Down, Moses" because they deal with Ike's and Roth's responsibilities to the Beauchamp family. Since the events of this chapter occur before those of "The Fire and the Hearth," it is clear that Roth has by no means relinquished his responsibilities to the black tenants on his plantation, even though those responsibilities are assumed—or perhaps extended—in "Go Down, Moses" by Gavin Stevens, the outsider who, like the deputy in "Pantaloon in Black," is largely ignorant of the relationships between Negroes in his own community.

Stevens is a more sensitive and compassionate human being than the deputy, but his perceptions of Negroes are largely abstract and patronizing. Upon learning that Molly is related to Hamp Worsham,

> he was not surprised. He had known Hamp Worsham all his life, though he had never seen the old Negress before. But even if he had, he still would not have been surprised. They were like that. You could know two of them for years...bearing different names. Then suddenly you learn by pure chance that they are brothers or sisters. (371–72)

Especially with "Pantaloon in Black" in mind, it is not possible to see Stevens's ignorance as merely his own. There are many things about Negro life "which no white man could have read" (135). As in Rider's case, Molly's concerns are viewed at a considerable remove from the world in which she lives. Stevens therefore treats very lightly Molly's accusation that Roth Edmonds sold her Benjamin into Egypt because he does not understand the significance of Roth's throwing Butch off of the plantation for breaking into the commissary store. From one point of view, this was no greater crime than Lucas's abduction of Roth's mule in "The Fire and the Hearth." From another perspective, however, the symbolic significance of

Butch's and Roth's acts is manifold. Butch offends against the laws of (white) property and against the established order represented by the commissary, but Roth is equally wrong in denying paternalistic responsibility for Butch's fate, so that both violate the plantation tradition of interdependence and mutual obligation.

That we are to remember in "Go Down, Moses" the themes of "The Fire and the Hearth" and "Pantaloon in Black" is apparent when Stevens visits Molly at the Worsham's house in order to inform her of his arrangements for Butch's funeral. The home "was still lighted with oil lamps and there was no running water in it" (379), but on the brick hearth "the ancient symbol of human coherence and solidarity smoldered" (380). Because Stevens is not part of and cannot share the traditions imbedded in the communal mourning of his black neighbors, he panics in a manner reminiscent of the white deputy's hysterical reaction to Rider. As Stevens rushes out, Faulkner emphasizes the "high, white, erect, old-time head" of Mrs. Worsham through the "old-time lamplight" (381). Nothing less than the "old times, the old days" are being evoked for the last time in *Go Down, Moses*.

At the funeral itself a

> number of people, Negroes and white both...the idle white men and youths and small boys and probably half a hundred Negroes, men and women too, [were] watching quietly, the Negro undertaker's men [as they] lifted the gray-and-silver casket from the train and carried it to the hearse and snatched the wreaths and floral symbols of man's ultimate and inevitable end briskly out and slid the casket in and flung the flowers back and clapped-to the door. (381–82)

The end of any human life has some interest to a cohesive community, simply because it is a blow to human solidarity. It is, in large measure, the casket as symbol, not the Butch Beauchamp within it, which engages the attention of this mixed group of watchers. The universality of their response to the corpse is comparable to Old Ben's death scene, where a great number of men, of all kinds from all parts of the countryside, gather round the slain bear much as the townspeople gather round Beauchamp, "the slain wolf" (382). Whatever threat the bear or the "wolf" posed to the existence of the community is now transcended by the greater fascination with death, with the cessation of energies that occurs at some time in all living things, no matter how good or evil.

Not that we are entirely allowed to forget Butch Beauchamp's crime: the "silver-and-gray casket" colors our view of Butch's role as "wolf," and on the penultimate page of the book he is referred to as the Negro murderer (382). At the close of the story Stevens realizes that Molly was not interested in hiding her grandson's evil life:

> *It doesn't matter to her now. Since it had to be and she couldn't stop it, and now that it's all over and done and finished, she doesn't care how he died. She just wanted him home, but she wanted him to come home right. She wanted that casket and those flowers and the hearse and she wanted to ride through town behind it in a car.* (383)[12]

Now that what Butch has done is past, Molly accepts her grandson simply because he was hers, regardless of his evil deeds. Her choice, then, is the reverse of Ike's. He repudiated a heritage, a past, rather than accept the evil that came with it, putting moral principle before love and devotion to family.

Yet Molly does not have the last word, nor is she the ultimate standard by which Ike is judged. No character enjoys such authority in *Go Down, Moses*. Gavin Stevens, for instance, helps us to see that in repudiating his patrimony, Ike also repudiates the community, but Stevens's words to his friend and ally suggest the inadequacy of his own response to blacks, and by extension, to those issues which divide the community: "'Come on,' he said. 'Let's get back to town. I haven't seen my desk in two days'" (383). It is important to remember at this point Buck's last words to Uncle Buddy in "Was": "'Go on and start breakfast. It seems to me I've been away from home a whole damn month'" (30). Buck was similarly out of his element in trying to cope with his Negro brother, Tomey's Turl.

The similarity in endings between "Was" and "Go Down, Moses" suggests, as Richard Adams says, that the last chapter is there "not as a denouement but rather as a contextual expansion of what has gone before."[13]

> This story performs at least the negative function of preventing perceptive readers of *Go Down, Moses* from settling into any simple formula as a note on which to conclude. We are made to feel, if we read the book from beginning to end and try to keep it all in mind, that events are very complicated, paradoxical, and contradictory. Life, or man, as Faulkner says, goes on, pragmatically, ruthlessly, often cruelly, as regardless of static moral formulas as of any other static ideas, smashing them when they get in the way and leaving them behind as they become obsolete. But there are dynamic moral principles emerging from change itself and requiring change on the part of responsible men. The static formulas are often emotionally more attractive, probably to Faulkner as well as to many of his readers, than this uncomfortable dynamic imperative; but they are not for that reason more highly approved either in Faulkner's recorded interviews or in his fiction. Change is the essence of Faulkner's work, in its moral as well as its artistic and technical aspects. The message is that we must go on with change, whether we like it or not.[14]

In the novel as a whole the many "shifts in period, setting, theme, and personnel," so "disturbing at a first reading,"[15] seem designed—when we try, in Adams's words, "to keep it all in mind"—precisely to make events seem "very complicated, paradoxical, and contradictory." The "moral formulas" and "static ideas" of Ike McCaslin are "smashed" and shown to be "obsolete" by juxtaposing him against those characters like Lucas Beauchamp who reject, or simply ignore, Ike's type of moralizing. Similarly, Faulkner's concern with change is embodied in the artistic and technical aspects of his work in the sense that he links character development to the processes of time. Here the historical dimension of Faulkner's imagination is the same as in *Absalom, Absalom!*, in which what a character's actions come to signify depends on the time from which they are viewed. Lengthen, shorten, or abolish the historical perspective, and the meaning of human actions and human character changes. How we perceive a character, then, depends very much upon how we adapt to the novel — upon, that is, the imaginative level reached. Faulkner always seems to imply in both novels that there is always another level, more intricate than the previous one, so that character creation becomes an historical exploration of the interaction between our past and present perceptions of specific figures. In this sense one can say that Faulkner has a great deal in common with an historian like Marc Bloch, who asserts that "the knowledge of the past is something progressive which is constantly transforming and perfecting itself."[16]

The progressive nature of Faulkner's exploration of the past is especially apparent toward the end of *Go Down, Moses*. For Parts Four and Five of "The Bear" and "Delta Autumn" all read like possible conclusions to the book which are superseded, each in its turn, by another attempt at closure. The book's meaning expands through these conceivable conclusions, but it does not end in any finite sense. Still another conclusion beyond "Go Down, Moses" is possible, although Faulkner obviously thought that with this ending he had achieved a structure for the whole work which would at the end be sufficiently apparent to return us to "Was" and to a sense of the past as still "transforming and perfecting itself" in our minds.

If we stand back from the seven individual chapters of *Go Down, Moses*, and from our interest in the ways they are connected to each other, we see a larger structural principle in operation. The first three chapters deal with plantation life in the South and with the history of race relations between the dominant white master class and their repressed Negro slaves. The wilderness out of which the white man carved this world is a minor theme. In the next three chapters the major and minor themes are reversed, and the world of white "civilization" is seen through the perspective of the wilderness as an encroaching set of future conditions. The resolution of this dialectic of wilderness and civilization is accomplished in the last chapter, briefly set in Chicago and then in Jefferson. In the town and the city, however, the same problems of white-black relationships occur, the same consequent question of what constitutes a genuine human community is posed.

The white man's invasions of (in turn) the wilderness, the plantation, the town and the city are successively the focal turning points which define his increasing distance from his own sources. For Ike, man's evil increases with the distance in time from man's initial violation of the wilderness. But *Go Down, Moses* itself seems to argue that good and evil are the basic, unquantifiable antinomies of all stages of history. Butch Beauchamp, for instance, is not corrupted in the city. He goes to the city because he is already corrupt, and because he has as a result been expelled from his native land. The census taker who inquires after his real name and background is just as shocked as a member of Jefferson would be to hear that Butch does not care about his family, and does not concern himself about the disposal of his body. Although the census taker is also in a "numbers racket," he does not treat Butch merely as a number, but responds to Butch's own inhumanity as might any sensitive human being. Gavin Stevens, with his Heidelberg Ph.D., is not less humane than Ike, who has been schooled in the wilderness. A sense of humanity, in short, is not tied to a particular place, and Ike's assumption to the contrary (that the wilderness is the special preserve of universal moral values) renders him powerless in a changing world.[17] As in *Absalom, Absalom!*, past and present are not joined by emphasizing the sameness of any two periods of time, but by dramatizing history as a human process that is going on at all times and all places.

6

Historical Research and the
Evolution of History in *Go Down, Moses*

Part Four of "The Bear" condenses the dialectic of past and present which goes on between the seven chapters of *Go Down, Moses* by embodying it in the debate between Ike and his cousin McCaslin. This section might be called the nuclear repository of the fundamental and unresolved historical issues of the novel, for it directly addresses the problem of how we can know history and to what extent we can claim to act upon such knowledge. These are questions the historian must confront, and therefore part of the discussion in this chapter will be devoted to the ways in which Ike becomes an historian, and to the value history itself has for him and for the reader who scrutinizes Faulkner's presentation of the past.

The commissary in which the debate occurs is both the symbol and the concrete manifestation of a social and economic system dominated by whites. It is the place where Negro labor is converted into economic profit, and where the very necessities of Negro existence are dispensed. It houses the archaic ledgers which record the transactions of the past, but it is also a living institution where blacks and whites continually meet on a day-by-day basis. The commissary, in sum, is the embodiment of the South's material and moral history.

We see the commissary's importance signalled throughout *Go Down, Moses* even before we focus on its special meaning for Ike and Cass in Part Four of "The Bear." Whenever Lucas, for example, tries to draw "anything extra in the way of cash or supplies from the commissary," Roth Edmonds suggests that Lucas "already had more money in the bank now than he would ever spend," more than he has himself (33–34). Roth is, of course, alluding to the money Ike gave Lucas on his twenty-first birthday and which derived from old Carothers's legacy to his unacknowledged black son, Tomey's Turl, Lucas's father. Obviously Lucas does not regard the commissary as merely his supply house; rather it represents for him part of his share in the plantation as a surviving McCaslin. He draws supplies "from the commissary as if he farmed, and at an outrageous and incredible profit, a thousand acres, having on the commissary books an account dating thirty years back which Edmonds knew he would never pay" (117).

When Lucas as a young man prepares to call Zack to account for taking Molly away from him, his first thought is to go to the commissary, where all transactions between blacks and whites traditionally take place (47). Many years later Lucas approaches Roth in the commissary to interest him in paying for the divining machine (78). Roth accuses him of not being willing to take a chance with his own money (80), but his insistence that Roth be included in the scheme also suggests a compulsive need to make it a family venture. The ultimate result of Lucas's fortune hunting is that Molly in her turn goes to see Roth in the commissary (he is, in fact, working on a ledger) to ask him to decree a divorce between herself and Lucas (99). In one way, her plea reinforces the fact that it is Roth who has the power to control the lives of the Negroes, but Roth also feels his total enslavement to the affairs of his tenants. Thus in spite of Roth's best efforts to detach himself from what he considers to be Lucas's foolish hunt for gold, he does become involved in the hunt because it becomes a family matter.

The commissary is also the place where the Negro tenants bank their money (138), where the hunters outfit themselves for their trips into the wilderness (169), "where on Saturday afternoons" Mannie in "Pantaloon in Black" "would walk...to buy their next week's supplies" (137), and where the weekly rations for all tenants and wagehands are dispensed (252). In "Go Down, Moses," Butch Beauchamp's "breaking into" the commissary store represents a fundamental repudiation of the institution by which his society is governed and results in Roth's ordering "him off the place" and forbidding him "ever to return" (373). There is a ceaseless inward and outward flow of crops, farming implements, foodstuffs, and currency. It is the life center, the "solar-plexus" (255) of the plantation, and it characterizes the life cycle of a civilization, as Cass himself notes when he compares the commissary to Rome as the center of an empire (257).

Thus the reader knows that Ike and McCaslin are debating a way of life, the organization of a society, that continues to flourish into the 1940s. Even in 1888, on Ike's twenty-first birthday, it is clear that Ike bears the burden of explaining how he can reject an institution that has at least endured and even prevailed against the grim background of Southern history. As Cass tells Ike, whether or not old Carothers had a right to the land is idle speculation in the face of his and his children's ability to hold and improve the land over a considerable number of years. Or as Faulkner once said in an interview, "To oppose a material fact with a moral truth is silly."[1]

Yet Ike persists in contending that the land was not old Carothers's property to bequeath to his family alone, but his only to hold "mutual and intact in the communal anonymity of brotherhood" (257). Therefore Ike cannot repudiate what his grandfather never owned, even though he can anticipate ("'I know what you are going to say'" [257]) Cass's insistence that his grandfather did own it, and was not the first man who laid claim to the land. Although Ike may appear to be willfully blind to the material facts, it is important to see that he is trying to vindicate a moral principle that has been buried underneath the material facts by articulating a "text" or statement that answers Cass's formidable defense of the precedent set by old Carothers.[2]

Not to be outdone by Ike's highfalutin' idea of history, Cass traces man's descent from Eden and God's chosen sprung from Abraham to Rome, the dark ages, and Columbus's (the "accidental egg") discovery of America, a "new hemisphere." Although he sees a cyclical pattern of birth, death, and renewal ending in America, he doubts that this cycle is divinely directed. God's purpose seems ambiguous, to say the least: "'This Arbiter, this Architect, this Umpire—condoned—or did He? looked down and saw—or did He? Or at least did nothing; saw, and could not, or did not see; saw, and would not, or perhaps He would not see—perverse, impotent, or blind: which?'" (258). The active force in history is not God, but man, and man has established his own relationship to the land.

But Ike replies that Cass's own historical account, read correctly, shows that man has been constantly dispossessed of the land he ravished. According to Ike, God's purpose in bringing men like old Carothers to the new world was to break the unbroken succession of Ikkemotubbe and his descendants and their hold over the land. Yet God has no special faith or preference for one race over another: "'He used the blood which had brought in the evil to destroy the evil as doctors use fever to burn up fever, poison to slay poison'" (259). How does Ike know this? "'The heart already knows,'" he says, "'and there is only one truth and it covers all things that touch the heart'" (260).

Cass counters Ike by pointing out man's genuine confusion as to what the Bible says, and Ike is placed in the uncomfortable position of explaining what he sees as God's clear intentions and man's muddled execution of them. He argues, on the one hand, that the heart cannot err, and on the other, that God's plan has only come clearly to Ike himself through the workings of time. Cass cannot see the plan manifesting itself in history and returns again to the confusion of history, to 1865, which was a disaster for his people, not a sign of divine redemption of erring mankind. Buck and Buddy, and a "thousand" others like them, Cass notes, tried to cope with what the Book said, and yet the war destroyed any opportunity they might have had to carry out what Ike calls God's plan. Why should Ike expect to do any better than they did, when there are not even two complete generations separating him from his grandfather old Carothers (261)?

Here the debate breaks off, leaving the two sides unreconciled and leaving the reader, I should think, either puzzled or simply incapable of choosing the better argument. Ike presumptuously speaks of a divine purpose transcending a loyalty to family heritage, while Cass stubbornly interprets history from the point at which his family took possession of the land. Ike invokes higher laws operating in contravention of his cousin's obsession with regional history, while Cass chides Ike for relinquishing his responsibility as the sole heir to the McCaslin plantation in favor of a faith in God's purposes that does not seem warranted in the light of the very history Ike invokes.

Though the debate itself remains unsettled, the issues are further explored in terms of the McCaslin family's commissary books, the common source for Ike's and Cass's views of the Southern past. As we might expect, these books, which are likened to "the Book," contain evidence supporting both sides of the debate, so that Ike's argument, as Cass says of his biblical references, can be proved or disproved by the same text. As we shall see, both Ike's and Cass's ideas of history are, in themselves, insufficiently commensurate with the history they attempt to describe and assess. Moreover, the ledgers suggest that any accounting of the past is by its very nature incomplete, and that any attempt to make full restitution for that past is thus doomed to failure.

In a sense Buck and Buddy had originated the debate that is carried on by Cass and Ike by both accepting and then trying to modify the legacy left to them by their father, old Carothers. They move out of the big house, the conspicuous symbol of a slave economy, and move into the one-room log cabin, "refusing to allow any slave to touch any timber of it other than the actual raising into place the logs which two men alone could not handle" (262). Even though slavery is in some sense repudiated by this unusual arrangement, Buck and Buddy still treat their slaves as animals, herding them "without question protest or recourse, into the tremendous abortive edifice scarcely yet out of embryo" (262), which was potentially symbolic of their attempt to abandon the fairly new tradition of slavery, but which in fact becomes symbolic of their own truncated efforts to wipe out a "tremendous" evil.

The commissary books themselves have an immense power to engage the reader in an intensive search for what it was like to live in the past because of their tangibility as documents, the very stuff out of which the historian makes his history, and because of their reevocation of "Was," that opening chapter which, Michael Millgate observes, "belongs to the

past — as its title insists — and to a particular moment in that past."[3] "Was,"
it is important to remember, is a narrative document based on Cass's
memory of past events and providing a remarkable insight into the atmosphere in which Buck and Buddy conducted the business of the plantation.
It is anecdotal or popular history rendered through the viewpoint of a nine-
year-old, but it has also been told at one time to Ike and is related to us
through still another voice representing a distillation of the story itself, a
story whose purity and smoothness reminds us of a legend, a family inheritance savored and no doubt elaborated during countless retellings. The
narrative, then, represents a society's way of looking at itself, not critically
but appreciatively, through the eye of one of its members, in this case a
child who holds no preconceptions about slavery, or about plantation life
in general. Cass accepts his circumstances as would any normal child of his
age. Consequently, an extraordinary sense of contemporaneity pervades
the story, in which the past can be accepted on its own terms and seen
pretty much from the vantage point of its historically unconscious
participants.

Ike, however, has not participated in these events, and no matter how
real they become in the telling, they remain, for him, hearsay. Thus when
he reads his father's and uncle's ledgers, he is provided for the first time
not only with concrete proof that the past once existed, but with the evidence of Buck's and Buddy's direct responses to their family heritage and
to their duties as plantation owners. The ledgers outline the history of the
McCaslin family and place "Was" within the framework of an entire age.
The ledgers themselves, therefore, are nearer in time than "Was" to the
events they describe — indeed as their faded ink and cracked bindings testi-
fy, they are actual products of the past and survivors from it. "Was," then,
from one point of view, is one step removed from these kind of written
records which, in G. J. Renier's words,

> give to the investigator a sense of immediacy which a narrative document can never
> produce. If we handle a bill, which is a private record, or a ledger, an order for the
> delivery of goods, we are in touch with traces of a commercial transaction that are more
> direct than the traces of the same event which we might find in the diary or the memoirs
> of the merchant who carried out this transaction. On the other hand, narrative
> documents often contain traces — but at one remove — of the atmosphere that accom-
> panied these transactions.[4]

The historian especially values written evidence because it "fixes a statement, and ensures its being transmitted faithfully."[5] Because the ledgers
are, in a sense, the past itself — "the yellowed pages and the brown thin ink
in which was recorded the injustice and a little at least of its amelioration
and restitution faded back forever into the anonymous communal original

dust" (261)—they give to Ike's investigation a sense of immediacy found nowhere else in *Go Down, Moses.* As Langlois and Seignobos suggest in their *Introduction to the Study of History:* "From the same document we derive facts bearing on handwriting, language, style, doctrines, customs, events."⁶ "A single page" from the ledgers, "not long and covering less than a year, not seven months in fact" (263), demonstrates how Buck and Buddy used the commissary books as business accounts, journals, diaries, and chronologies. In the process of accustoming ourselves to the varied uses of the ledgers we are also accustoming ourselves to the thought patterns, the sense of history, and indeed the heritage which Ike and Cass have theorized about in their debate.

The first entry on this "single page" is Buck's detailed account of his purchase of

> *Percavil Brownly 26yr Old. cleark @ Bookepper. bought from N.B. Forest at Cold Water 3 Mar 1856 $265.dolars* (264)

Buck's purchase of a fellow human being is set down just like any other commercial transaction, and in that respect reminiscent of his treatment of Tomey's Turl as his property in "Was." Although Buck's actual intentions are never known, his frequent misspellings and infrequent, inconsistent use of punctuation eloquently suggest that he needed someone to assist him in keeping the records of the plantation in order. It is significant, of course, that Buck is not compelled to state any reason for his purchase. His assurance, Edmond Volpe observes, derives from the "formalized and accepted pattern of Negro-white relations" in the antebellum South.⁷ Yet, as in "Was," which occurs approximately three years after the purchase of Brownlee, this "formalized and accepted pattern" is rather humorously wrecked by the slave, who proves resistant to the white man's system of control.

Just two days after the purchase of Brownlee, Buck writes:

> *5 mar 1856 No bookepper any way Cant read. Can write his Name but I already put that down My self Says he can Plough but dont look like it to Me. sent to Feild to day Mar 5 1856* (264)

Buck's assumption that he could "buy" a "*bookepper*" for "265 dolars" is contrasted with the problems of slave ownership. Notice that the formal recording of fact in the first entry has been replaced by a diary-like record revealing in terse and understated language Buck's puzzled attempts to figure out this individual black man's interests and capacities, which the two men seem to have discussed. From the discussion it becomes apparent to Buck that he had not even "bought" the services of a fieldhand, which was at least a more likely job for a slave.

The more Buck tries to suit the slave's temperament to the work he is supposed to do, the more it becomes evident, especially to his brother Buddy, that Brownlee just does not fit anywhere in the plantation system:

> [Buck] *6 Mar 1856 Cant plough either Says he aims to be a Precher so may be he can lead live stock to Crick to Drink*

and this time it was the other, the hand which he [Ike] now recognized as his uncle's when he could see them both on the same page:

> *Mar 23th 1856 Cant do that either Except one at a Time Get shut of him*

then the first again:

> *24 Mar 1856 Who in hell would buy him*

then the second:

> *19th of Apr 1856 Nobody You put yourself out of Market at Cold Water two months ago I never said sell him Free him*

the first:

> *22 Apr 1856 Ill get it out of him* (264)

As Ike learns to distinguish between his father's and uncle's almost identical handwriting he also learns to distinguish between their similar and yet distinct reactions to the Negro, which, in turn, are reflective of a number of other differences between the brothers that are noted in passing by Cass in "Was" but only become fully significant as Ike reads the ledgers. Buck is the more venturesome brother who dares to fetch Tomey's Turl from Hubert Beauchamp's plantation, where Miss Sophonsiba is ready to capture a husband. Uncle Buddy never goes anywhere (6). Even more than Buck, Buddy avoids contact with women, and both brothers use Buck's necktie "just as another way of daring people to say they looked like twins." Buddy is the better poker player (7). Unlike Buck, he never drinks and is not "woman-weak," as Hubert Beauchamp puts it (26). Buddy never takes chances; when he gambles, he always wins. He seems less human than Buck for this very reason. Because he avoids all complex human relationships, he never becomes involved in the contradictory and frustrating attempts of Buck to establish relationships, no matter how limited or even unjust, with the slaves and with whatever neighbors Buck comes into contact. Neither brother is outgoing, and both regard Brownlee as a bad business investment, but whereas Buddy would simply write off the transaction as a loss, Buck would try the harder, and as it turns out, more dangerous alternative of somehow recouping the value of his purchase.

In answer to Buck's desperate assertion, *"Ill get it out of him,"* Buddy says almost two months later:

> *Jun 13th 1856 How $1 per yer 265$ 265 yrs Wholl sign his Free paper* (265)

For Buddy the question is merely ludicrous, but for Buck, writing three-and-a-half months later, it is clear that the arrangement with Brownlee has resulted in total disaster:

> *1 Oct 1856 Mule josephine Broke Leg @ shot Wrong stall wrong niger wrong everything $100. dolars* (265)

After calming down, Buck's entry the next day simulates the matter-of-factness of his first entry, as if he were trying to forget the trouble he has brought upon himself, and go back to the action recommended by Buddy:

> *2 Oct 1856 Freed Debit McCaslin @ McCaslin $265. dolars* (265)

Buddy's next comment not only refuses to accept any share of the responsibility or cost himself but also reminds Buck that Brownlee has cost almost half as much again as Buck originally paid for him and reveals the confusion Buck has interjected into the plantation system by bargaining and negotiating with Brownlee:

> *Oct 3th Debit Theophilus McCaslin Niger 265$ Mule 100$ 365$ He hasnt gone yet Father should be here* (265)

Buddy is preparing the ground for his humorous suggestion for the renaming of Brownlee, but the invocation of old Carothers's name serves to recall that he had ruled his plantation with a firm hand, and would never have allowed such an episode to go on for so many months. He also had an absolute sense of what the relationship between Master and slave should be, so that there was never any ambiguity about the procedures and rules of slave ownership.

The reference to "Father" also reminds us that Buck and Buddy are the products of their age, struggling with a limited vocabulary and limited concepts to define their options in dealing with an "anomaly" (263) who does not fit into the slave system they have inherited. Above all, they must think in terms of the day-to-day realities and responsibilities of running the plantation. Along with Ike, we see how much Buck and Buddy are caught up in the "unavoidable business of the compulsion which had traversed all the waste wilderness of North Mississippi in 1830 and '40 and singled them out to drive" (263). Brownlee's own career, as we later learn, fittingly follows the erratic course of the twins' reforms. Shortly after the war he appears as a preacher on the McCaslin plantation, then as a member of the "entourage of a travelling Army paymaster," and finally as the "well-to-do proprietor of a select New Orleans brothel" (292–93) — as the master, ironically enough, of an institution which, like slavery, uses human beings for economic profit and sexual exploitation. Thus Brownlee has proven himself capable of manipulating the situation on the plantation and the "system" as a whole to his advantage, so that the white men are, so to speak, mastered by their slave.

The amusing manner in which Buck and Buddy tolerate this strange slave is, however, far more important than the slave himself. In spite of the frustration and pecuniary losses, Buddy is not willing to make a serious issue of his brother's mistake; instead Brownlee becomes a crude joke. He is renamed "Spintrius," an allusion to his effeminacy and probable homosexuality, since the *spintriae* were the practitioners of perversion.[8] What the joke and the whole Brownlee episode brilliantly convey is not a sense of slavery as a weighty issue or a moral crime but as a way of life; we see how Buck and Buddy coped with and sometimes even enjoyed the anomalies of their world, and we get a momentary insight into the past as it was experienced by its contemporaries.

The extreme brevity of the entries shows that Buck and Buddy were not primarily thinkers or observers of their contemporary scene; it also tantalizes us with just a fleeting glimpse of, so to speak, the past in motion, argued and articulated in its own words. Like all such evidence of past life, these words capture part of what it must have felt like to live there and then, but the words themselves are not enough to evoke past life as a whole. For Ike, reading the one page of entries on Brownlee, the past "took substance and even a sort of shadowy life" (265), but it is by no means fully alive. Similarly, in *Absalom, Absalom!* the words of Charles Bon's letter begin to take on a kind of shadowy life for Quentin. Like Quentin, Ike is placed in the position of having to generate through reason and imagination a complete portrayal of the past. Here Ike's task is similar to the historian's as defined by Langlois and Seignobos:

> The facts of the past are only known to us by the traces of them which have been preserved. These traces, it is true, are directly observed by the historian, but, after that, he has nothing more to observe; what remains is the work of reasoning, in which he endeavors to infer, with the greatest possible exactness, the facts from the traces.[9]

The interpretation of the past at which Ike eventually arrives is based on a chain of reasoning, far removed from the events themselves and dependent on imperfect records of those events the eyewitnesses have left. Like the historian, Ike has pages and pages of documents which tell not only of "general and condoned injustice and its slow amortization" but also of "the specific tragedy which had not been condoned and could never be amortized." For Ike, this specific tragedy is found on the "new page and the new ledger" (266), from which we learn that Old Carothers McCaslin had been dead almost twenty years when Buck and Buddy were asking themselves what their father would have done with Percavil Brownlee. On the very day of their father's death the brothers had tried to free his slaves, even offering their family's chattels money, or in one case, a "10acre peace." The mispelling of "piece" ironically underlines the fact that the twins had no "peace" when it came to amortizing what they seem to have considered as a family debt incurred by their father. As chattels the slaves had no idea of what they were being offered, and could no more become free of old Carothers than could Buck and Buddy.

Unlike the earlier entries concerning Brownlee, which constituted a kind of diary or journal of a specific period of time in the twins' adminis-tration of the plantation, this second entry (266) bunches together events of a long period of time in something like the manner of a genealogy or set of annals. The dates and places of old Carothers's birth, death, and burial are recorded. Also recorded are the names, births (often without a date), and deaths of slaves whom old Carothers inherited, bought, and "rased." It seems that Buck and Buddy were doing their best to put together a com-plete account of what they knew about their family as it had been estab-lished by their father and grandfather. After their father's death, the twin McCaslins were conscientiously attempting to free their family's slaves in the only way they knew how—through business transactions recorded in the family ledgers. That the slaves were more than just property, more than just a part of plantation "business" to Buck and Buddy is clear from the entries in which Buck notes that neither Fibby nor Roskus wanted to leave the plantation and that Thucydus felt that he had to earn his free-dom. Moreover, if Buck is ignorant of some of the important dates in his family's history, and if his knowledge of others is incomplete or perhaps inaccurate, he makes sure that the 27th and 28th of June 1837, the days on which "*A.@T. McCaslin*" tried to free their slaves after their father's death, are fully and precisely recorded. The very making of the genealogy is evidence that the McCaslins viewed the care of their family as a grave responsibility. Thus Buck and Buddy's attitude toward Brownlee, which may have seemed to be only humorous, is placed into the context of the McCaslin family's experience in the antebellum period as it is recorded in

Buck's genealogy from 1772, the year in which their father was born in "*Callina*," to "*1 Aug 1849*," the year in which "Fibby Roskus Wife, *bought by granfather in Callina*," "*dide*" and was "*burd*" (266).

Beneath this genealogy, it is reported, are five pages in the ledger which represent neither an episode in plantation life nor a chronicle of the system but rather an accounting of "the slow day-by-day accrument of wages allowed" Thucydus and of "the food and clothing" charged to this slave who had insisted on staying on the plantation and "working out" the cash offer of the two McCaslins. Ike imagines the black man as hopelessly dependent on his white master. The slave could never be free so long as he had to think of the white man as the giver of his freedom (266–67). It seems that Buck had invested, not in the black man's freedom, but in his continued slavery. Yet Ike's father persisted in entering the results of his and his brother's patient attempts to honor the provisions of old Carothers's will (267).

Two entries in the ledger, one by Buck and one by Buddy, seem to have been Ike's first insight into why it was so important to free Thucydus on the very day after old Carothers died:

> *Eunice Bought by Father in New Orleans 1807 $650. dolars. Marrid to Thucydus 1809 Drownd in Crick Christmas Day 1832* (267)

Buddy's entry is easily the most dramatic in all of the ledgers, for it is made without preface or explanation and reaffirmed after Buck's skeptical reactions two days later:

> *June 21th 1833 Drownd herself*
>
> *23 Jun 1833 Who in hell ever heard of a niger drownding him self*
>
> *Aug 13th 1833 Drownd herself* (267)

Buck brings out the truly shocking nature of Buddy's statement by expressing an implicit assumption of his time, that a slave had no life of his own which he could think of ending. Buck is not reflecting on the particular circumstances of Eunice's death (note his change from "*herself*" to "*him self*"), but is betraying his notions about Negroes in general.

Ike, however, does not share his father's attitudes toward Negroes, and because his world view is different the nature of his questions is also somewhat different. It is not quite so surprising to him that Eunice should commit suicide, but he is puzzled by Uncle Buddy's insistence on the point (268). By inquiring into the conditions which prompted Buddy to be so adamant, making his belief known in "two identical entries" which, although they are separated by almost two months, "might have been made

with a rubber stamp save for the date" (267), Ike is unconsciously following a principle of historiography holding that in the reading of all historical
documents the context in which a statement is made is as important as the
statement itself.[10] Buddy's brief, repeated statements are indeed what historians call a "psychological trace," which is not the historical fact itself
and

> not even the immediate impression made by the fact upon the witness's mind, but only a
> conventional symbol of that impression.... This granted...in order to ascertain the
> relation which connects the document with the fact [which was its remote cause], it is
> necessary to reproduce the whole series of intermediate causes which have given rise to
> the document. It is necessary to revive in imagination the whole of that series of acts
> performed by the author of the document which begins with the fact observed by him
> and ends with the manuscript (or printed volume), in order to arrive at the original
> event.[11]

As part of the intermediate causes which give rise to Buddy's written assertion of Eunice's suicide nearly seven months after the event itself, Ike finds
two additional entries in the ledger:

> *Tomasina called Tomy Daughter of Thucydus @ Eunice Born 1810 dide in Child bed
> June 1833 and Burd. Yr stars fell* (269)

> *Turl Son of Thucydus @ Eunice Tomy born Jun 1833 yr stars fell Fathers will* (269)

Eunice died seven months before her daughter was to give birth to a child.
On June 21, 1833, perhaps after the birth of Tomey's Turl, Buddy realized
that her death was suicide. On June 28, 1837, four years later, and a day
after old Carothers died, Thucydus, Eunice's husband, was offered his
freedom.

Once Ike looks at his grandfather's will, he realizes that old Carothers
"made no effort either to explain or obfuscate the thousand-dollar legacy
to the son [Tomey's Turl] of an unmarried slave-girl" (269). If never stated
by old Carothers, it is nevertheless clear to Ike, as presumably to Buddy,
that old Carothers would have left such a legacy only to his own son, and
that he shifted the burden and the consequences of his sin to the next two
generations of his family rather than directly acknowledge his responsibility to his black son (269–70).

But precisely because Buck's "genealogy" has treated the freeing of the
slaves as a family matter, not simply a business transaction, Ike is forced to
consider what may have been his grandfather's feelings. Ike's extenuating
inference is that his grandfather may in some sense have loved the girl and
that her mother may have acquiesced in Old Carothers's desires because
she and her husband were not "field hands" but an important part of the

family—after all, "the husband and his father and mother too had been inherited by the white man from his father" (270). Old Carothers's genuine affection for his slaves is also apparent to Ike when he thinks of his grandfather travelling "the three hundred miles and better to New Orleans in a day when men travelled by horseback or steamboat" (270), just to obtain Eunice, a very expensive slave ($650), as a wife for Thucydus.

That Ike's train of thought is now beginning to follow the actual pattern of past events appears to be suggested by "the old frail pages" themselves which "seemed to turn of their own accord even while he thought *His own daughter His own daughter. No No Not even him*" (270). It has suddenly occurred to Ike that old Carothers impregnated his own daughter and that is why he could not directly acknowledge his son. The only way for Ike to corroborate his shocking inference is to return again to the fact that his grandfather "(not even a widower then) who never went anywhere any more than his sons in their time ever did and who did not need another slave, had gone all the way to New Orleans and bought one" (270). In ostensibly seeking a mate for Thucydus, old Carothers had evidently obtained a mistress for himself. Ike then shifts to the only other concrete evidence he has: since Tomey's Turl "was still alive" when Ike was ten years old, Ike "knew from his own observation and memory that there had already been some white in Tomey's Terrel's blood before his father gave him the rest of it" (271). Buddy's insistence on Eunice's suicide finally makes sense. Tomey's Turl received his white blood from Carothers's intercourse not only with Tomasina but also with her mother, Eunice. Ike can now achieve an imaginative recreation on the basis of his Uncle Buddy's brief but insistent record of Eunice's suicide:

> He seemed to see her actually walking into the icy creek on that Christmas day six months before her daughter's and her lover's (*Her first lover's* he thought. *Her first*) child was born, solitary, inflexible, griefless, ceremonial, in formal and succinct repudiation of grief and despair who had already had to repudiate belief and hope. (271)

Ike invests Eunice with a dignity and integrity that are only hinted at in the historical record, and that Buck and Buddy seem to have only partially recognized. Indeed our only assurance that Ike's portrait approximates what actually happened is based on our faith in the process of historical interpretation which we have undertaken along with him. His appreciation of circumstances, his constant alertness to the way in which human actions arise out of the pressures of day-to-day existence, are revealed in his evocation of old Carothers's loneliness and arrogance, the references in the ledgers to "father's will," and then Buddy's abrupt announcement that Eunice has drowned herself—all of which draw his attention to the "significant detail," that break in the pattern of business as usual on the planta-tion.[12] It is the peculiar circumstances which become the "essential facts"[13] for Ike as historian.

Thus we gradually form our reading of the McCaslin story through the actual experience of historical interpretation, becoming experts, together with Ike, in the interpretation of the past. Were this not the case, then we would not understand that old Carothers committed incest and miscegenation, for nowhere are those sins so labeled. Indeed an inattentive or simply uncomprehending reader could, conceivably, have no idea of how Ike arrived at his conclusions. In fact one critic has gone so far as to maintain that although Ike's interpretation has "aesthetic persuasiveness,"[14] it is not "necessarily the 'correct one,'"[15] because the so-called facts he arrives at "are not ascertainable" in "objectively verifiable data." This critic does not doubt that Ike's version is "convincing," "believable," and "realistic," but these terms apply, so the argument goes, to the truthfulness of a novel, not, it is implied, to the truthfulness of history.[16] We cannot be sure that Ike is "right" or indeed that there is any such condition as "right"—for Ike, like the historian, can only make the best sense he can out of the evidence that survives. "Facts" and "objectively verifiable data" can-not exist independently of or apart from the historian or character-narrator who views them. How the facts of the past come to light are, as I will argue later, dependent on Ike's peculiar consciousness, and John Lukacs, in his study of historical consciousness, suggests that this is also true of any his-torian:

> While it is certainly arguable that what happened is more important than what we think happened, it is hardly arguable that these are separate matters—that, in other words, a fact can be isolated not only from other facts but from our thinking about it.[17]

Not only can a fact not be isolated from our thinking about it, but the historian knows that

> the amount of verifying a researcher does depends not only on his own curiosity but also on the grasp of his subject that he possesses at the start. The more he understands at the beginning, the more he finds to question and ascertain.[18]

At sixteen, when Ike first reads the ledgers, we are told that his act is the culmination of several years of growing interest in what the books might contain. Ike knew, even as a child of nine, that he would examine the ledgers one day, and "he knew what he was going to find before he found it" (268). He knew because, like Quentin Compson in *Absalom, Absalom!*, he had lived all his life with the heritage that he would have to confront some day as an adult. Just as Quentin knew, in a sense, that he would find

Henry Sutpen in the attic at Sutpen's Hundred, so Ike knew, in a sense, of his grandfather's incest and miscegenation even before he had read the ledgers.

There almost seems to be a reference back to *Absalom, Absalom!* in the narrator's description of the "rank dead icy air" (268) in which Ike asks himself why Eunice drowned herself; so Quentin in the cold tomb-like Harvard room asks himself why Henry killed Bon. For both young men the past—however remote and shadowy it may seem at times—is of immense importance to their sense of identity; they cannot live in the present without coming to terms with the past, which is to say that they are actually asking the historian's question: "How has this world as it now exists come to be what it is?"[19] The past has obviously left its traces upon the present in the form of the evidence which is the starting point for Ike's investigation.[20]

Like R. G. Collingwood's critical historian, Ike does not simply assemble, scrutinize, and interpret conflicting primary sources; he asks his own questions about what he feels is most important in the problem he is studying. In other words, he becomes his own authority,[21] and we too become experts insofar as we can duplicate and ratify the soundness of his method. Ike's facts cannot be abstracted from the context in which he fits them. As Carl Becker observes, facts are not material substances which,

> like bricks or scantlings, possess definite shape and clear, persistent outline. To set forth historical facts is not comparable to dumping a barrow of bricks. A brick retains its form and pressure wherever placed; but the form and substance of historical facts, having a negotiable existence only in literary discourse, vary with the words employed to convey them. Since history is not part of the external material world, but an imaginative reconstruction of vanished events, its form and substance are inseparable; in the realm of literary discourse substance, being an idea, is form; and form, conveying the idea, is substance. It is thus not the undiscriminated fact, but the perceiving mind of the historian that speaks: the special meaning which the facts are made to convey emerges from the substance-form which the historian employs to recreate imaginatively a series of events not present to perception.[22]

In other words, we are profoundly impressed with the whole sum of Ike's interpretation of the evidence because he has found a form which gives substance to the past, and which is internally consistent and accurate in its rendering of details. His interpretation is not simply compatible with the evidence; rather his story constitutes the "best reading—the reading that captures most succinctly what the evidence has to say."[23]

Part Four of "The Bear" thus resembles Quentin and Shreve's reconstruction of the past in Chapter VIII of *Absalom, Absalom!* insofar as it makes the narration of events up to the confrontation between Ike and Cass in the commissary *evidence* for Ike's and Cass's interpretations of history. Our total readings of *Go Down, Moses* and *Absalom, Absalom!* are simultaneously expanded and condensed in Ike's reading of the commissary books and in Quentin and Shreve's interpretation of Bon's life. In other words, Ike's and Cass's views, and Quentin's and Shreve's, literally grow out of the "stories" or different versions of history which now have a cumulative impact on our own understanding of the entire novel, and we, in a sense, become just as responsible for the "history" in *Absalom, Absalom!* and *Go Down, Moses* as the characters are.

In *Absalom, Absalom!* we must follow Quentin and Shreve in filling in the gaps of Sutpen's autobiography and in making the necessary inferences from Bon's letter and from Quentin's interview with Henry. So too in *Go Down, Moses* we are never told that old Carothers made out his will the same year Eunice committed suicide—Buddy never says why he suspected Eunice of committing suicide—yet all of these "facts" emerge from our juxtaposing and ordering the various entries in the ledgers. From there we go on to review the evidence from earlier sections to see what light it casts on Buck's and Buddy's jottings. Moreover, with our own painstakingly earned historical perspective we can, in turn, place Ike and Cass within the context of the history they interpret, as the narrator in Chapter VIII of *Absalom, Absalom!* places Quentin and Shreve in the context of the Sutpen story. Finally, the focus of both novels narrows down to Quentin and Ike, the only members of their families who have pieced together a relatively full account of the past, and who agonize over the massive implications of their discoveries.

Quentin and Ike are each juxtaposed against a figure from the past who possesses titanic energy, and who is the founder of a dynasty. The constant references to old Carothers's ruthless "will" (meaning both the legal document which established a legacy for his black offspring and his own innate assertive power) remind one of Thomas Sutpen's ruthless design to establish a dynasty, no matter at what cost to himself or to others, or even to his own family. For, like Sutpen, old Carothers denied his own son. Quentin's discovery of Henry in the Sutpen house and of the meaning of the Sutpen story is tantamount to acceding to the irremovable presence of the past in his own life. Ike's discovery of the ledgers and of the meaning of his grandfather's legacy remains forever as part of his consciousness: "He would never need look at the ledgers again nor did he; the yellowed pages in their fading and implacable succession were as much a part of his consciousness and would remain so forever, as the fact of his own nativity" (271).

Nonetheless, Ike is not faced with exactly the situation that Quentin inherits. Ike's is an evil but not a moribund heritage. Unlike Sutpen, old Carothers did leave a legacy for his black son, even if he could not directly acknowledge him. In contrast to Quentin, Ike thinks that he can make good the past by using his grandfather's legacy to "free" the black McCaslins—though even here his use of the legacy commits him, as it committed Buck and Buddy, to perpetuating the terms set by old Carothers's will.

Ike's various attempts to redeem the past should all be seen as a preparation for the renunciation scene with his cousin Cass when he turns twenty-one. At eighteen, just two years after the deaths of Lion, Old Ben, and Sam Fathers, and two years after his momentous discovery of his grandfather's refusal to openly acknowledge his own black son, Ike tries to track down Tennie's Jim, the eldest surviving child of Tomey's Turl and Tennie Beauchamp, who disappeared from the plantation on the day of his twenty-first birthday. In spite of strenuous efforts Tennie's Jim cannot be found, perhaps because he does not want to be found. In "The Fire and the Hearth" the narrator suggests:

> It was as though he had not only (as his sister was later to do) put running water between himself and the land of his grandmother's betrayal and his father's nameless birth, but he had interposed latitude and geography too, shaking from his feet forever the very dust of the land where his white ancestor could acknowledge or repudiate him from one day to another, according to his whim, but where he dared not even repudiate the white ancestor save when it met the white man's humor of the moment. (105)

Evidently Tennie's Jim does not want his acknowledgment contingent on what he perhaps considers the "whim" of Ike, who is himself, after all, a grandson of old Carothers. In any case, he is the first black McCaslin to leave the plantation of his own free will. Perhaps this choice in itself is what constitutes his freedom. Ike seems to have misread the lesson of the ledgers, for the real problem, perhaps, is not so much *how* the Negro is to be freed but *what* freedom the Negro can possibly have. The limitations of Ike's own conception of freedom are defined by his subsequent attempt to "free" Fonsiba, who has already achieved with her Northern husband a kind of freedom which is in its sterility strikingly reminiscent of Ike's own situation, and by his failure to see that Lucas, the last of Tennie's children, has come to terms with his position as a black McCaslin in a way that is peculiarly his own. Instead of leaving the plantation as his brother and sister had done, he simply refuses to act according to the patterns established for blacks by a white-dominated society, symbolizing his choice by changing his first name from Lucius, which had been old Carothers's name, to Lucas, "making it no longer the white man's but his own, by himself composed, himself selfprogentive and nominate, by himself ancestored, as, for all the old ledgers recorded to the contrary, old Carothers himself was" (281). Lucas, as we saw in "The Fire and the Hearth," has old Carothers's ruthlessness and pride, and while these qualities do not make him free, they make him a man in the same sense that old Carothers was a man, who at least exercised his will, his power over life. He is not free because, as Ike himself realized when he had to give Lucas his share of the legacy, "no man is ever free and probably could not bear it if he were" (281).

Part Four of "The Bear" shifts back at this point to the debate in the commissary between Cass and Ike, and we see that the latter, in contrast to Lucas, views himself as a "chosen, symbolic figure—a Moses charged with the tablets of the law," invoking a view of history that depends "heavily upon the actions of individual heroic figures and interventions by God himself."[24] Indeed one reason why Cass has so much trouble in understanding Ike's God is that "Ike's views of history are...a projection of his personality and situation."[25] His portrayal of God wrestling with matters of conscience in "His lonely and paramount heaven" (282) is also a good portrayal of himself. Ike's projection here is far greater than that of the narrators in *Absalom, Absalom!*, to whom he has been compared,[26] because he claims to know not only why God let the South lose the war but also that he himself has been especially chosen by God to repudiate the evil: "'If He could see Father and Uncle Buddy in Grandfather He must have seen me too'" (283). It is not surprising, then, that Cass should accuse both God and Ike of betraying his family and the South (258, 283).

Again Cass returns to the incompatibility between Ike's ideas and what actually happened in 1865. How can Ike see history as part of God's continuous plan, when such a ghastly disaster wrecked the efforts of Buck and Buddy, who were presumably preparing for Ike's regeneration of an evil system? Ike's answer is that Buck and Buddy alone were not "enough"—a judgment based, soundly enough, on a reading of the commissary books, where it is clear that Buck and Buddy could not have significantly remedied a pervasive evil. Ike goes on to say that only the war, a total assault on a whole way of life, was "enough." What alternative to war was there, Ike wonders. Certainly the politicians "passing resolutions about horror and outrage in warm and airproof halls" affected the actual lives of slaves not a jot. Certainly the manufacturers engaged in the production of cotton would never have stopped the "whirling wheels" of their machines long enough to obliterate the system from which they derived their profits (283-84).

Only one man during this time receives Ike's praise, John Brown, who was "just one simple enough to believe that horror and outrage were first and last simply horror and outrage and was crude enough to act upon that, illiterate and had no words for talking or perhaps was just busy and had no time to..." (284). Brown is one of those simple people who, Ike had earlier said, absorb the simple truths of the Bible, which are directed to the unerring heart. Ike's point can be understood in terms of Reinhold Niebuhr's statement in *The Irony of American History* that "there may be a wholeness of view among the simple which grasps ultimate truths, not seen by the sophisticated."²⁷ Because of such men God turned "'once more to this land which He still intended to save because He had done so much for it'" (285). Again, however, Ike's emphasis on Brown's simple act and simple faith and uncompromising stance against evil is a good characterization of his own simple rejection of evil, which sometimes degenerates into a fanaticism of principle rather like Brown's. For Ike's act of repudiation, like Brown's suicidal raid on Harper's Ferry, is a desperate act, as desperate as Ike's portrayal of Eunice's "formal and succinct repudiation" (271).

Yet some readers have found Ike's repudiation admirable, and I suspect that it is for the same reasons that Brown has been admired. To unequivocally state one's position, to identify the evil and to refuse to cooperate with an unjust order, is a virtuous, and often a courageous act.²⁸ The demand for freedom, in whatever context, be it public or private, the Civil War or Molly's wish to be released from Lucas's intolerable obsession with treasure hunting ("'I gots to be free'" [121]), is a moral imperative. To go against the past, to stand against the whole weight of tradition as Ike must, is surely an act of unusual courage. Perhaps in the context of his own time this one act is enough to make Ike a hero; it certainly makes him a very lonely, exiled, and much misunderstood figure.

But does Ike's act of repudiation stem only from the purity and the courage of his principles? Notwithstanding his insistence that his "simple" act accords with God's own design, Ike provokes our skepticism at the moment when Cass presses him especially closely on the matter of reconciling his providential view of the Civil War with the war's apparent purposelessness. With his back up against the wall Ike confesses:

I'm trying to explain to the head of my family something which I have got to do which I dont quite understand myself, not in justification of it but to explain it if I can. I could say I dont know why I must do it but that I do know I have got to because I have got myself to have to live with for the rest of my life and all I want is peace to do it in. (288)

Ike disarms Cass through candor, and through an appeal to deeply felt emotional impulses which his rationalizations cannot explain. In effect he is saying that he cannot be argued out of his position because he did not arrive at it through argument alone. Cass is never given an opportunity to respond to Ike's confession because Ike cuts off his interjections and moves on to the subject of the war again. But Cass does later imply that Ike's position is selfish (299), for Ike really wants peace, not the frustrating and unremitting confrontation with plantation life which Cass, and Buck and Buddy before him, had so bitterly experienced in the antebellum South, during the Civil War, and during Reconstruction. Like Hightower in *Light in August*, all of Ike's responses to the past are imaginary and vicarious,

never practical or concrete—in the sense that a commitment to the present
and its problems is an effective response to the burdens of the past. Ike's is
"essentially 'a fugitive and cloistered virtue, unexercised and unbreathed.'"[29]
Ike further slips out of Cass's dialectical grasp by appealing to truths
both he and Cass can celebrate. He shows how the war united the divergent
peoples of the South, slave-owners, small farmers, and poor whites alike,
into a force which terrorized the North and forced the Northerners to re-
consider just what the Union meant to them. Cass, for his part, is at least
willing to consider that the Civil War was what God "'wanted. At least
that's what He got'" (289). The cousins also share a passionate concern for
a land which has had to suffer so much. To the Northern military occupa-
tion, the Ku Klux Klan, the carpetbaggers, the inept Reconstruction government staffed by poorly prepared blacks, is added, for the McCaslins,
the dispersion of a family that had once been unified at least in terms of
location:

> Tennie's Jim gone, nobody knew where, and Fonsiba in Arkansas with her three dollars
> each month and the scholar-husband with his lenseless spectacles and frock coat and his
> plans for the spring; and only Lucas was left, the baby, the last save himself [Ike] of old
> Carothers' doomed and fatal blood which in the male derivation seemed to destroy all it
> touched, and even he was repudiating and at least hoping to escape it (293).

What is referred to in particular here are the personal tragedies of Tomey's
Turl and Tennie Beauchamp, who lost two children during the war years:

> *Dauter Tomes Turl and tenny 1862*
>
> *Child of tomes Turl and Tenny 1863* (272)

The birth of Tennie's Jim in 1864, Ike noticed, was "more carefully written
and spelled...as if the old man [Ike's uncle]...had taken as an omen for
renewed hope the fact that this nameless inheritor of slaves was at least
remaining alive long enough to receive a name" (272). But Tennie's Jim,
grown to manhood, had repudiated his legacy and disappeared.

All of these confusing and sometimes ironic turns of events suggest the
turmoil out of which both Ike and Cass try to fashion a coherent
explanation of what happened to the South. Cass, who has lived through
all of these years, cannot very well dissociate himself from them, or from
the plantation which restored order to a chaotic situation. Ike, who cannot
be sure of what he remembers and what he has been told, finds it easier to
maintain a critical view of the plantation, and to make it part of his sacrifice for a better future. In the very face of his cousin's endurance Ike dares,
after a moment's hesitation, to praise the Negro's capability to endure

(294). Perhaps Ike falters because he knows that his perverse (for a McCaslin) favoring of the Negro over the white is not based on faith in the Negro himself, but on a need to identify with the victims of his grandfather's sin. It is another, if merely symbolic, way for Ike to compensate his black kin. But such compensation amounts to little more than old Carothers's legacy, for it still does not recognize the Negro as an independent human being, but only as a projection of white guilt. Ike is still assuming black inferiority.

Yet the inheritance is evil, no matter how good or bad Ike's reasons are for rejecting it may be. The Negroes he favors do not share the culpability of the whites for the destruction of the wilderness or, obviously, for slavery. They have borne everything with endurance, "'pity and tolerance and forbearance and fidelity and love of children,'" "'from the old free fathers a longer time free than us because we have never been free'" (295). This cadence of Negro virtues, plus the possible allusion to Sam Fathers, instantaneously transports Ike and Cass into a joint memory of a scene which had taken place in "that summer twilight seven years ago" when Cass tried to explain to Ike, then a fourteen-year-old boy, why he had failed to shoot Old Ben.

Cass, in that remembered scene, quotes Keats's lines, "*She cannot fade, though thou hath not thy bliss...Forever wilt thou love, and she be fair,*'" to reveal that Ike refrained from shooting during the "*interminable minute*" in which the "*fyce covered the twenty yards to where the bear waited*" because the pursuit of the bear had shown him the meaning of "*Courage and honor and pride, and pity and love of justice and liberty*" which all "*touch the heart*" (297). In that fraction of time, which was like a vision of eternity, Ike secured the idea of total freedom. But this total freedom is not a condition realizable in history. It is a state of mind, experienced in a minute, though this minute may seem "interminable." The point of quoting Keats is to show that the bear itself is not to be confused with the truth Ike discovered, for the truth exists in other contexts, not only in the wilderness but also in Keats's poem. When Ike misses Cass's point, and says that Keats is "'*talking about a girl,*'" Cass replies "'*He had to talk about something*'" (297). What Ike does not understand is that the girl of the poem, like the bear itself, is merely the "something" which stimulates the poet or Ike to perceive timeless truths. As Cass insists seven years later, however, Ike must deal with time as well as with his state of mind, with the imperfect condition of his life as well as with the "freedom of the heart."[30] Thus when Ike declares at the age of twenty-one that he is free (299), one is just as likely to think of the hollowness of Fonsiba's identical claim (280) as of Ike's momentary perception of what it means to be completely free in the wilderness. This is where he goes wrong of course: the wilderness experiences are essentially out of time (as his relinquishment of his watch aptly symbolizes), but one cannot be out of time in the real world.

It is tragic that Ike does not see the relevance of his cousin's references to Keat's poem,[31] because Ike, in effect, tries to live the poem,[32] the "dream of perfection."[33] Ike is caught between the ideality of art and the reality of life: "Art and life are antithetical, then, insofar as the subject of art — truth — implies permanence and unity, while the condition of life is change and multiplicity."[34] It is not that Cass cannot see the "truth" Ike seized by stopping for an "interminable minute" the actions of the hunt; rather he advises Ike that life, history, the seven years which separate Ike's refusal to shoot Old Ben and his repudiation of his tragically flawed heritage, demonstrate that time, unlike truth, cannot stand still, even though the wilderness fostered the illusion that it might.

At the end of "The Old People" Cass had accepted Ike's version of the dead buck "walking out of the very sound of the horn which related its death" (184), but he questioned whether what Ike saw had a "substance" which could "cast a shadow" (187). Because Sam had initiated him into the same experience many years before (187), Cass was able to draw upon his subsequent experience of the real, working world and juxtapose a valid momentary vision in which time is emptied of its motion toward death against the whole dimension of history itself, in which this momentary vision plays only a small part. Without damaging the reality of Ike's momentary vision of the *dead* buck, Cass emphasized that "you cant be alive forever, and you always wear out life long before you have exhausted the possibilities of living" (186). Implicit in his counsel to Ike is the belief that life changes, as Cass himself had changed, and that no experience should be credited with more than its share of importance in the total process of life.

Unfortunately Ike is, in a sense, obsessed with shadows, with the past which no longer has a "substance." To know the past, the old times and the old people, is an important and necessary part of both Cass's and Ike's educations, but Ike has tried to live in the past through his more than seventy years (see, for example, 171, 354). Although Ike is aware of history as the record of human change and development, he tends to retard this dynamic process in his own mind by fixing on his imaginative recreation of the past and by insisting on God's predetermined design of the world.

In his debate with Cass, which is resumed after their joint memory of the hunt for Old Ben, Ike reaffirms that the land has been "cursed" (298). Thenceforth he returns to his argument that history has a goal, that its meaning is eschatological, in that it has led to his repudiation. Cass cannot understand Ike's mode of thinking, because for him history is a universal condition affecting all men equally. He will concede that there may be something like progress in history, but if so, it is wasteful and so drawn out in achieving its goal that it is irrelevant to current circumstances:

> "And it took Him a bear and an old man and four years just for you. And it took you fourteen years to reach that point and about that many, maybe more, for Old Ben, and more than seventy for Sam Fathers. And you are just one. How long then?" (299)

Ike addresses himself only to the part of the question concerning time. He readily admits that it will be a long time between his individual regeneration and the total regeneration of the South. But because Ike is so obsessed with the moral nature of his repudiation, he never contemplates what Cass sees as his appalling isolation: "'And you are just one.'" Cass knows how he himself has translated his personal loyalty to his family into service to the communal institution of the plantation, and he wants to know how Ike's personal faith in the Negro people will correlate with the attitudes of a whole society. Thus it is not surprising that Cass should avoid a direct argument with Ike on moral issues, shifting instead to Ike's connection with Sam Fathers and the prehistoric past. Is not Ike's descent from Sam all the more reason to accept the land? Who could possibly have a better claim to it? How can Ike repudiate his white man's heritage without simultaneously repudiating the heritage of Sam Fathers? If there is a direct line extending from Sam to Ike, then only Ike can break it. Cass presents a shrewd argument, but Ike, not surprisingly, seems to miss the point of his questions. Although he has the last word in the debate, Ike does not really answer his cousin but simply affirms: "'Yes. Sam Fathers set me free'" (300). In Ike's view, apparently, he is free *from* Cass's duties and responsibilities rather than free to carry them out.[35]

But in winning this last round, Cass does not necessarily win the debate. It is difficult to say who does. Cass is often a Southern apologist who defends the status quo. His argument derives much of its strength from its function as a counter to Ike's extreme faith in the efficacy of the moral act. But material facts of the kind that Cass is constantly referring to do not of themselves negate the moral truth for which Ike is searching. Without the tension Ike introduces into the debate by his willingness to strike out into the whole vast panorama of history, Cass's views would surely seem static and unimaginative. This is perhaps why the debate is so much more satisfying when viewed as one argument, in which Ike jointly explores with Cass all the possible responses the individual can make to the evolution of history. By having Ike repeat Cass's catalogue of virtues seven years later in the commissary, for example, Faulkner implies that this debate between cousins is very much a matter of the conflicting tendencies of what is really one mind.³⁶ Ike is trying to reach out and encompass the whole of history, but the whole is always disintegrating under Cass's particular attacks. Ike is right in attempting to obtain a survey of history in its entirety, and Cass is wrong in supposing that it is not worthwhile to seek such a whole. But he is right in believing that no man can adequately explain his insight into the wholeness of history, and Ike is wrong in supposing that he knows enough to repudiate his inheritance. As Marc Bloch, the French historian, has said, history "is an endeavor toward better understanding and, consequently, a thing in movement."³⁷

The debate is not resolved, but is carried on, in another form, in the story of Uncle Hubert Beauchamp's bequest to Ike of a silver cup, filled with gold pieces, which is to be opened on Ike's twenty-first birthday. In contrast to Ike and Cass's debate about the meaning of their heritage, the silver cup is not an idea but a "thing, possessing weight to the hand and bulk to the eye and even audible" (301). Uncle Hubert would pass the cup around to the family, even to Tennie (304), then Ike's nurse, in order that it be shaken, as though the succession of shakes confirmed the continuity of the family. Though it may have seemed in "Was" that Hubert Beauchamp did not share his sister's illusions about the nobility of their family, which was supposedly descended from an old English house, he now proves otherwise by creating the cup ceremony and by writing notes of hand first dated at "Warwick" (Sophonsiba's pretentious name for the Beauchamp plantation) and signed "Beauchamp" with "no location save that in time and signed by the single not name but word as the old proud earl himself might have scrawled Nevile" (307).

What seems to have stimulated Beauchamp's interest in the preservation of his family (his first intention was simply to marry his sister off to Buck) is the palpable degeneration of his plantation. The child Ike vividly remembers its shabby and overgrown appearance, and partially recalls the moment when his mother ejected from it his uncle's black mistress—a scene which offers still another comment on the debate between Ike and Cass on the nature of freedom for both blacks and whites.³⁸ The departure of Hubert Beauchamp's Negro mistress coincides with the dissipation of the legacy. Soon Beauchamp allows only Ike to "obediently" shake what is now not a silver cup, as we later learn, but a tin coffee pot, substituted for the cup as the notes of hand and the copper coins are substituted for the gold pieces. The cup ceremony now takes place before a "cold unswept hearth," the antithesis of Lucas Beauchamp's hearth that continued to warm his home for forty-five years. For Hubert Beauchamp, however, the parcel still conveys his faith in a family inheritance. Ike remembers his uncle at his death, "the eyes still trying to tell him even when he took the parcel so that was still not it, the hands still clinging to the parcel even while relinquishing it, the eyes more urgent than ever trying to tell him but they never did" (306). The use of "relinquishing" in this context must refer back to Ike's own attitude toward his patrimony as well as his uncle's toward the legacy. Just as his uncle clings to the parcel "even while relinquishing it," so Ike will cling to his heritage "even while relinquishing it."

Once the legacy is opened, Ike and Cass find the "unstained tin coffee pot." Though it is "unstained" and "brand new," the coffee pot is, in one sense, a common token of daily life similar to the scarred and cracked ledgers of the commissary which are also part of Ike's legacy. In another sense, the coffee pot symbolizes the innocence and amazement of Hubert Beauchamp, who tried to leave his nephew an "unstained" legacy. In fact, if we compare Beauchamp's notes of hand found in the coffee pot with Buck and Buddy's cryptic jottings in the ledgers, we see the same brevity, the same lack of excuse for his behavior, the same pattern of constantly diminishing explanations of the time, place, and circumstances in which the "notes" were written:

> a collection of minutely-folded scraps of paper sufficient almost for a rat's nest, of good linen bond, of the crude ruled paper such as negroes use, of raggedly-torn ledger-pages and the margins of newspapers and once the paper label from a new pair of over-alls, all dated and all signed...written in the shaky hand not of a beaten old man because he had never been beaten to know it but of a tired old man maybe and even at that tired only on the outside and still indomitable, the simplicity of the last one the simplicity not of resignation but merely of amazement, like a simple comment or remark, and not very much of that:
> *One silver cup. Hubert Beauchamp.* (306–8)
>
> once more in the ledger and then not again and more illegible than ever, almost inde-cipherable at all from the rheumatism which now crippled him [Buck] and almost com-pletely innocent now even of any sort of spelling as well as punctuation, as if the four years during which he had followed the sword of the only man ever breathing who ever sold him a negro, let alone beat him in a trade, had convinced him not only of the vanity of faith and hope but of orthography too.
> *Miss sophonsiba b dtr t t @ t 1869*
> but not of belief and will because it was there, written, as McCaslin had told him, with the left hand, but there in the ledger one time more and then not again. (273)

Hubert Beauchamp's and Buck McCaslin's persistent efforts to chronicle human life in conditions inimical to their own survival, and to record what they owe to the future, are undercut by their "almost indecipherable" and lifeless statements. Buck's last entry can be understood only by using one's accumulated experience in interpreting previous entries: Miss sophonsiba born dauter tomes turl @ tennie 1869. Like Hubert Beauchamp's last words, "One silver cup," Buck's last words have lost almost all power to specify what he means. Both men lapse into near silence; whatever tangible legacy they meant to leave behind has crumbled away.

Ike and the reader can recover Beauchamp's and McCaslin's intentions, their hopes for the future, and their bewilderment in confronting their own past, but the past itself is already turning to dust. "Dide and burid" is the familiar refrain of many of the ledger entries, but Ike never admits that the past is indeed dead. As Professor Millgate points out, this prevents him from "rethinking his position or from learning anything fresh about himself or about mankind."[39] Instead he envelops himself in the stale and rank odors of past human transactions in the commissary store.

Near the end of his life all Ike can say in acknowledgment of his kinship with Roth's mistress is "'Tennie's Jim...Tennie's Jim'" (362). It is hardly more than Buddy's brief acknowledgment of Eunice's suicide, "Drowned herself," or the obsessive repetition of *"Father's will"* in the commissary books. And the obviously amazed tone of Ike's voice (361) precisely parallels Hubert Beauchamp's "amazement, like a simple comment or remark, and not very much of that: *One silver cup*" (308). All Ike has to offer the young black woman and her child is one silver hunting horn. And though the horn is presumably meant to be a gesture of acknowledgment to both the woman and her child, representing the best of the wilderness world,[40] in the Northern world to which Ike advises her to return it will probably have even less value, practical or symbolic, than the coffee pot. Both the horn and old Carothers's thousand dollars are mere substitutes for the "simple comment or remark" — the "my cousin" which Ike should have said to the girl, the "my son" which old Carothers should have said, as Ike once realized, to his black offspring.[41] Ike has indeed forgotten the "primacy of the heart."[42]

Ike, then, is doomed not only to an obsession with the past, but to an ironic repetition of it. As the coffee pot sits "one night later [after Ike's debate with Cass] on the mantel above what was not even a fireplace in the little cramped icelike room in Jefferson" (308), we see just how much Ike has in common with his uncle, who sat before a "cold unswept hearth" and bade the young boy shake the silver cup. Certainly we are meant to recall that other ice-like room, the commissary, where Ike had stood before Cass trying to repudiate his heritage. This time Cass has come not to argue but to deliver Ike's first pension installment. Ike, knowing full well how deeply his decision has hurt his cousin, reflects back on the Beauchamp legacy, and ponders:

how much it takes to compound a man (Isaac McCaslin for instance) and of the devious intricate choosing yet unerring path that man's (Isaac McCaslin's for instance) spirit takes among all that mass to make him at last what he is to be, not only to the astonishment of them (the ones who sired the McCaslin who sired his father and Uncle Buddy and their sister, and the ones who sired the Beauchamp who sired his Uncle Hubert and his Uncle Hubert's sister) who believed they had shaped him, but to Isaac McCaslin too. (308-9)

Ike's unusual life is like that of the "plantation in its mazed and intricate entirety" (298), in terms of which all of the McCaslins must sort out their responsibilities to their heritage and establish their independence from it, so that they can take, from among all that mass of experience, just those particulars which make them what they are. The closeness between Ike and Cass, and yet their utter alienation from each other, is not something Ike could have predicted, though he can perhaps understand it after hearing Cass reject his invitation to stay in his rented room instead of going back the seventeen miles on horseback and in the cold to the plantation: "'Why should I sleep here in my house when you wont sleep yonder in yours?'" (308).

Cass's bitter words prepare us for Ike's similar estrangement from his wife. Perhaps because of his father's constant compromises with the evils of slavery, especially after his marriage, when he capitulated to Sophonsiba's demand that they reoccupy the big house, Ike feels he must resist his own wife's demand that they move onto the plantation and assume full responsibility for owning the land and governing the lives of those who dwell and work upon it. In this respect, Ike is very like his bachelor uncle Buddy who refused to move into the big house when Sophonsiba and Buck were married. Instead Buddy remains in a small cabin, estranged from his family (he never accompanied the young Ike and his mother to the Beauchamp plantation), and, in general, living an isolated existence anticipating Ike's (301). Moreover, Buddy's increasing isolation was related to his separation from Buck as Ike's is linked to his alienation from McCaslin, for like the twins, Ike and McCaslin—"rather his brother than cousin and rather his father than either" (4)—constitute a complementary team, encompassing between them many possible responses to the past, and to the McCaslin heritage. When these teams are internally divided, so too are their attitudes toward the past divided and incomplete. Thus in his marriage Ike acts without Cass's counsel; indeed one might say that his denial of his wife's wishes is a result of his dispute with Cass. Knowing that the plantation's evils still persist in spite of his family's efforts to change the foundation of evil upon which it was built, Ike decides to remain absolutely outside of any participation in the system. As Blanche H. Gelfant observes: "Just as he saw in the wilderness that truth is one, so he [believes he] sees in the commissary that evil is indivisible."[43]

At various points in his life Ike has briefly intuited the possibility that through marriage, or at least through the relationship of man and woman, truth can become one as in the wilderness. But as with his ambiguous recognition that history is a process of change, he shies away from the full implication of the idea that forms of life other than the wilderness might provide him with a sense of continuity. Nearing the age of eighteen, and on his last visit to Major de Spain's hunting camp in Part Five of "The Bear," he thinks:

> he would marry someday and they too would own for their brief while that brief unsubstanced glory which inherently of itself cannot last and hence why glory: and they would, might, carry even the remembrance of it into the time when flesh no longer talks to flesh because memory at least does last: but still the woods would be his mistress and his wife. (326)

Before it is clear that his marriage is going to fail, Ike again affirms:

> each must share with another in order to come into it [the human heritage] and in sharing they become one: for that while, one: for that little while at least, one: indivisible, that while at least irrevocable and unrecoverable. (311)

At the time when Lucas comes for his share of the legacy, and after Ike's marriage had indeed failed, Ike still believes in

> that one long ago instant at least out of the long and shabby stretch of their human lives, even though they knew at the time it wouldn't and couldn't last, they had touched and become as God when they voluntarily and in advance forgave one another for all that each knew the other could never be. (107–8)

Even as an old man Ike retains his faith that in the act of coupling man and woman can overcome alienation and evil:

> "I think that every man and woman, at the instant when it dont even matter whether they marry or not, I think that whether they marry then or afterward or dont never, at that instant the two of them together were God." (348)

All of these affirmations, however, resemble Ike's perceptions of the timelessness of the wilderness, wherein he escapes the human cycle of birth, procreation, and death. "The woods would be his mistress and his wife" because he believes, more than he probably knows, that the woods offer a refuge from his indivisible ties not just to evil but to family responsibilities involving some degree of repudiation of self for the sake of producing future generations.

Ike's wife's parting words—"'And that's all. That's all from me. If this dont get you that son you talk about, it wont be mine: 'lying on her side, her back to the empty rented room laughing and laughing" (315)—are like an eternal damnation of his efforts to escape the evil of the past. The scene concludes Part Four, but the absence of a final period allows it to extend infinitely into Ike's future, and simultaneously stretch back to that sentenceless prologue to "Was" in which Ike is described as "uncle to half a county and father to no one" (3). From the perspective of Part Four we can see that the emphasis that is placed in the prologue on Ike's repudiation of property, of the notion that man can own anything (land or slaves), is precisely associated with the fact that he is "father to no one." We are told that Ike is an "only child," and that his only close relation (both brother and father) is McCaslin, his cousin (4). In rejecting Cass's position in Part Four of "The Bear," then, Ike divests himself of what amounts to the only family he had known. His further estrangement from his wife, and hence his childlessness, naturally follows from his repudiation of the land to which his cousin was so deeply committed, and to which his wife attached so much importance as the common property of their marriage.

Furthermore, after reading Part Four, the meaning of Ike's childless marriage and its relationship to "Was" and "The Fire and the Hearth," where Ike seems to be only a peripheral figure, is now clear. Although the sixty-year-old Buck did eventually produce a son (Ike himself), Buck's extreme reluctance to marry Sophonsiba, a reluctance which threatened to end the McCaslin line, and Tomey's Turl's contrasted eagerness to have Tennie are eventually paralleled by Ike's failed marriage and long bachelorhood and Lucas's forty-five-year union with Molly. Thus the juxtaposition of Ike and Lucas against the history of their family, already noted in discussing "The Fire and the Hearth" and Part Four of "The Bear," becomes absolutely crucial to an ultimate assessment both of Ike and of what *Go Down, Moses* itself has to say about the evolution of history.

Among the Negroes Lucas carries the honorary title of "Uncle" (138), as Ike does among the other half of the county, the whites. While these titles are a sign of the community's respect for these two old men, such titles also define their remoteness from the present. Each man is something of an anachronism, and each is rather selfish in his devotion to the old times. Just as Ike regrets the encroachment of an industrial civilization on his beloved woods, so Lucas scorns all mechanical contrivances (such as a tractor, or the plane that sprays the crops) upon the land he has known intimately for seventy years.

But, unlike Ike, Lucas has a penchant for possession and a strong sense of family responsibility. Whereas Ike invokes God, Lucas invokes the memory of old Carothers. Though it may be said that Lucas's materialism corrupts him, as when he nearly destroys his and his daughter Nat's marriages by running a still and hunting for gold, that same materialism, like that of his McCaslin forebears, is nevertheless associated with and strengthened by his devotion to family life. As Cass insists over and over again, it is Ike's *grandfather* who owned the land, and the land cannot be relinquished without also losing the identity which its possession has given to the McCaslin family. Although Lucas is wrong in supposing that Cass ruthlessly took the land away from Ike (36), he understands that "say what a man would," Ike "had turned apostate to his name and lineage by weakly relinquishing the land which was rightfully his to live in town on the charity of his great-nephew" (39–40). This is, in fact, precisely what Cass tells Ike when the pseudophilosophizing of the debate in the commissary is stripped away. Of course Lucas has no conception of Ike's noble if futile efforts to offer an alternative reading of history, a kind of minority report, which seeks to obviate the necessity of repeating many of the sins of the past. Lucas's conception of history is simpleminded, in some ways, when compared to Ike's, but it is grounded in the day-to-day complexities of life. Lucas *is* a father, so that in the process of protecting the old patterns and routines of his life, he is forced to employ a shrewdness and flexibility equalled only by his daughter, who thereby illustrates the theme of continuity in family life—a continuity which the Negroes so prize in this novel and which accounts for their attaining in their lives an equilibrium between past and present such as Ike never masters.

It is Nat's idea to make sure that the police find Lucas's as well as George's still (67). At the inevitable confrontation with her father, she shows that she shares his ability to dicker and bargain for just what she wants out of life (68–70). Distraught, defiant, "alert and speculative," suiting her voice to meet her father's now calmer consideration of her wants, upping the terms on which she will now accept George, and then keeping silent when she sees that she has won her point, only restating a key term in their agreement, and finally settling for just a little less than she demanded, Nat reveals a mind as agile and intelligent as her father's—in spite of her youth, her inexperience, and her subordinate position as a woman and a daughter, a position which corresponds, in a way, to Lucas's own subordinate position as a black man in a white-dominated society. In fact, Nat must play the role of hunted animal, as her grandfather Tomey's Turl had done: when Lucas realizes that she has been watching him bury the still, she is likened to "the quarry fleeing like a deer across a field and into that still night-bound woods beyond" (41). Then Nat is able to turn the race around and beat Lucas at his own game as Tomey's Turl beat Buck.

Father and daughter are, in a sense, like master and slave. For like Nat, Tomey's Turl was at least able to force Uncle Buck, his white brother, to recognize that he and Tennie had created their own relationship—and Lucas's success in forcing Roth to recognize his independence is essentially similar. As in Uncle Buck's pursuit of Lucas's father, so in Roth's enraged tracking down of Lucas, who has stolen his mule, it is the black man who controls the situation—in spite of the white man's apparent superiority. Like his father, Lucas knows just how far he can go in ignoring Roth's commands, and he can correctly estimate what Roth's response will be to any given situation in which the plantation code is threatened (36). Lucas has, in the terminology Buck once applied to Tomey's Turl, "stole away": that is, he has defied the plantation code by acting on his own impulses. In this case Lucas's easy usurpation of Roth's mule as security for the divining machine is an assertion of his claim on it as plantation property. In this ironic reversal of the traditional code, it is the black man who forcibly takes the white man's property. Indeed Roth's tremendous rage against Lucas is a result of what he sees as part of a long historical pattern of such attacks against the authority of the white McCaslins: "He was raging—an abrupt boiling-over of an accumulation of floutings and outrages covering not only his span but his father's lifetime too, back into the time of his grandfather McCaslin Edmonds" (104).

Ike, unfortunately, discounts the Negro's ability to control his life in conditions which are admittedly inimical to, but which by no means absolutely abrogate, his freedom. By having Roth remember the frustrating times of his grandfather McCaslin Edmonds, and by using Cass as the unreflecting recorder of "Was," Faulkner fashions a perspective on Ike's later (in terms of the structure of the novel) reading of the commissary books. Most critics have seen it the other way: Ike's experiences revalue what we have seen in "Was." True, but Ike's interpretation must nevertheless be balanced by the experiences of those who lived the past which the commissary books record and of those who now carry on the administration of the plantation. While it can be argued that "Was" is as much Ike's property as Cass's and constitutes Ike's initiation into family and Southern history,[44] in stressing the fact that Ike did not participate in these events, Faulkner may already be suggesting that Ike's is not the best, and certainly not the only, perspective on the past.

The commissary books, which become so important a part of Ike's consciousness, give in a page, or a series of pages, a vivid but strictly limited impression of what it was like to live in the past. The ledgers are not inaccurate, and they contain their own kind of immediacy and relevance for the present, but they are incomplete. They never record, for example, Lucas Beauchamp's birth, because by that time (1874) Buck and Buddy were dead (281). Life, then, is too protean to be sandwiched between the covers of the ledgers, and those men who recorded the life of the past on those pages could not have foreseen "the ledgers, new ones now and filled rapidly, succeeding one another rapidly and containing more names than old Carothers or even his [Ike's] father and Uncle Buddy had ever dreamed of" (292). The ledgers represent only one perspective on the past, the perspective that shows what remains after individual human vitality has been stilled. But in order to infuse the dusty books with life, one must use one's energies and keep in mind that the study of the past is an activity carried on in the present by an interpreter who must recognize that the past is, in one sense, a projection of his own mind and, at least to that extent, a changing phenomenon.

In chapter 5, I suggested we have to adjust in *Go Down, Moses* to the histories that are formulated, interpreted, and enacted by different characters and narrators in different times and places, and to the constant changes in structure from chapter to chapter. In conclusion, it must be further suggested that we have to adjust to the numerous changes in tone, style, and point of view, to the various "voices" or patterns of narration, within and between the novel's seven chapters.[45] The easygoing comic presentation of the various "races" in "Was" (1859), the tragicomic portrayal of Lucas's relations with the white and black McCaslins in "The Fire and the Hearth" (1895, 1898, 1941), the unrelenting evocation of Rider's despair and the deputy's hysteria in "Pantaloon in Black" (August 1941), the celebration of the beauty and the mystery of the wilderness in "The Old People" (1879), the evolution of the tortuous logic of the debate between Ike and Cass in Part Four of "The Bear" (1888), the juxtaposition of the grim arguments of Ike and Roth in "Delta Autumn" (Autumn 1940), and the sober account of the well-meaning but somewhat inept efforts of Gavin Stevens in the concluding chapter, "Go Down, Moses" (July 1940) — all suggest an encyclopaedic exploration of the development of human experience as an historical process.

The complexity of that process is dramatized by the novel's narrative momentum, which changes from chapter to chapter, in such a way that we find ourselves projected forward by or abruptly thrust into certain passages and slowed down by others. For example, in "Was" we are primarily moved along by an interest in Buck's pursuit of Tomey's Turl and Miss Sophonsiba's pursuit of Buck. In "The Bear," however, which deals with many of the same themes, we have not only the action of the hunt but the long descriptive passages on the wilderness and the carefully constructed tableaux — such as the one discussed in chapter 5 in which the representatives of a passing frontier society gather around the body of Old Ben. As we accustom ourselves to the narrative pace of each chapter, so too are we learning to experience different kinds of time which vary from (at the one extreme) the day-to-day work on the plantation to (at the other extreme) those moments in the wilderness where time seems frozen, obliterated, or in which the motion of time seems reversed by Ike's projections of himself into prehistory.

Our position in regard to the characters and events is never quite the same in any of the chapters. Sometimes we have an intimate and immediate point of view. We hear the deputy talking to his wife; his failure to understand Rider's despair is revealed in his own excited words, in his own bravado, which is meant to dismiss Rider's story even as it makes apparent how deeply he has been disturbed by what he has seen and heard. Sometimes we feel somewhat distant and removed from a character — as with Ike McCaslin when his life is briefly summarized and alluded to in the first three chapters of the novel, so that we are forced to try to relate him to the lives of the characters who occupy the foreground. Moreover, by making Ike a minor character in the beginning, Faulkner shows us the consequences of his decision to isolate himself from those very situations in his society in which he would have been called upon to act had he accepted his place as head of the plantation. Sometimes our view of characters and events is intermediate — that is, neither entirely inside or outside of the minds of the characters and the times which we are experiencing. Thus we often see life through Lucas's or Ike's eyes, but seldom get their reactions to experience in precisely their own words. Instead the narrator articulates their points of view. We know, for example, exactly what Lucas thinks of George Wilkins, even though he never fully expresses his feelings either in direct speech or in a stream-of-consciousness rendering of his thoughts.

Like *Absalom, Absalom!*, then, *Go Down, Moses* is not primarily a novel about a specific historical past but a novel about man's perception of historical process. To a certain extent, it resembles historical novels which offer a theory or reading of history,[46] but it seems that Faulkner along with other twentieth-century novelists, historians, and philosophers of history[47] is especially concerned with the study of the past as a hermeneutical discipline, a discipline concerned with the various ways in which past events are interpreted in different times and places, and from different points of view. In his essay on *Nostromo* David Daiches suggests that

> the breaking-up of the narrative, the shifting of times and places and points of view, helps to build up that sense of utter conviction, as though this were not a mere story to be told straight off in a chronological line, but part of the complex pattern of life, which we can look at only through a mixture of retrospect and anticipation, of memory and desire, of the endless intertwining of cause and effect.[48]

We cannot regard the novel as presenting a "story" in any simple sense because the original sequence of events is broken up and witnessed through conflicting points of view; and since there is no consistent chronological or narrative line, we are forced to become collaborators in the making of history.[49]

Conrad's breaking-up of the chronological narrative clearly fore-shadows Faulkner's way of forcing us to become our own historians. Chapter 2 of *Nostromo*, for example, emphasizes the interpenetration of past and present by beginning a description of Sulaco in the present tense, as though it were being approached for the first time, and then slipping into the past perfect tense for an historical account of what we have just seen:

> The only sign of commercial activity within the harbour, visible from the beach of the Great Isabel, *is* the square blunt end of the wooden jetty which the Oceanic Steam Navigation Company (the O.S.N. of familiar speech) *had thrown* over the shallow part of the bay soon after they *had resolved* to make of Sulaco one of their ports of call for the Republic of Costaguana. (my italics)[50]

Because present and past merge so swiftly and so smoothly, the impression is conveyed that only by taking in both Sulaco's present and past can the town be fully *seen* and understood. Faulkner perhaps emphasizes the indivisibility of present and past more than Conrad does by making Part One of "Was" a fragment, incomplete by itself but serving as an introduction to Ike's listening to his cousin's story which comes out of "the old time, the old days" (4).

Avrom Fleishman has spoken of the rapid time shifts and changes of point of view in *Nostromo* as a "set of notes recording discrete observations in or on the past, out of which a continuous and coherent sequence must be constructed."[51] In Part One, we have not only the narrator, speaking briefly as an eyewitness to history (80) and as its rather reserved recorder, but also a series of participant-observers—Captain Mitchell, Charles Gould, his wife, and the reported impressions of numerous minor characters—all of whom "make up history", so to speak, in the process of perceiving it. As in *Go Down, Moses*, Parts Two and Three of *Nostromo* engage in a kind of historical revisionism, for the views of characters like Charles Gould (idealist) are supplanted by Martin Decoud (skeptic), who is, in turn, countered by Dr. Monygham (cynic). History hinges on these partial perspectives, the structure of Conrad's novel implies, even as it is somehow greater than their sum and less controllable than the idealists, cynics, and those of various persuasions between these extremes, imagine. The pattern of history in both novels is cyclical; that is, the past repeats itself in the present *with a difference*. If Chapters 2 and 8 in Part One of *Nostromo* inscribe a circle around the failure of government in Costaguana—exemplifed in the flight of its President—there is a sense, by the end of the novel, of a new, comprehensible stage of development if not of progress,[52] for in both Conrad and Faulkner the idea of progress is always problematic. How could it be otherwise when history is mediated — indeed compromised — by those who wish to know it, to fix its uncertain flow.

In *Go Down, Moses* Faulkner's "notes" on history are even more fragmented because of their embodiment in separate chapters, which, even if rearranged, would not yield a single narrative line. Conrad is more apt to remind us of the way his fragments fit together because of his repeated allusions to the same events. In Faulkner we have to strain, especially on that first difficult reading, to *see* how those individually titled chapters of *Go Down, Moses* are related to each other. Although certain fundamental facts are repeated in the manner of Conrad, we must make all of the transitions between these facts for ourselves. In this way successive chapters do not simply fill in gaps between one period of time or point of view and another, but are in themselves versions of the history that is held in dialectical tension throughout the novel, so that Stevens's actions in *Go Down, Moses* are not simply a continuation of the actions of Buck in "Was" and of the deputy in "Pantaloon in Black," but are actions which arise out of a highly individual response to a common history shared by his community. The point of such a method is not only to make us realize that our perception of a character, place, or action is relative to the time in which we perceive it, but to force us to feel that we are part of that time, delimited by its perspective, until a shift is made to another time, and so forth. As we gradually accustom ourselves to these sudden juxtapositions of time, character, and place, we acquire an overview of the history of the whole novel, without sacrificing a detailed knowledge of its individual parts. We have a sense of the past, present, and future, and yet all three are amalgamated into our minds as one solid form.

Faulkner follows Conrad's aim to get as close as possible to the texture of the historical process as it is actually lived,[53] a process in which we use the same skills as help us to negotiate the twists and turns of our own life histories. As Carl Becker has said, the research methods of the historian are very close to the methods every man uses to organize the pattern of his daily life — though the historian may be more conscious of what he is doing. History, as Becker defines it, is the "pattern of remembered things"[54] and a form of discourse taking place between the individual and the world he interprets, so that the historian's or "every man's" so-called "facts" are arrived at through circumstances and purposes uniquely relevant to that individual. Hence those very "facts" are extremely malleable.[55] As novelists, Conrad and Faulkner go beyond the historians by making us experience the immediate context in which these malleable facts are fashioned; and they show us that errors and failures of perception are unavoidable, no matter what the point of view may be. In other words, they do not simply give us the results of their research but rather force us to participate in the historian's task of investigating the primary sources of historical knowledge. It is in this sense that their novels can be described as history in the making, as an interpretative process that is going on simultaneously in the minds of the characters and the readers alike.

Above all, therefore, *Go Down, Moses* is an experimental novel which explores the manifold ways of interpreting human character and history. Unlike *Absalom, Absalom!*, *Go Down, Moses* is not centered solely on an historical study of a single story, although the story of old Carothers's repudiation of his black son is an integral part of the novel. Rather *Go Down, Moses* goes even further than *Absalom, Absalom!* in making the evolution of history itself a major concern. Only in *Requiem for a Nun* does Faulkner consistently confront and define the past and the historical process in terms which are more explicit than, even while they grow out of, those of *Go Down, Moses*.

7

The Relationship Between Historical Fact and Historical Fiction in the Yoknapatawpha Novels

Though Faulkner did not consider himself to be an historian or sociologist of the South,[1] and though he said that his novels were not written in accordance with any chronological or genealogical plan,[2] his profound sense of history seems inseparable from a long-standing concern with the past of his own region — a concern which led him to develop a complex understanding of historical process, of the fundamental repetitions and ironies of history, and of the ways in which the necessary recognition and acceptance of change must be reconciled with an appreciation of what is fundamental and permanent in human experience.

I

As several critics point out, Faulkner's conception of Yoknapatawpha, its past, and its relationship to the actuality of northern Mississippi developed only gradually.[3] James B. Meriwether notes that in *Sartoris* Faulkner was not "very eager. . .to tie the county of his fiction to his native region."[4] Elizabeth M. Kerr observes that he neither emphasized the overall design of his novels as a portrait of his region by dividing them "into 'Scenes' like Balzac's or into family sagas," nor gave external clues to the relationships between his works except by his map of Yoknapatawpha and by the explicit trilogy form of *Snopes*.[5]

Both the map and the trilogy, however, like *Collected Stories* (1950) and *Requiem for a Nun* (1951), tend to suggest that the author had a firm idea of the geographical and historical dimensions of his imaginative world, and of that world's essential integrity and unity. Certainly Faulkner was receptive to Malcolm Cowley's plan to present "The Saga of Yoknapatawpha County, 1820-1945, Being the First Chronological Picture of Faulkner's Mythical County in Mississippi"[6]: "By all means let us make a Golden Book of my apocryphal county."[7] In admitting that he had "thought of spending my old age doing something of that nature: an alphabetical, rambling genealogy of the people, father to son to son,"[8] Faulkner may also have been thinking of his brief attempt in 1932 to write "The Golden Book / of Jefferson & Yoknapatawpha County / in Mississippi / as compiled by / William Faulkner of Rowanoak"[9] — an attempt which clearly indicates that Cowley's idea, though welcome, was not new to him. Joseph Blotner's description of this "chronicle" written "on a piece of letter-size looseleaf notebook paper" reveals Faulkner's early interest in producing a history of Yoknapatawpha of a relatively systematic kind:

> Having thus suggested something of the medieval scholar, genealogist, and gentleman, Faulkner went on to write a 700-word biography of John Sartoris, born July 14, 1823, in South Carolina, and murdered in Jefferson after the war by Redlaw, his one-time partner turned rival. He added new lore to that which had already appeared in *Flags in the Dust* and *Sartoris*. It appears that he was doing this five-page chronicle for his own pleasure, unless he thought of it as raw material for fiction or as an appendix one day, possibly, to another work about the Sartoris family.[10]

Writing to Cowley about the finished anthology, *The Portable Faulkner*, Faulkner spoke approvingly and even admiringly of what was in part Cowley's achievement rather than his own: "The job is splendid. Damn you to hell anyway. But even if I had beat you to the idea, mine wouldn't have been this good. By God, I didn't know myself what I had tried to do, and how much I had succeeded."[11] Evidently the "saga" of Yoknapatawpha had been an important but only implicit and not even fully conscious part of Faulkner's fiction. Though the author had once thought about a chronicle of Cowley's type, the works themselves were not conceived as a systematic or formal history of his imaginative world.

In order to make that history explicit and uniform Cowley had to edit Faulkner's fiction and do the kind of cross-referencing that Faulkner had always demanded of his readers. Cowley was, in a sense, establishing a point of view for the reader who sought to come to terms with Faulkner's work as a whole, but in the process *The Portable Faulkner* became false in many ways to the kinds of experiments in structure and point of view and in the manipulation of time which distinguish Faulkner's novels individually. Moreover, the author differed from the critic in the way he defined his role as the creator of Yoknapatawpha. In attempting to extract an historical pattern from Faulkner's fiction, Cowley asked him about certain discrepancies between the *Compson Appendix* (originally intended only for the *The Portable Faulkner*) and *The Sound and the Fury*. In his reply Faulkner revealed that he did not think of his fiction as a history based on recorded and immutable fact but as a realm of experience continually changing, perpetually growing out of the renewed process of creation in each new and independent work:

Would rather let the appendix stand with the inconsistencies, perhaps make a statement (quotable) at the end of the introduction, viz.: The inconsistencies in the appendix prove that to me the book is still alive after 15 years, and being still alive is growing, changing; the appendix was done at the same heat as the book, even though 15 years later, and so it is the book itself which is inconsistent: not the appendix. That is, at the age of 30 I did not know these people as at 45 I now do; that I was even wrong now and then in the very conclusions I drew from watching them, and the information in which I once believed. (I believe I was 28 when I wrote the book. That's almost 20 years.)[12]

In reflecting back upon his life Faulkner suggested that there had taken place certain changes in himself (note his parenthetical return to the matter of his age at the end of his statement) which made his present reading of *The Sound and the Fury* different from his initial conception of the novel. In order to achieve this new perspective on his own work, Faulkner had to create it anew, rather than address himself to what he had already written and thus tamper with a statement which had had its own integrity at the time when it was written. Only in this way could he insure his approach to the original material of *The Sound and the Fury* at "the same heat."

The *Appendix* differs markedly from *The Sound and the Fury* in that it approaches the form of a chronicle. It specifically dates the period of time it covers (1699–1945), and it includes accounts of Ikkemotubbe ("A dispossessed American king"),[13] of Jackson ("A Great White Father with a sword" [404]), and of the generations of Compsons which precede the Compsons of the novel. By beginning his "chronicle" just before the beginning of the eighteenth century and carrying it down to the middle of the twentieth (exactly two hundred years after Quentin MacLachan "fled to Carolina from Culloden Moor" [404]), Faulkner reverses the method of *The Sound and the Fury* in which the family's history is discovered and interpreted solely from the family's point of view. That history is now seen as a larger process out of which the family has developed (or failed to develop) as one particular unit.

It is, then, the historical connections and contexts missing in *The Sound and the Fury* that Faulkner explores in the *Appendix*. As Mary Jane Dickerson observes:

> The past and present mesh in a comprehensive manner in the Compson Appendix, a method Faulkner probably deliberately eschewed in the novel, instinctively realizing the primary necessity of concentrating on the inner lives of his characters and achieving the mastery of a technique that serves so richly in later works. . . . [T]he Compson Appendix. . . is essentially a story of origins, extending beyond the genealogy of the Compson family to distil [sic] much of the original historical and legendary experience of a region and of a nation.[14]

In retrospect, Mr. Compson's fatalism, for example, has its historical as well as personal place, for in the *Appendix* it is a fact, not just a feeling, that the family has been allied to lost causes. Its struggle for victory—indeed its very propensity to do battle—must seem to a latter-day Compson an illusion revelatory of man's "folly and despair." With the *Appendix* in mind, one also has a sharper appreciation of how the Compson failure to cope with history has become mystified and melodramatic in the novel. The mother, for example, speaks of "dreading to see this Compson blood beginning to show" in her favorite, her second son, the fourth Jason. "Who can fight against bad blood," she wonders as she dwells on Caddy's misbehavior, and looks for a way to help Jason escape "this curse" (128). All the children absorb the mother's hapless surrender to fate even as they try to resist it. "[T]here's a curse on us its not our fault is it our fault" Quentin tells (asks?) Caddy. "I'm bad anyway you can't help it" she resignedly confides to Quentin (196). In *The Sound and the Fury*, the family cannot get outside of itself, cannot put its own history in perspective, or see itself in a complex historical process. Instead, Compsons try to assign blame, to mete out punishment to the self and to each other in the narrowest, most prejudicial terms:

[Caddy to Quentin:] "It was all your fault. . . . I hope we do get whipped." (14)

"I know, I know." Mother said. "It's all my fault." (73)

[Dalton Ames to Quentin:] "Listen no good taking it so hard its not your fault kid[.]" (199)

[Quentin to Jason:] "Whatever I do, it's your fault," she says. "If I'm bad, it's because I had to be. You made me. I wish I was dead. I wish we were all dead." (324) (see also 22, 87, 140, 167, 169, 196, 304, 305, 323, 327, 348)

The Compsons in *The Sound and the Fury* lack Ike McCaslin's awareness of historical development, of how intricately their actions fit into patterns begun in the past, and of "how much it takes to compound a man" (308), as Ike puts it. Certainly the fault-finding prevalent in Compson thinking deters any consideration of the sources of their failure. "I wish I was dead"—the anguished cry of Caddy's daughter echoes Caddy's brother, although no one in the family seems to realize it. On the contrary, Mrs. Compson can only cry over the female Quentin and talk "about how her own flesh and blood rose up to curse her" (224). Ironically, Jason, who is supposed to feel the least like a Compson, nevertheless acts cornered and cramped by time without knowing how closely his sense of futility links him to the time-obsessed Compsons who, he supposes, have had it easier than himself: "Damn little time to do anything in, but then I am used to that. I never had to go to Harvard to learn that" (292-93). As Dickerson observes, Jason and Quentin—regarded within the historical context of the *Appendix*—are not so much "the antitheses in temperament of their name-sakes" as they are "absurd extremes of qualities incipient in their name-sakes."[15] Furthermore, she points out that Quentin has evolved not only out of the Compson saga but out of the national history evoked in the *Appendix*, for his obsession with Caddy has its historical analogue in the portrayal of Andrew Jackson, a "rough-edged-soldier with a chivalric streak," determined to protect his wife and "the principle that honor must be defended whether it was or not because defended it was whether or not" (404).[16] Jason Compson, for example, is defined in the *Appendix* in rela-tion to an actual historical event. He is described as "the first sane Comp-son since before Culloden and (a childless bachelor) hence the last" (420). He is the "first sane Compson" because he accepts what is inevitable and refuses to keep fighting the lost battle of Culloden—standing for all doomed romantic causes—and in so doing partially frees himself from the fatality and helplessness of the latter-day Compsons. Having abandoned principle and tradition in the interest of "practicality," he is able to compete and hold his own with the Snopeses, the new economic men. But Jason's selling of the Compson house and property not only characterizes his attitude toward the past, it also marks the culmination of an historical process, of which the Compsons are only a part. The *Appendix* also deals with the dispossession of the Indians and portrays all of the manifold yet interrelated changes that occur as a result of that dispossession. Thus we see the successive transformation of the "solid square mile" of land from the time when Ikkemotubbe, "a dispossessed American king" (403), swapped it for the racehorse belonging to Jason Lycurgus Compson, "the grandson of a Scottish refugee who had lost his own birthright by casting his lot with a king who himself had been dispossessed" (403). Then the mile was "almost in the center of the town of Jefferson" (407) when Brigadier Jason Lycurgus II put the "first mortgage on the still intact square mile to a New England carpetbagger in '66" (408). Then we are given a description of "what was left of the old square mile" in the time of the "Old Governor": "the weedchoked traces of the old ruined lawns and promenades, the house which had needed painting too long already" (409). Finally, part of the mile was sold by Quentin's father to pay for Caddy's wedding and Quentin's last year at Harvard, and the remainder by Jason, Quentin's brother (420). Nevertheless the square mile was still "intact again in row after row of small crowded jerrybuilt individuallyowned demiurban bun-galows" (411), still identifiable as the land Jason Lycurgus Compson obtained through a horse trade. Indeed the fate of the Compson house itself as a "boardinghouse for juries and horse-and mule-traders" (410) recalls, in an ironic way, that first horse trade. Thus in spite of all of the changes that have been catalogued, the Compson mile retains its basic shape as a physical reminder of the past. Even after Ikkemotubbe's "lost domain" (403) has become the "Compson Domain" (408) and then been divided into even smaller units, Jason IV still retains his own "particular domain," a "railed enclosure" in the farmers' supply store (414). In Jason's arrogation of his own "domain" — no matter how small or insignificant it might seem — we see the continuity of the historical process: though Jason rejects the past, the very form of his rejection fits ironically into the pattern of history as it unfolds in the *Appendix*.

II

In the Quentin section of the *Appendix*, it is clear that his intense sense of dislocation from the mainstream of history is exacerbated by his family's loss of land, which is tantamount to its loss of honor, the honor it created by acquiring, holding, and defending its land. Caddy thus becomes Quentin's substitute for land, for the locus of his identity:

> Who loved not his sister's body but some concept of Compson honor precariously and (he knew well) only temporarily supported by the minute fragile membrane of her maidenhead as a miniature replica of all the whole vast globy earth may be poised on the nose of a trained seal. (411)

Caddy is, in fact, "a miniature replica" of Compson land, honor, and identity — a compact symbol for the overwhelming history of defeats that Quentin cannot begin to reverse. She is Quentin's virgin wilderness,[17] like the one out of which the family fashioned a "Compson mile," and she is just as fragile, just as prone to violation as the land and the Compsons have been all along. Quentin, then, is doomed from the start by poising the meaning of existence on that "membrane." His sense of family honor cannot originate with her; he cannot precede, as it were, his forebears and begin history anew because, as John Irwin puts it, "there is no virgin space within which one can be first. And for the same reason Quentin's obsession with Candace's loss of virginity is necessarily an obsession with his own impotence, since the absence of the virgin space renders him powerless."[18] As Dickerson reminds us, in *Absalom, Absalom!* Quentin has apparently given up on the land itself, for he sees "it's going to turn and destroy us all some day, whether our name happens to be Sutpen or Coldfield or not" (12).[19] Lest there be any doubt that in the *Appendix* Faulkner means us to make the historical connections between the intact Compson Mile "sold to pay for his [Quentin's] sister's wedding and his year at Harvard" (412) and Quentin's obsession with Caddy's intactness, note that the brother

> loved not the idea of the incest which he would not commit, but some presbyterian concept of its eternal punishment: he, not God, could by that means cast himself and his

sister both into hell, where he could guard her forever and keep her forevermore *intact* amid the eternal fires. (411, my emphasis)

"Intact" (a word never used in *The Sound and the Fury*) is chosen to imply, I believe, the way Quentin has tried to center all of Compson history into the figure of his sister. This, I take it, is what Lewis Simpson is responding to when he suggests that "like Herman Melville, Thomas Mann, Robinson Jeffers, and Eugene O'Neill, Faulkner was attracted to the relationship between brother and sister as a profound symbol of the modern internalization of history."[20]

In the *Appendix*, Simpson concludes, "Faulkner presumably moves as far outside his novel as he could ever have gotten without starting over and rewriting it."[21] The movement outward, I would add, is profoundly historical, is—indeed—an inquiry into the structure of history out of which (Faulkner saw in retrospect) the novel emerged. For not only does he continue Caddy's biography, he also implies "the story of the Compson family ends in Caddy's identification with the unspeakable Nazi endeavor to effect a final purification of history. Serene in her prolonged beauty, Caddy knows her damnation."[22] As she said so many years before to Quentin in the novel, "I'm bad anyway." Simpson observes that Caddy understands "somehow her role in Quentin's struggle with history."[23] This understanding, incipient in *The Sound and the Fury*, is fulfilled in the *Appendix* by putting Caddy not only in Quentin's mind but firmly in documented history, in the photographs of her with a "German staffgeneral" (415). She has followed her doomed brother's example, the example of "a world historical neurotic and self-defeated historian."[24] In ranging so far beyond Yoknapatawpha, Faulkner at once confirms the universality of its history and shows that his County is a part of a greater history which Yoknapatawpha—that "keystone in the universe"—has helped to shape.

III

The pattern of history in the *Appendix*, however, is not the same as Malcolm Cowley's idea of the "saga of Yoknapatawpha County." The *Appendix* itself does not derive from a preconceived history of Yoknapatawpha but is an independent work in which the author creates new "facts" and sometimes contradicts old ones. Faulkner seems to have regarded Yoknapatawpha's past, present, and future as continually developing out of each new act of creation: "I would have preferred nothing at all prior to the instant I began to write, as though Faulkner and Typewriter were concomitant, coadjutant and without past on the moment they first faced each other at the suitable (nameless) table."[25] In the broadest sense his imaginative world has a unified and coherent history; we can trace its development as we can trace the development of his native region. But Faulkner was not interested in the narrower senses in which his imaginative world might be called a saga or a history. He did not especially care about the contradictions and inconsistencies between his accounts of the same events and characters in different novels. Even in *Snopes,* where one might suppose that he would want to emphasize the unity of the trilogy, he failed to correct the inconsistencies and contradictions in the presentation of those characters and events which appear in more than one novel.[26]

In an introductory note to *The Mansion,* published in 1959, Faulkner expanded on the view of his work he had conveyed to Cowley thirteen years earlier:

> This book is the final chapter of, and the summation of a work conceived and begun in 1925. Since the author likes to believe, hopes that his entire life's work is a part of a living literature, and since "living" is motion, and "motion" is change and alteration and therefore the only alternative to motion is unmotion, stasis, death, there will be found discrepancies and contradictions in the thirty-four-year progress of this particular chronicle; the purpose of this note is simply to notify the reader that the author has already found more discrepancies and contradictions than he hopes the reader will—contradictions and discrepancies due to the fact that the author has learned, he believes, more about the human heart and its dilemma than he knew thirty-four years ago; and is sure that, having lived with them that long time, he knows the characters in this chronicle better than he did then.[27]

Even though he calls his trilogy a "chronicle," Faulkner does not subjugate his imagination to the factual consistency and continuity normally associated with a chronicle; instead the facts change over the years as the author approaches the people he created with new understanding. The "discrepancies and contradictions" do not matter because the author feels that his knowledge of his imaginative world is progressive; that world is continuous and alive and coherent because he has not ceased to see it dynamically, from new and more mature perspectives.

IV

No doubt Cowley's "saga of Yoknapatawpha County" stimulated Faulkner to reflect upon the historical process portrayed in his fiction. Certainly the *Appendix* and the novels following it, especially *Requiem for a Nun,* deal with that process in a much more explicit way than *The Sound and the Fury* and other early novels. But the historical process presented in the *Appendix* is not specifically Southern, and Faulkner never acceded to the proposition that he was recording or creating a "legend of the South." His perception of history may well have grown out of his concern with the Southern past, but the process itself is more fundamental and universal — as can be seen from an examination of Quentin's attitude toward the Southern past in *The Sound and the Fury.*

Quentin tries to live in accordance with his rather abstract notions of what the Southern past must have been like. Rather than attuning himself to the realities of the present, he seeks refuge in an outmoded chivalric code. When his sister Caddy fails to conform to Quentin's idea of virginity, and when Quentin himself fails in his defense of that ideal, he withdraws into himself, transforming the present events of his life into no more than reenactments of his past experiences. As he walks through one of the suburbs of Cambridge, wrapped entirely in his own thoughts and trying to avoid the shadow that reminds him that he cannot ultimately escape into his own private world, he registers — but does not react to — the heterogeneous and vivid immigrant community (162). But Quentin's withdrawal from the concrete conditions of life, his inability to establish continuity between past and present, is but an intensification of an attitude toward experience that is prevalent among the suburbanites, to whom the Italian immigrants are simply "'Them furriners. I cant tell one from another'" (162),[28] and who cannot see through the poverty and disorder of the immigrant community to its vitality, its color, and its individuality — like the "garment of vivid pink" hanging from an upper window (162–63). The Cambridge suburbanites — and Quentin with them — seem to have forgotten that they too, like all Americans, come from immigrant stock, that the "weathered" the "unpainted houses," the "fence of gaping and broken pickets," the "ancient lop-sided surrey," and the barn "broken-backed" and "decaying" (165) are cast-off remnants of their suburb's past, and that there was once a wilderness where there are now "quiet lawns and houses neat among the trees." The street that is "empty both ways" (160) seems suggestive of its inhabitants, for they see neither what their own past has been nor what the future will be for these immigrants: they have lost their sense of time and live only in the present, where all they see of the immigrants is their shabbiness and untidiness.

It is ironic that Mrs. Bland, who thinks her son is the perfect gentleman, should despise those "ignorant lowclass Yankees" (181), even as those Yankees are despising the immigrants. Mrs. Bland touts her son's gentlemanly demeanor and behavior and ludicrously assumes an aristocratic pose in a manner reminiscent of Lady Hammeline in *Quentin Durward.* Gerald Bland's degradation of women reminds Quentin so much of the scene with Dalton Ames that he attacks Bland and fails, for the second time, to defend his idealized conception of women. As Richard Gray has recently observed, Bland represents a parody of Quentin's "pretensions to gentility."[29] Thus neither in his own person, nor in the world in which he situates himself, can Quentin locate and affirm a serious demonstration of the chivalric code.[30] Having passed out in front of the sympathetic Ames, and having been bloodied up by the egomaniac Bland before he has had a chance to land a blow on either of them, Quentin seems immobilized and enervated; he capitulates to the family's sense of gloom and doom. He is never able to reconcile Caddy's individual needs with the unrealistic and unfair stipulations of family tradition and the myth of Southern woman-hood. He repeatedly fails to accept life on its own terms and is hounded by an absurd ethical imperative which constantly compares what ought to be against what is.

Quentin himself characterizes what he sees as "Land of the kike home of the wop" (155). This kind of attitude has produced the prim woman in the bakery who gives the deformity she has made in her oven to the little immigrant girl (158), thinking that the "gnarled" and unsaleable cake is good enough for her, and who is herself sharply divorced from the colorful reality which the immigrants represent. She has a "neat grey face" and "hair tight and sparse" above "her neat grey skull." She is a cold person, a dry materialist, and a bigot who lives in a world of "ordered certitudes long divorced from reality" (155). No wonder she fails to respond to any new experiences or insights. In contrast to the immigrants, she is barely alive.

Quentin is the only character who expresses any real sympathy for the "dirty" little Italian girl, perhaps because she evokes his feeling about his defiled sister Caddy:

> "You going to give her that bun?" the woman said. "Yessum," I said. "I expect your cooking smells as good to her as it does to me." (157)

In a curious way, Quentin himself establishes a closeness between himself and the little girl by calling her "sister" and "lady"—again perhaps because he is thinking of his sister. Certainly there is an atmosphere of decay envel-oping both the immigrants' and the Compsons' houses (165, 355), but the Compsons are, so to speak, at the end of an historical cycle whereas the immigrants are just at the beginning, just finding their place in America as the Compsons had once found theirs. Yet Quentin is like the immigrant girl in that he too is a displaced person. At one point he is suspected of being a foreigner (148), and as he enters the bakery the doorbell rings for both himself and the immigrant girl (156), who acts indeed at this point as that shadow which Quentin is unable to get rid of (160, 166).[31] Quentin is accused of stealing the girl just as she is accused of stealing the bread, and while he thinks about femaleness and its "delicate equilibrium of periodical filth" (159), she clutches a "half-naked" loaf until it is pushed out of its package and becomes dirty and wet (172).

Despite all the differences between them, Quentin, the little Italian girl and her fellow immigrants, the woman in the bakery, the Cambridge suburbanites, and Mrs. Bland are (in these various ironic ways) connected to each other in a complex historical pattern of which they are themselves unaware. As has been suggested earlier, there is in Faulkner's work an immense historical strength which inheres not in the handling of specific historical events nor in fidelity to chronology — or, it should be added here, in an exclusive concern with a regional past — but simply in his profound understanding of historical process, of the way in which, as Ortega y Gasset puts it, all human beings are linked together in a "single, inexorable chain."[32]

V

In much of the fiction written after the *Appendix* Faulkner tends to make the connections between his imaginative world, his region, and the much larger world to which that region is attached more explicit than was customary in his earlier novels. In *Collected Stories* (1950) he complemented the *Appendix*, representing "an historical catalogue" of his world, with "an overview of its geography. While the *Appendix* can be seen as a condensed ordering of the time of Yoknapatawpha County, *Collected Stories* represents a more sustained and perhaps — for Faulkner — a more successful systematizing of its space."[33] Especially important, as Paddock points out, is the volume's effort to recompose his fiction: "In order to articulate his conception of Yoknapatawpha as a microcosm not just of the South, but of existence itself, Faulkner apparently found it necessary to juxtapose fictions set in his imaginary county with fictions set elsewhere."[34] Similarly, *Requiem for a Nun* (1951) goes beyond the *Appendix* as historical synopsis and emphasizes the interdependence of fiction and fact by including both the author's imaginary Jefferson and Mississippi's actual capital, Jackson, in its presentation of the geographical and historical development of the state, even though Faulkner stops short of identifying the state with the setting of those dramatic portions in which only his fictional characters appear: "On the wall behind and above the chair, is the emblem, official badge, of the State, sovereignty (a mythical one, since this is rather the State of which Yoknapatawpha County is a unit)."[35] *Requiem* also tends to identify the historical process going on in Faulkner's fiction with the historical process going on not only in his region but in the modern world and confronts that process more directly than ever before by specifying a response to the problems of change and of man's relationship to the past. As in *Go Down, Moses*, the dramatic portions of *Requiem* debate and define in the form of a dialogue between two main characters the whole range of responses to the past and to the present. The narrative passages gather together references to past, present, and future, "as vast backdrop to a compressed action,"[36] "a specific moment in time," which is the drama marking "the accretive end-result of the historical events and processes which the prose chronicles."[37] Hence a consideration of *Requiem* in the light of what already has been said about Faulkner's uses of the past may help to determine what in the broadest sense Faulkner thinks our attitude toward history and the past should be.

Requiem follows the method of the *Compson Appendix* by simultaneously updating the lives of characters who appear in earlier novels and extending the historical reach of the narrative to a past that is more remote than that found in the author's previous works, until the very beginnings of the county are revealed. In the *Appendix* Jefferson begins as "one long rambling onestory mudchinked log building housing the Chickasaw Agent and his tradingpost store" (403); in *Requiem* the town is at first hardly more than a "postoffice—tradingpost-store" (3). In the *Appendix*, as soon as Jason Lycurgus Compson obtains possession of the land, that "square mile" begins to go through increasingly radical transformations; in *Requiem*, as soon as the people of Jefferson begin to think of themselves as inhabiting a town which requires a number of separate and progressively larger institutions, both the rate and the complexity of change are so great that

> overnight it would become a town without having been a village; one day in about a hundred years it would wake frantically from its communal slumber into a rash of Rotary and Lion Clubs and Chambers of Commerce and City Beautifuls...a fever, a delirium in which it would confound forever seething with motion and motion with progress. (4)

In *Requiem* the successive changes in Faulkner's mythical county are directly associated with an historical process that is endemic to the world as a whole. Not just Jefferson but the world itself begins in an extremely chaotic form: "the steamy chiaroscuro, untimed unseasoned winterless miasma not any one of water or earth or life yet all of each, inextricable and indivisible" (99). Just as Jefferson must have its courthouse and jail, then a school, and then its "rash" of organizations, so the world itself becomes cluttered with more and more agencies and institutions, "changing the face of the earth." As the prologues approach the present time of the novel, dates begin to proliferate and become more specific. In particular, the second prologue ends with a comprehensive list of names, a roster of cities, lists of forms of transportation, accommodation, and diversion—all of which emphasize the multiplication of man's activities and the acceleration of his motion through time. The changes are so swiftly accomplished that a hundred years after its foundation the members of the town "no longer even knew" who Doctor Habersham and old Alec Holston and Louis Grenier, the founders of the town, were (47). The original character of the land, which was forested in the "old days," is replaced by "formal synthetic shrubs contrived and schooled in Wisconsin greenhouses" (243).

As if to ascertain what meaning the past might still have in the present, when most of the visible evidence of its existence has disappeared, the reader is suddenly addressed as "you, a stranger, an outlander say from the East or the North or the Far West" who chances upon Jefferson, or comes to see a "relation or acquaintance or friend of one of the outland families which had moved into one of the pristine and recent subdivisions"— as someone trying "to learn, comprehend, understand what had brought your cousin or friend or acquaintance to elect to live here—not specifically here, of course, not specifically Jefferson, but such as here, such as Jefferson" (252). What the reader of *Requiem* and what the visitor to a town "such as Jefferson" recognize is that as the past recedes before the ongoing rush of time, the more strongly the town's citizens seem to remember and cherish that past:

> Suddenly you would realise that something curious was happening or had happened here: that instead of dying off as they should as time passed, it was as though these old irreconcilables [who represented "that steadfast and durable and unhurryable continuity against or across which the vain and glittering ephemerae of progress and alteration washed in substanceless repetitive evanescent scarless waves" (250)] were actually increasing in number; as though with each interment of one, two more shared that vacancy: where in 1900, only thirty-five years afterward, there could not have been more than two or three capable of it, either by knowledge or memory of leisure, or even simple willingness and inclination, now in 1951, eighty-six years afterward, they could be counted in dozens (and in 1965, a hundred years afterward, in hundreds). (252)

In Jefferson, and in all towns such as Jefferson, an awareness of the past increases at the same rapid rate as the changes which efface its traces: indeed the changes seem ephemeral when compared to the tenacity of those who hold on to the past. So sure is he of this historical process that the narrator can project beyond the time frame of his own present into the future, to 1965.

The reason given for the increasing consciousness of the past seems, at first, incredible—for it is no more than "one small rectangle of wavy, crudely-pressed, almost opaque glass, bearing a few faint scratches apparently no more durable than the thin dried slime left by the passage of a snail...which, after a moment, you will descry to be a name and a date" (253-54). As in *Absalom, Absalom!* and *Go Down, Moses* we witness directly the evidence of the past—which is "almost opaque"—and try to decipher its meaning. We carefully follow a perceptual pattern in which we first see the shape of the glass, then note its texture and the elements which contribute to that texture, and finally detect "after a moment," after a certain amount of time has elapsed in our investigation, "a name and a date"—the signs of a human record.

After we experience what it is like to discover and interpret those signs on the glass, we are told that they comprise "that tender ownerless obsolete girl's name [Cecilia Farmer] and the old dead date in April almost a century ago—speaking, murmuring, back from, out of, across from, a time as old as lavender, older than album or stereopticon, as old as daguerreotype itself" (254). The pane of glass evokes the girl's glimpse of the soldier whom "she had not known or even spoken to long enough to have learned his middle name or his preference in food, or told him hers" (257), and of her riding away with him after the war toward

> a country she had never seen, to begin a life which was not even simple frontier, engaged only with wilderness and shoeless savages and the tender hand of God, but one which had been rendered into a desert (assuming that it was still there at all to be returned to) by the iron and fire of civilization. (257)

In some ways, our knowledge of the past is just like Cecilia Farmer's knowledge of the soldier, for the past too is a country we have never seen, and yet we, like Quentin and Shreve in *Absalom, Absalom!*, ride persistently toward it in our imaginations. We yearn to know and to name the past; we identify with it from a distance as Cecilia Farmer identifies with the soldier, as Quentin and Shreve identify with the two young men they have never seen or spoken to. Finally, we know no more about our destination than the girl does who travels "into a desert (assuming that it was still there at all to be returned to)." Although the girl's gesture seems so pathetic, it is really no more so than the labors of the settlers as they "clawed punily" a "tiny clearing" out of the "pathless wilderness" (32), or than the very creation of the "broad blank mid-continental page for the first scratch of orderly recording" (100). All attempts at communication, at defining the world and its history, begin in a seemingly feeble way. Nevertheless, the girl has made her own "scratch of orderly recording," and we are made to feel it, in all of its tangibility, as the message of one human being to all human beings who will follow her: "*'Listen, stranger; this was myself: this was I'*" (262).

This passage perhaps contains the best explanation in Faulkner's fiction of the value of all those tombstones, documents, and other objects from the past that have the power to evoke in our present consciousness a sense of history as the record of human life. In the course of time, many of the "facts," the specific conditions of the past to which these objects refer, are erased and replaced by speculation: "in the town's remembering after a hundred years" the girl's hair "has changed that many times from blonde to dark and back to blonde again" (256). But what stimulates such specula- tion, the search for imaginative specificity, is the simple fact that this frail girl lived at all, that she "was" (261), alive then as we are alive now. As long as the past is considered simply as a scanty collection of facts and artifacts — as Mr. Compson regards the past — then it is all just incredible; it does not make sense. There must, therefore, come a point at which we use our own experience as human beings in order to interpret the past, and this is why in *Requiem* we are addressed so directly as "you." What the narrator calls the "rubble dross of fact and probability" provokes our interest in the past, but our imagination must disperse that dross and burn it away, "leav- ing only truth and dream" (261).

Our arrival at "truth and dream" is the universal experience which binds us to the past and to the continuum of time. Somewhat earlier in the novel it is suggested that all men want to live, to say "no to death" (215), and because they have the dream of living forever, all men wish to project themselves into history, back into the past of 1865 and forward into the future of 1965. Through a concentrated act of human will we try to endow the past with motion, with life, and with those particulars of existence which have been disintegrated in the course of time: "perhaps by turning your head aside you will see from the corner of your eye the turn of a mov- ing limb — a gleam of crinoline, a laced wrist, perhaps even a Cavalier plume — who knows? provided there is will enough, perhaps even the face itself three hundred years after it was dust" (215). Near the end of the novel it is said that "all you had to do was look at it [the pane of glass] a while; all you have to do now is remember it" and then "you" will hear the "clear undistanced voice as though out of the delicate antenna-skeins of radio" (261-62). Our sense of the past may be activated by an exposure to its physical remains, but that sense endures through an act of the creative and interpretative imagination capable of overcoming "even the technology of amplified sound itself," and all of the noises of modern chaotic change threatening to overwhelm human individuality.[38] "The delicate antenna- skeins of radio," representing the roar of modernity Faulkner abhorred — since it tended to drown out the artist's voice[39] — paradoxically, metaphori- cally, are used to suggest that the lines of communication are still open, still continuous, like the Compson mile, in spite of, and partly because of, radical change.

Karl Zender has argued that a significant shift is made in Faulkner's sense of the past on pages 261-62. Whereas in *Go Down, Moses* "Ike's act of reading is an effort to discover objectively verifiable truths," in *Requiem* the stranger "moves beyond the text," and "truth can no longer be revivified fact. It must instead be a dream, and the success of the act of reading, as now defined, is measured in its ability to overcome 'fact and probability.'"[40] I question Zender's idea that Faulkner depicts in *Requiem* "a world turned chaotic and meaningless."[41] On the contrary, however unruly and anarchic change appears to be, the very instruments of change ("the delicate antenna-skeins of radio") become serviceable parts of an historically durable point of view. Cecilia Farmer's story is a kind of worst-case scenario that vindicates rather than vitiates a reading of the past that is not so different from what it is in *Absalom, Absalom!* and *Go Down, Moses.* Even where the past has seemingly vanished completely into folklore, the symbolic and tangible efforts of this frail woman to leave a sign of herself stimulate the stranger and the narrator to sift through legend and fact. The knowability of history may be more problematic in *Requiem* than in Faulkner's earlier works, yet nowhere else does his narrator function more like a historian, carefully trying to discriminate between fact and legend even while conceding they are difficult to separate and must ultimately be fired into the "truth" and "dream" of a coherent, unified, transcendent history. As Noel Polk puts it, the narrator "becomes the culture itself, relating its collective and imperfectly synthesized memories of its own beginnings, memories mystical in character, compounded of fact, legend, and hope, which have been transformed into myth by the workings of the numerous imaginations that have passed them down from generation to generation."[42] It is the consciousness of history as myth that distinguishes the narrator, however, so that he also stands outside of the culture appealing to "you," "the outlander." As an historian, then, the narrator tries "to discern the most likely sequence of, and explanation for, events."[43] As an historiographer, he is at pains to trace history "more or less as it occurred" and as it is "perceived in the present." He is, then, a self-conscious organizer of historical narrative,[44] who is far more acute, more scrupulously scholarly than any character in the novel—even Gavin Stevens, who dominates the dramatic sections with his elaborate narratives of the past. The narrator is not omniscient, but he does unite "his general knowledge of human and natural history with his specific familiarity with the townspeople."[45] As Hugh Ruppersburg has ably demonstrated, "*Requiem*'s narrator speaks with one of the most versatile, powerful lyric voices in Faulkner's fiction."[46] In fact, in terms of the way Faulkner has economically deployed his narrator's versatility *Requiem* stands alone among his works, since it ranges all the way from full familiarity and identification with Jefferson's citizens to a detached, fully withdrawn narrative of their evolving identity through time. From eyewitness reporter, to speculator, to synthesizer, the narrator condenses and dramatizes different rhythms of past and present—and the points of view held by different individuals in a way unrivalled by any other novel except *Go Down, Moses.*

As in *Absalom, Absalom!*, the narrator in *Requiem* intervenes to lend credence to conjecture. He is an authority, a superbly informed historian, in an invented historical world. Even more than in *Absalom, Absalom!*, the narrator in *Requiem* is a shrewd observer, but he is less tentative and apparently more familiar with his evidence. In contrast to his counterpart in the earlier novel, he does not convey the impression that he is guarded in his judgments, even though he frequently admits — perhaps even relishes — discrepancies in the community's accounting of itself. It is not just that the narrator of *Requiem* knows more about the past (in spite of much he does not know) but that he is presented throughout the prologues as an aggressively interpretative voice calling much more attention to itself than is true of any other historian in Faulkner. The narratives of *Requiem*, in other words, are ostentatiously shaped by the figure of the historian.[47]

Another feature of this interpretative voice that sets it apart from Faulkner's earlier narrators even as it builds upon their historiographical prowess is its use of abstractions, of terms like "history" and "time" which are defined and summarized rather than obliquely rendered in metaphors (as in Quentin's understanding of history in the umbilical water-cord passage). Thus the very term history takes its place in a sequence of terms, as in "legend and record and history" (249). The "history of a community" (214) is not only given, it is referred to as a concept in itself, a concept best approached not in "church registers and the courthouse records, but beneath the successive layers of calcimine and creosote and whitewash on the walls of the jail" where — in addition to "the scrawled illiterate repetitive unimaginative doggerel and the perspectiveless almost prehistoric sexual picture-writing" — one will find "the images, the panorama not only of the town but of its days and years until a century and better had been accomplished..." (214). The abstraction history, concretized on jail walls, is a study in itself of a kind of process going on but not defined so explicitly in earlier novels, except insofar as time is explicitly analyzed in *The Sound and the Fury*, *As I Lay Dying*, *Absalom, Absalom!*, and *The Wild Palms*, for example. Even references to time, however, have a somewhat different function in *Requiem*, where there are not only phrases like "an old dead time and a dead age" (39) to remind us of *Absalom, Absalom!* and *Go Down, Moses*, but also explicit, more abstract formulations of a "millennium's beginning" (104), of "an older time already on its rapid way out too" (223), of "frontier, pioneer times" (6), and of "reconstruction times" (242). The labeling and layering of time frames, the pointed recognition that "after a hundred years it [the town's remembering of Cecilia Farmer] has changed that many times" (256), make *Requiem* Faulkner's most avowedly historical work, the one in which he comes closest to formal historical narrative.

Requiem reflects Faulkner's expanded sense of the past, a sense of the past that is just one measure of man's progressive encompassment of time, of his attempt to say "no to death." As man takes in more of his past (like the old irreconcilables in Jefferson who increase in number each year), he also produces a plethora of new forms and shapes for his future as part of a continuing creative and dramatic process—like the "next act and scene" of a play,

> itself clearing its own stage without waiting for propertymen; or rather, not even bothering to clear the stage but commencing the new act and scene right in the midst of the phantoms, the fading wraiths of that old time which had been exhausted, used up, to be no more and never return. (222)

Rather than having the historical process developed obliquely through the consciousness of his characters as in earlier novels, Faulkner in *Requiem* directly presents the acts and scenes of that process as the setting in which the drama of Temple Drake's life takes place. Thus in preparing his book for publication Faulkner directed his editor to "Set all the acts like this: the number designations of each *act* to *precede* the prose prologue," and emphasized that "to me the prose is not at all a prologue, but is an integrated part of the act itself." In his typescript, Faulkner further emphasized the integral connection between his narrative and drama by having scene 1 of Act I immediately follow on the same page the ending of the first prologue.[48] After a reading of the entire novel, it seems that the prologues mediate between, and must be seen in the perspective of, Temple Drake's insistence that her life now is what constitutes her identity and Gavin Stevens's contrary insistence that her life now be viewed within the context of her past.

The very absoluteness of Stevens's statement—"The past is never dead. It's not even past" (92)—must give us pause, for in the prologues it is abundantly clear that the narrator's evocation of life as motion means that there are a succession of pasts that are all abandoned in turn, shattered by the tremendous velocity of man's own energies. Not only is each successive moment superseded, it is all but forgotten and effaced from the earth. The past only lives to the extent that in living in the here and now man can imagine what it was like to live there and then. At the very least, Stevens is giving a reductive version of a complex truth, as Richard Gray recognizes when he suggests that Stevens's argument is "rather too much like a sermon in which the idea is abstracted from the experience and necessarily simplified in the process."[49] At the same time, Stevens's statement contains more than a grain of truth, for the prologues also show that there is more than a trace of the past in the present, and that the present grows out of the past.

As Brooks says so well, "the past does continue to live in the present, not only in the sense that it is alive in our memories, but also because we ourselves have been shaped by the past."⁵⁰ As soon as the people of the Chickasaw trading post decide to name their place of habitation Jefferson and call it a town, they hitch themselves to the racing engine of history, and the analogue in Temple's life to Jefferson's development, to the sense that the present emerges out of the past, is her belief that her child's death has been caused by her liking for evil (135), by her involvement eight years before the present time of *Requiem* with the gangster Popeye, and a lover, Red, in a Memphis whorehouse, after her boyfriend Gowan, now her husband, got drunk and passed out. Of course the events of *Sanctuary* are not the precise and the immediate cause of Nancy's killing of Temple's six-month-old child any more than the decision of the men at the Chickasaw trading post to call themselves a town is the precise and immediate cause of the modern city of Jefferson. But each of these initial events sets in motion a train of cause and effect which leads to the situation in the present time of the novel. To that extent Temple is neither more nor less responsible for Nancy's actions than the founding fathers of Jefferson are responsible for the present state of life in Jefferson.

Instead of admitting Temple's right to exist as Mrs. Gowan Stevens, Gavin Stevens insists on referring to her as Temple Drake, which is tantamount to thinking of the town of Jefferson as no different from the Chickasaw trading post. Eight years have elapsed in which Temple has tried to be a good wife, to raise a family, to live with her guilt feelings concerning her own past and with her husband's constantly forgiving her for that past. Of course it is important to remember that Nancy killed Temple's child in order to prevent Temple from returning to her past and that Temple's whole relationship with Nancy suggests that she herself has never been willing to abandon that past entirely.⁵¹ Nevertheless, in his attempt to uncover the original causes which led to the death of Temple's child, Stevens is surely placing a greater burden on her than is necessary or wise for a human being who must go on living after a terrible tragedy. In Stevens's view the past completely eclipses the present, and Temple's obsessively repeated question as to whether she will have to reveal all of her past to the Governor must elicit our sympathy as well as expose, in Millgate's words, "Stevens's increasingly arid pursuit of an abstract conception of justice and truth, his obsessive concern with a dead past, and his insensitivity towards the present."⁵² Like Nancy's misguided killing of the child, Stevens's interrogation of Temple suggests an inhuman isolation from life's complexities.

The drama, then, juxtaposes Stevens and Temple as the rather neatly contrasted representatives of two ways of looking at history. The past is never past, in that it has shaped the present, but it is man in the present who determines the way in which he will react to the past, and if he chooses to attempt to live in that past his capacity for present action is fatally impaired. Like Bayard Sartoris in *The Unvanquished*, Temple is attempting to deal with her personal past on her own terms in the present. Stevens's exclusive concern with that past provides Temple with very little opportunity to break out of her old pattern of action. Thus his obstinate refusal to set aside any part of her past is as unrealistic and self-defeating as Drusilla Hawk's rigid unwillingness in *The Unvanquished* to set aside any part of Bayard's past.

Like some of the exchanges between Quentin and Shreve in *Absalom, Absalom!*, the debate between Stevens and Temple is at times extremely cruel and almost unbearable. Like Shreve, Stevens likes to launch out on long-winded, hypothetical reconstructions of the past, but in so doing he is usually making a direct attack on Temple, establishing a case against her, whereas Shreve's criticism of Quentin is often modified in the course of their joint exploration. Nevertheless, Stevens, like Shreve, is the only one who is able to develop the story. Beck reminds us of Temple's evasiveness,[53] and like Quentin she cannot bear to uncover by herself events which are so much a part of herself. As Mary Dunlap observes: "Stevens poetizes here, as he has to, in order to explain motivations which the major actor could not tell, being incapacitated by the inherent lack of objectivity."[54]

Because Faulkner is dealing with people and not just with ideas, the debate develops out of the very different personalities of its participants. We are forced not to choose sides, but to see the way in which each side responds to the historical process that is presented in the prologues of the novel. In a curious way, Stevens and Temple depend upon each other, like the old general and his son in *A Fable*. Of their conflict, Irwin comments: "Since the two opposing principles exist by means of the very opposition between them, like left and right, high and low, father and son, they are always and everywhere implicated in one another."[55] Out of the dialogue between Stevens and Temple comes that tension between divergent views of the past and present which also marks the debates between Ike McCaslin and McCaslin Edmonds in *Go Down, Moses* and between Stevens and Chick Mallison in *Intruder in the Dust*.[56] The chief distinction of *Requiem*, especially in the prologues, is the way in which it manages so directly to juxtapose the development of Yoknapatawpha and the modern world as a whole with the development of the individuals who live in it.

Nowhere is this clearer than in the new treatment of the French architect. In *Absalom, Absalom!* he is created as an adjunct of Sutpen's demonizing in Miss Rosa's account, and in Mr. Compson's as a complex abettor and obstructor of Sutpen's outrageous design. In *Requiem*, he is first introduced as Sutpen's "tame Parisian architect—or captive rather." But "the settlement had only to see him once to know that he was no dociler than his captor" (37). Not a mythological figure but a man, the architect speaks to a community's desire to build an edifice of itself: "'You do not need advice, You are too poor. You have only your hands, and clay to make good brick. You dont have any money. You dont even have anything to copy: how can you go wrong?'" Jefferson takes its shape from his molds and kilns (45). Even the destructiveness of war fails to disturb "one hair even out of the Paris architect's almost forgotten plumb" (46). The architect's imprint remains, more than a hundred years later, "not on just the courthouse and the jail, but on the whole town" (225), for he has built and made possible the community's own drive to preserve and perpetuate itself, a drive more narrowly conceived in *Absalom, Absalom!* in relation to Sutpen's ambitions. In *Requiem*, even after the community apparently loses much of its historical identity—"gone now from the fronts of the stores are the old brick made of native clay in Sutpen's architect's old molds" (244)—still there is a surviving remnant of memory and of place found in the "thin durable continuity" of the jail itself and what it stands for (250).

The chief failing of *Requiem* resides in its dialogue that is not as flexible or as ventilated by narrative commentary as in *Absalom, Absalom!* and *Go Down, Moses*. By constricting the exchanges between Temple and Stevens, so that they are isolated and exist "solely in the context of their private emotions, thoughts, and dilemmas," Faulkner deftly intensifies the burden of history on "the individual human will,"[57] but at the same time he overburdens his characters' speeches, making their words serve the antithetical functions of narration and dramatization. Occasionally the two support each other as in Temple's account of Rider's lonely despair, which is very much like her own (198-99). Warren Beck notes that Temple's memory of Rider reveals the "play of reactive influence in a closeness of community among its members, despite racial and socioeconomic stratifications."[58] In other words, Temple's anguish is almost unbearably hers alone to suffer, yet she is aware that it is not unprecedented in her community; and to that extent the drama of her life is simultaneously a part of her people's history, entangling all of them—as Nancy tried to demonstrate in her demented murder of Temple's child. It is significant, I think, that Rider's name is not mentioned, since Temple is recalling a past separate from her own but similar enough to stimulate her communal, historical, consciousness. It is a kind of consciousness—the historian-narrator shows in the prologues—that may simplify or otherwise distort details while preserving the essential meaning of past events. Temple's struggle to recall Rider's story becomes particularly poignant when one reflects on the deputy in "Pantaloon in Black" who missed the meaning of the black man's hysteria. By making Temple a witness to Rider's suffering, Faulkner finds yet another way of making Yoknapatawpha morally and historically coherent.

More often, however, the dialogue is tiresome as Stevens works overtime to narrate Temple's life and interrogate her as well. He holds the stage too long and acts like history's spokesman. Even when his prominence in the telling of Temple's past may be diminished by the insufficiency of his own language or by a dramatic scene that apparently undercuts his version of events,[59] Stevens's desire for dialogue with Temple makes his role honorific—unless one cares to argue that Temple should be left alone. The prose prologues, however, suggest that such a withdrawal from community, from history, is self-defeating, if not self-destructive. So Temple and Stevens must talk, must air their views on cause and effect and on what individuals owe to each other. Without a firm narrative presence in these scenes—as in the debate over the problem of the missing lock in the first prologue (18–35)—exposition and character development in the drama get clogged and clotted with rhetoric.

It is as if the dialogue in *Requiem* were Faulkner's innovative replacement of the italics used in the previous novels, the italics representing an intensification of thought and emotion immediately set off from slower narrative. *Requiem* reads like a brilliant effort to take apart, to strip down a style, and then reassemble it along two tracks: one in the form of an incredibly supple voice equal to tracing the enormous ramifications of historical process, and the other not quite able to reify consistently that process in individual lives. The two tracks converge thematically but are never fully integrated into the novel. The drama is too often curiously static; yet the prologues rush with life, pregnant with those acts and scenes of history alluded to in *Go Down, Moses*, chronicled in the *Appendix*, spatialized in the sections of *Collected Stories*, and finally synchronized by Faulkner's narrator-historian in *Requiem for a Nun*.

8

Conclusion

All of Faulkner's uses of the past are prompted by his search for the meaning of history. He is more than a regionalist in that he sees the Southern past as a way of getting at the universal causes and consequences of history, different from the historian in that he is not primarily concerned with authenticating facts about the past, and unlike the historical novelist in that he rarely separates the past and the present and never exclusively concentrates on the manners of a past period of time. In Faulkner the facts about the past are always imaginatively created and recreated and therefore always subject to change. In Faulkner's mature fiction the experience of the past is the product of human consciousness; as consciousness awakens and develops, so too does a sense of the past awaken and develop.[1]

Of course both the historian and the historical novelist are interested in more than authenticating historical facts and in portraying the manners of a past period of time. Such twentieth-century historians as Carl Becker and R. G. Collingwood have been very much concerned with man's consciousness of the past and with the way in which that consciousness alters the presentation of the so-called historical facts. Becker has said that every man is his own historian insofar as every man interprets for himself the meaning of his own life, just as the historian, on a higher and more disciplined level, interprets the significance of the past in the light of his own experience as an historian.[2] Historical facts are not easily discoverable objective quantities—as Collingwood acknowledges when he says that the historian's perspective on the past is inevitably influenced by who he is and by what his contemporary world is like, so that "all history is contemporary history."[3]

Similarly, Avrom Fleishman has recently argued that the historical novelist, whatever the extent of his interest in the past may be, is inevitably concerned with what the past means in relation to his own present time.[4] Even if the historical novelist avoids any reference to his own time, he must, by and large, render his understanding of the past in terms of the present—if only so that his readers will understand and identify with the past. Otherwise the past is of little more than antiquarian interest. Thackeray and Scott, for example, do not concentrate exclusively on the past but on their characters' recollection and understanding of it. The characters then relay that understanding to other characters and to us. The experience of the past, then, is not simple, direct, and uniform but complex, oblique, and ultimately unified by our organization of the different kinds of testimony given to us by what Collingwood would call our "authorities." These "authorities"—whether we are speaking of those in an historical novel or in an actual historical account—are not be be taken at their word. We do not simply piece together their statements into what Collingwood calls "scissors and paste history";[5] on the contrary, historical interpretation is an active and vigorous questioning of all the evidence, a product of the inquiring mind.

In his best work Faulkner goes beyond most historians and historical novelists in making the past and present, historical fact and human imagination, the inseparable parts of a single process: the understanding of the meaning of history. Though the historian may concede his interest in the present as well as in the past, and though the historical novelist may state or imply his interest in both, Faulkner is the rare example of a writer who is able to dramatize the process of understanding the past even as the past's relationship to the present is being revealed. As Quentin and Shreve progress in their understanding of the past, they also grow closer together in their understanding of each other. As Ike and Cass jointly explore the meaning of their heritage, they also come to realize more clearly than ever before the similarities and the differences between them. While other novelists, such as Scott, have also been able to juxtapose past and present in this way, and while the dialogue form Faulkner so often uses is at least as old as Plato, Faulkner seems almost alone in making the dialectical relationship between past and present absolutely crucial to the structures of his novels and in so manipulating that relationship as to necessitate our own involvement as readers in the process of historical interpretation.

It would be absurd, of course, to claim any absolute originality in Faulkner's approach, for part of his strength derives from his absorption and extension of the methods employed by his distinguished predecessors. It is not surprising, then, to find that Faulkner's work resembles the type of historical novel which, as Herbert Butterfield says, invents all of its characters and events in order to reveal "history in its workings in an imaginary life set in it; in the same way as a teacher may illustrate the force of gravity to children by talking about its workings on an imaginary apple. It may be in a way true to history without being true to fact."[6]

Butterfield's distinction between being "true to history" if not "true to fact" comes close to the very heart of Faulkner's uses of the past. I have already cited his nonfiction statements on the truth/fact dichotomy, but in their elliptical, truncated nature they do not do justice to his fiction's complexity. He was not much interested in academic analyses of his work, although he would sit more or less patiently through interviews and attempt to answer questions thoughtfully. He came from a culture, as Cleanth Brooks informs us, harboring "a genuine distrust of abstractions of every kind."[7] As a result, Faulkner could not be drawn very far into the kind of historiographical discussion pursued in this book. Nevertheless, one would be mistaken, I think, to assume that he did not have a profound grasp of all that the abstraction "history" stands for. He was, when he wanted to be, scholarly and academic in a somewhat circumspect and surreptitious way—as Joseph Blotner shows in his account of a conversation between Faulkner and Robert Penn Warren.[8] Perhaps, as Blotner surmises, Faulkner felt the need to make up for his "qualified praise" of *All The King's Men*, or perhaps, as I surmise, he saw in Warren one to whom "the distinction between the fact of a thing and the truth of a thing" would be crucial. All through dinner together Faulkner "kept working at it," relating the distinction to Warren's fiction, "point[ing] out cases and [going] off on tangential references, not citing other writers by name but referring to many narratives for illustration."[9]

Critics who tend to discount Faulkner's interest in history also minimize the linkage *between* fact and fable, fact and truth in his work. Fact has its severe limitations, but it also must be sifted carefully before "you" can transcend it for "truth and dream." Just as there is dialogue between characters, there is also a dialectic between the data of the past and the imaginative reception of it; and dialectic implies dependence. In other words, Faulkner had to shift constantly between "the fact of a thing" and "the truth of a thing" in his conversation with Warren, and he does the same in his fiction.

Clearly, the making of narratives fascinated Faulkner, for only through narratives, and his study of them, could he bridge the gap between facts and truth. Narrative, indeed, is a bridging process in his fiction. So it is in works of formal history such as Shelby Foote's three volumes on the Civil War, subtitled *A Narrative*. Although certain kinds of academic history have discredited narrative as too artful, too biased and fictional, and have tried to take the measure of the past scientifically, Cleanth Brooks is surely right to say that historians seeking a scrupulous, lifelike, meaningful rendering of the past will necessarily write it as a story:

> Our professional historians are thus set a difficult task: to try to eliminate at least the more fanciful myths, and to ground history, as nearly as possible, on fact; and yet to

provide an interpretation of history—not just a dry chronicle of facts—something that will possess the dynamics of myth even though based on actual happenings.[10]

Faulkner partakes of this scholarly scrupulosity as well, for as Wesley Morris notes, in the midst of his most powerful stories he uses, quite self-consciously, tentative terms like "as if" to call attention to "the narrow gap that exists between fiction and factual history."[11]

Without an esthetic sense of shape, of form, and of story, there could be no history, the structures of Faulkner's novels imply. In this respect, his work follows in the tradition of Scott, who for all of his reverence for documented history nevertheless relies on "the imagination [which] fills the framework of historical fact with the picture of dramatic human confrontations," so that "events are freed from their fixed abode in the past, and are brought back to life with the attendant diversification that characterizes all real events."[12] As Iser observes, "there are moments when Waverley experiences an exciting convergence of reality and imagination," when he actually meets a seventeen-year-old girl who has already experienced what he has only dreamed about and associated with a remote past. "Past and Present seem to have become interchangeable for Waverley, for a scene conjured up by his imagination does not, in fact, belong to some distant age but is happening here and now," Iser points out.[13] Precisely the same words can be applied to the scene between Quentin and Henry in *Absalom, Absalom!*, although the connection between past and present is not made nearly so explicit or so comforting. Like narrative in works of formal history, Faulkner's literary narrative is found to have "gaps," and meaning "resides tenuously in these gaps...."[14]

As a novelist, Faulkner is much freer to acknowledge these gaps than historians. Martin Duberman, who is both a playwright and an historian, puts the dilemma succinctly in his drama *The Memory Bank*, when he has an interviewee (Andrews) suddenly turn on the interviewer-historian (Smyth) to demand an explanation of the narrative he is assembling:

Andrews: Then what will you say?
Smyth: Well, to the extent that I understand it —
Andrews: Don't be modest. It's unbecoming in an historian. Makes people doubt your word.
Smyth: Well, it seems to me —
Andrews: Bad start.[15]

Andrews is not satisfied until Smyth drops all qualifying phrases and recites a confident narrative that is clearly based as much on intuition as it is on fact, and on Andrews's life as much as on the unnamed and evidently deceased historical figure Andrews knew.

Three extraordinary examples of historians' efforts to write the kind of narrative found in Faulkner's novels also help to define just where he is unique in his presentation of history. In his rendering of Lincoln's assassination, Shelby Foote, a novelist and historian, perhaps comes as close as possible in a work of formal history, based on a copious assortment of primary and secondary sources, to Faulkner's dramatization of the past:

> Then it came, a half-muffled explosion, somewhere between a boom and a thump, loud but by no means so loud as it sounded in the theater, then a boil and bulge of bluish smoke in the presidential box, an exhalation as of brimstone from the curtained mouth, and a man coming out through the bank and swirl of it, white-faced and dark-haired in a black suit and riding boots, eyes aglitter, brandishing a knife. He mounted the ledge, presented his back to the rows of people seated below, and let himself down by the handrail for the ten-foot drop to the stage. Falling, he turned, and as he did so caught the spur of his right boot in the folds of a flag draped over the lower front of the high box. It ripped but offered enough resistance to bring all the weight of his fall on his left leg, which buckled and pitched him forward onto his hands. He rose, thrust the knife overhead in a broad theatrical gesture, and addressed the outward darkness of the pit. "Sic semper tyrannis," he said in a voice so low and projected with so little clarity that few recognized the state motto of Virginia or could later agree that he had spoken in Latin. "Revenge for the South!" or "The South is avenged!" some thought they heard him cry, while others said that he simply muttered "Freedom." In any case he then turned again, hobbled left across the stage past the lone actor standing astonished in its center, and vanished into the wings.[16]

The tension in this scene between what is known and not known is reminiscent of *Absalom, Absalom!*. Did Booth "cry" or did he "mutter"? And what *exactly* did he say? Phrases like "somewhere between" and "but by no means so loud as" convey the subtle shifting between precise and not so precise assessments of atmosphere, which verges on staged melodrama — Booth "brandishing a knife...*presented* his back to the rows of people...thrust the knife overhead in a broad theatrical gesture and *addressed* the outward darkness of the pit." The momentousness and inevitability of the assassination have reached such a pitch of expectation in Foote's narrative that he has only to say "then it came," and to carry us in a long sweeping sentence a third of the way into the paragraph, the deed already done as swiftly as in reality. Sentence by sentence there is a fine blend of immediacy and retrospection, as there always is in the best of Faulkner. The alliteration and the onomatopoeic effects are balanced by the language of surmise. Image and metaphor are countered by supposition and analogy. Foote conjectures "an exhalation as of brimstone from the curtained mouth," which is a kind of bridging phrase between fact and fiction, for his "as of" is akin to Faulkner's "as if." As in Faulkner, the narrative is cumulative, basing itself on authorities but breathing with its own life, its own management of the past, sustained by the incremental nature of its tropes.

Phillip Shaw Paludan's book *Victims* demonstrates far less narrative power than Foote's but more of Faulkner's speculative drive. Paludan sees the need for showing how he has brought all of his interpretative powers to bear on the story of a massacre in Shelton Laurel, North Carolina during the Civil War. He prefaces his history with a denial of Aristotle's distinction between the historian and the poet, between a concern for particulars and universals:

> Historians want also to know what happens to mankind generally, what historical perspective can contribute to understanding enduring elements in human experience. I have been drawn to study Shelton Laurel because I am concerned with My Lai and the Holocaust, in the tragic capacity that humans have shown throughout history—the capacity to commit atrocity.[17]

Paludan then goes on to describe his interest in an "incident" about which there is a "scarcity of pertinent materials." He has supplemented primary evidence of the past with "oral interviews with current residents" of Shelton Laurel, applied "generalizations drawn from the sociology of communities" and from "psychological studies of soldiers in Vietnam and elsewhere in seeking to understand the dynamics of the atrocity-producing situation." His search has been "not just for documents but also for angles of vision that might expand my understanding," and he has had to "go up to and perhaps beyond the boundaries of traditional historical research." Sounding much like the narrators of *Absalom, Absalom!*, in spite of his professional training, he speaks of getting involved with "primary emotions that are less a part of a certain moment in history and more a part of the human personality." He writes in "a style that calls for the reader's emotional resources as an aid to understanding."[18]

Although Paludan's voice never becomes as colorful as the voices in *Absalom, Absalom!*, his meditative and sometimes keenly anxious tone approximates the different narrative keys and registers of the novel. In his power to move from a focus on individuals to the concerns of a whole community and of an age, he resembles the resourceful narrator of *Requiem*[19]:

> Something in James Keith would not rest. He had to be improving himself, working his way up, becoming somebody. For him the land was not enough. The seasons and the harmony with the place did not satisfy him. Maybe his father, a Baptist preacher, had something to do with that. Sometimes preachers taught more than resignation. Sometimes the idea crept in that a man had a calling and should see about that calling, that God had given each person gifts and a man did not waste God's gift by letting it lie fallow. Keith's father was an example to him—doing his duty for his flock, seeking them

out, moving from place to place to spread the word of the Lord, going about His work striving, always striving, to be better in His eyes. And maybe there was something in having books around and being able to read them and having to study the Word, not just hear it spoken.[20]

Paludan does not have Faulkner's awesome talent for compressed narrative, for quick character delineation, or for the intricate layering of one point of view on another, but his presence—moving in and out of the past, probing it, shaping it, and filling in gaps while allowing the gaps to show—is everywhere apparent and very Faulknerian. He grapples with "something" in James Keith that (in the second sentence) gets defined as a kind of ambition, derived "maybe" from his striving father, a preacher, and preachers—so Paludan generalizes—sometimes "taught more than resignation." Then Paludan switches to considering the circumstances and the environment that may have "driven," Paludan says in the next paragraph, Keith's ambition. In four paragraphs Paludan constantly modulates between facts and speculations to summaries of inferences and circumstances, occasionally generalizing from the conditions he has studied in a variety of sources in the past and the present. His technique is really not so different from Mr. Compson's attempts to animate the past, to rectify rents in the evidence, to philosophize not in the abstract but in relation to a culture intimately experienced and deliberately scrutinized.[21] Like Mr. Compson, Paludan looks for angles of vision, and like Quentin and Shreve he tries to insinuate himself into the historical figure's point of view, imagining at one point that Keith "could look forward to a life of influence and responsibility."[22] In point of fact, Keith will be largely responsible for the massacre that ruins his career, and like the narrators in *Absalom, Absalom!*, Paludan sets out to see how Keith and others became irrevocably caught up in the murders.

In *Black Mountain: An Exploration in Community* Martin Duberman describes and analyzes his sense of identification with the community of Black Mountain College. As Quentin talked with Henry Sutpen, the survivor of the past, so Duberman talks and feels a kinship with many of the former students and faculty members of the defunct college. He gives excerpts from his dated journal in which he reflects on his own place in time in relation to Black Mountain, and from the standpoint of 1971 projects himself into a faculty meeting which took place September 28, 1936.[23] In short, Duberman has attempted to respond to the rather harsh criticisms of those like Olga Vickery who hold that

the historian deliberately removes the human aspect from history; his collection of data is intellectually ordered in terms of laws which are as general and abstract as possible. The result is, of course, intellectually convincing, but such a pattern cannot command emotional allegiance since it misses the core of truth and reality. When the Civil War is reduced to names of battles, military strategy, and lists of casualties, it loses all its stirring, evocative power and becomes simply information fixed in dead words.[24]

Duberman's attempts to involve us in his increasing identification with the people of Black Mountain College are not a consistent element of the overall style and structure of the book — as they are in Faulkner's attempts in *Absalom, Absalom!* to involve us in Quentin's and Shreve's increasing identification with Henry Sutpen and Charles Bon. Duberman has used the methods of the professional historian: carefully recorded interviews, extensive notes, and a massive bibliography of sources. He has researched and authenticated facts of the past in ways that neither Faulkner nor his characters are particularly interested in doing. As an historian, Duberman must be faithful to the particulars of the specific past he studies; as a novelist, Faulkner, beyond his basic need to sustain the reader's suspension of disbelief, is faithful to the particulars of a specific past only to the extent that such particulars reveal what is universally true in all times and in all places.

However one finally judges the extent of Duberman's success in showing the way in which an historian interacts with past events, the ending of *Black Mountain* points up his desire to set up a dialogue between himself and what he calls his "data," and to portray time, past and present, as a continuum of human experiences:

> I completed the book a few minutes ago. I'm strangely, idiotically, near tears. So many completions are involved, my own and Black Mountain's, that they blend into some indistinguishable sadness.... And what I'm trying to do right now is *not* conclude, not damage (further?) the particularity of their struggle with some sanctifying, cheapening formula that would too neatly link their labors to an emerging world.[25]

This conclusion resembles the open-ended conclusions of Faulkner's novels, especially those of *Absalom, Absalom!* and *Go Down, Moses,* which try to keep the experience of living in history fluid in the sense that no final answer to the issues debated in the dialogues is possible. Thus the dialectical momentum of the exchanges in point of view between the characters is preserved, and the novels themselves do "*not* conclude, not damage...the particularity of their struggle with some sanctifying, cheapening formula that would too neatly link their labors to an emerging world."

Since the "authorities" on the past cannot be wholly trusted, and since the novels themselves refuse to yield a definitive and conclusive "formula" that would neatly link up the conflicting testimony, it is imperative that we assemble our own evidence, become our own historians, and interact, personally and individually, with the experience of the past. Otherwise we have to accept the past, as some of Faulkner's characters do, as a hard and fast phenomenon that preempts and blocks off our action in the present, and retards, if it does not stop, our motion in time. In Faulkner's novels the search for the meaning of history immerses us in a ceaseless and often ambiguous process of trying to establish an identification between human experiences in the past, the present, and the future. Out of our intense and intimate participation in historical interpretation comes the realization that in spite of the limitations of our own time and place and the manifold changes in the course of time which separate us from the past, we are, like the characters of the novels, the products and extensions of historical process, and that underlying that process are certain perennial and abiding human experiences which make history meaningful as a whole.

Notes

Chapter 1

1. José Ortega y Gasset, *History as a System and other Essays Toward a Philosophy of History* (New York: W. W. Norton, 1962), p. 213. For a critic who views Faulkner's fiction in terms similar to Ortega y Gasset's, see Olga Vickery, *The Novels of William Faulkner: A Critical Interpretation,* revised edition (Baton Rouge: Louisiana State University Press, 1964), p. 257.

2. *Flags in the Dust,* ed. Douglas Day (New York: Random House, 1973), has been discussed rather than *Sartoris* because the former is closer to the novel which Faulkner originally submitted for publication. As both Michael Millgate in *The Achievement of William Faulkner* (London: Constable, 1966), p. 84, and Day (p. viii) note, almost a fourth of Faulkner's typescript was excised as the result of Harcourt, Brace's request for an "extensive cutting job" (Day, viii). In his "introduction" to *Flags* Day states that the text "aims at being a faithful reproduction" of Faulkner's composite typescript (ix). Nevertheless, it must be emphasized that the text is less than satisfactory. In Day's own words: "The final complete typescript, which must have served as setting copy for the Harcourt, Brace edition of *Sartoris* (and which must have been the draft in which Wasson made his cuts), has not survived. Nor have any galley proofs. All we had to work from, then, was the composite typescript, by any scholar's standards a suspect source. There was no way, finally, to tell which of the many differences between *Flags in the Dust* and *Sartoris* were the result of Faulkner's emendations in the hypothetical setting copy and the galley proofs, and which belonged to Wasson. If there were to be any publication of *Flags in the Dust* at all, then, it had to be what we have here provided" (ix-x). Richard P. Adams, in "At Long Last, *Flags in the Dust,*" *Southern Review* 10 (1974):880, disagrees with Day and mentions the manuscript version, "which might possibly contain some clues as to what Faulkner intended." Adams does, however, conclude that it is better to have this "dubiously reliable text" (881) than none at all; for a more detailed critique of Day's text, see George Hayhoe, "William Faulkner's *Flags in the Dust,*" *Mississippi Quarterly* 28 (1975):370-86, and Merle Wallace Keiser, "*Flags in the Dust* and *Sartoris,*" in *Fifty Years of Yoknapatawpha,* eds. Doreen Fowler and Ann J. Abadie (Jackson: University Press of Mississippi, 1980), pp. 44-69.

3. Frederick L. Gwynn and Joseph L. Blotner, eds., *Faulkner in the University* (New York: Vintage Books, n.d.), p. 277.

4. Malcolm Cowley, *The Faulkner-Cowley File, Letters and Memories 1944-1962* (New York: The Viking Press, 1966), p. 112.

5. Jean-Paul Sartre, "On *The Sound and the Fury*: Time in the Work of Faulkner," *Faulkner: A Collection of Critical Essays*, ed. Robert Penn Warren (Englewood Cliffs, New Jersey: Prentice-Hall, 1966), p. 89.

6. See, for example: John Hunt, *William Faulkner: Art in Theological Tension* (Syracuse: Syracuse University Press, 1965), p. 7; and George C. Bedell, *Kierkegaard and Faulkner: Modalities of Existence* (Baton Rouge: Louisiana State University Press, 1972), pp. 184–90.

7. William Faulkner, *Absalom, Absalom!* (New York: Random House, 1936), p. 131. Page references to this photographic reprinting of the 1936 first edition are subsequently incorporated in the text within parentheses.

8. *Faulkner in the University*, p. 84. See also pp. 47–48.

9. Millgate, p. 287. See also Vickery, p. 262.

10. *Faulkner in the University*, p. 139.

11. James B. Meriwether and Michael Millgate, eds., *Lion in the Garden: Interviews with William Faulkner 1926–1962* (New York: Random House, 1968), p. 255.

12. *Lion in the Garden*, p. 70.

13. Robert Hemenway, "Enigmas of Being in *As I Lay Dying*," *Modern Fiction Studies* 26 (1970):142.

14. See, for example: Robert Penn Warren, "Faulkner: The South, The Negro, and Time," *Faulkner: A Collection of Critical Essays*, p. 267; Bedell, pp. 223–24, 227–28; Michael Millgate, "'The Firmament of Man's History': Faulkner's Treatment of the Past," *Mississippi Quarterly* 25 (1972):32.

15. Warren Beck, *Man in Motion: Faulkner's Trilogy* (Madison: University of Wisconsin Press, 1963); and Richard P. Adams, *Faulkner: Myth and Motion* (Princeton: Princeton University Press, 1968).

16. Joseph Blotner, ed., *Selected Letters of William Faulkner* (New York: Random House, 1977), p. 239.

17. *The History of Henry Esmond* is an excellent example of an historical novel which attempts to give a portrait of an age. As John Sutherland notes in his introduction to the novel (Baltimore: Penguin Books, 1970), p. 27, the first edition, published in 1852 in "three volumes, printed in an eighteenth-century type-face, and sprinkled with archaisms, masqueraded as the memoirs of Colonel Esmond, published in 1778." In part, the novel was the product of Thackeray's extensive reading over many years in eighteenth-century history, and he was indebted to Macaulay's *History of England* not only for facts but for Esmond's "Whig historical thesis" (Sutherland, p. 25). The personalities and politics of Generals Marlborough and Webb, of Addison, Steele, and Swift are carefully delineated by their contemporary, Henry Esmond, who also gives brief descriptions of St. John, Harley, Congreve, Pope, and other political and literary figures as well as a detailed portrayal of the Stuart Pretender. Besides dealing with these historical figures, Thackeray is at pains to make Esmond's memoirs more like a genuine historical document. The memoirs are introduced with a "preface" written by Esmond's daughter, Rachel Esmond Warrington, who comments on her father's personality and on the contents of his memoirs. At various points throughout the novel both Esmond's

daughter and wife comment on and attempt to correct or explicate his interpretations of human motivations and historical figures and events.

18. Oscar Handlin, *Chance or Destiny: Turning Points in American History* (New York: Atlantic-Little, Brown, 1955).

19. Hugh M. Ruppersburg, *Voice and Eye in Faulkner's Fiction* (Athens: University of Georgia Press, 1983), p. 19.

20. Ruppersburg, p. 100.

21. See Martin Kreiswirth, *William Faulkner: The Making of a Novelist* (Athens: University of Georgia Press, 1983), pp. 38, 61.

22. Lisa Paddock, "'Sublimating the actual into apocryphal': The Case for Faulkner's *Collected Stories,*" unpublished essay, pp. 5, 7. For an elaboration of her argument, see "Contrapuntal in Integration: A Study of Three Faulkner Short Story Volumes" (University of Toronto, Ph.D. dissertation, 1979).

23. Paddock, p. 13, is not specifically concerned with Faulkner's uses of the past, but I have found her comments supportive of my argument.

24. Wesley Morris, *Friday's Footprint: Structuralism and the Articulated Text* (Columbus: Ohio State University Press, 1979), pp. 21-23. I draw heavily on Morris's view of "Was" in my subsequent remarks.

25. Cowley, p. 109.

26. Aristotle, "On the Art of Fiction (From Poetics)," *Aspects of the Drama: A Handbook,* eds. Sylvan Barnet, Morton Berman, William Burto (Boston: Little Brown, 1962), p. 23.

27. See *Faulkner in the University,* p. 9.

28. *Lion in the Garden,* p. 120.

29. Michael Millgate, "Faulkner and History," *The South and Faulkner's Yoknapatawpha: The Actual and the Apocryphal,* eds. Evans Harrington and Ann J. Abadie (Jackson: University Press of Mississippi, 1977), p. 35.

30. Millgate, "Faulkner and History," p. 35.

31. Quoted in Millgate, "Faulkner and History," p. 35.

32. Millgate, "Faulkner and History," p. 36.

33. Millgate, "Faulkner and History," p. 36.

34. See Michael Millgate, "'A Cosmos of My Own': The Evolution of Yoknapatawpha," *Fifty Years of Yoknapatawpha,* p. 41.

35. Joseph Turner, "The Kinds of Historical Fiction: An Essay in Definition and Methodology," *Genre* 12 (1979):340, 335.

36. Turner, p. 343.

37. Robert Penn Warren, "Faulkner: Past and Future," *Faulkner: A Collection of Critical Essays,* p. 17. On the Contents page the title reads "Faulkner: Past and Present."

38. Brent Harold, "The Value and Limitations of Faulkner's Fictional Method," *American Literature* 47 (1975):229.

39. *Selected Letters,* p. 239.

40. *Selected Letters,* p. 239.

41. Michael Millgate, "Faulkner's Masters," *Tulane Studies in English* 23 (1978):152.

42. *Lion in the Garden,* p. 110.

43. See James C. Simmons, *The Novelist as Historian: Essays on the Victorian Historical Novel* (The Hague: Mouton, 1973).

44. *Selected Letters,* p. 79.

45. Thackeray appears on a list of books Faulkner prepared for his grandchildren. See a reproduction of the list opposite page 7 of Joseph Blotner, *William Faulkner's Library: A Catalogue* (Charlottesville: University Press of Virginia, 1964).

46. Cowley, p. 115.

47. Cleanth Brooks, "Faulkner and the Muse of History," *Mississippi Quarterly* 28 (1975):266–67.

48. Brooks, "Faulkner and the Muse of History," p. 267.

49. Andrew Sanders, *The Victorian Historical Novel 1840–1880* (New York: St. Martin's Press, 1979), pp. 16–17.

50. A number of critics have pointed out similarities between Scott and Faulkner: Bruce Harkness, "Faulkner and Scott," *Mississippi Quarterly* 20 (1967):164; Elmo Howell, "William Faulkner's Caledonia: A Note on *Intruder in the Dust,*" *Studies in Scottish Literature* 3 (1966):248–51; Elmo Howell, "Faulkner and Scott and the Legacy of the Lost Cause," *Georgia Review* 26 (1972):314–25; Millgate, *Achievement,* p. 314; Millgate, "'The Firmament of Man's History,'" pp. 25–26; Edgar Johnson, *Sir Walter Scott: The Great Unknown* (New York: Macmillan, 1970), p. 923; Richard Milum, "Faulkner, Scott and Another Source for Drusilla," *Mississippi Quarterly* 31 (1978):425–28.

   Almost nothing has been written on the relationship between Thackeray and Faulkner. Arnold Goldman briefly compares *Absalom, Absalom!* and *The Virginians.* See "Introduction," *Twentieth Century Interpretations of Absalom, Absalom!,* ed. Arnold Goldman (Englewood Cliffs, New Jersey: Prentice-Hall, 1971), p. 10. For those books by Scott and Thackeray which Faulkner owned see Blotner, *William Faulkner's Library,* pp. 71, 74.

51. See Chapter Six of "The Uses of the Past in the Novels of William Faulkner" (University of Toronto, Ph.D. dissertation, 1975). Faulkner's indebtedness to Conrad is certain. The comparisons between them are too numerous and widespread to cite, but see, for example, Albert J. Guerard, *Conrad the Novelist* (New York: Atheneum, 1967); Richard P. Adams, "The Apprenticeship of William Faulkner," *William Faulkner: Four Decades of Criticism,* ed. Linda Welshimer Wagner (East Lansing: Michigan State University Press, 1973), pp. 20–25; Millgate, "Faulkner's Masters," pp. 149–50.

52. Wolfgang Iser, *The Implied Reader* (Baltimore: Johns Hopkins University Press, 1974), pp. 87–89, 100, points out that Scott is well aware of the "problems attending comprehension and perception of historical reality." Since "it is no longer possible to find a single, ideal position that will command a total panorama," Scott's narrative in *Waverley* fans "out of history into sections of the past, depending on the age and standpoint of

the eye-witness.... Thus from several points of view, comprising several different social levels, we are presented with historical rituals and rhythms of life within a single clan." Yet, Iser concludes, "we cannot equate Scott's 'perspectivism' with that of the modern novel since Flaubert and Henry James. Scott's splitting of his subject matter into perspectives always serves the specific aim of communicating historical events. While the modern novel seeks to create its subject through a profusion of perspectives, Scott's subject is already present and is divided up purely for the sake of achieving enhanced vividness." Scott is devalued too greatly by the phrase "enhanced vividness," since he is ambitiously trying to show how the deepest understanding of history is created out of the conflict between points of view, but Iser is right in detecting history as something "already present and divided up." In other words, Scott does not radically question the nature of point of view itself, of how history and a consciousness of it arise at the same time. He lacks the rigorous self-reflexiveness of modernist writers.

53. Beck, pp. 16, 23–24.

54. Warren, p. 256.

55. Plato, *Euthyphro, Apology, Crito,* translated by F. J. Church, translation revised, with an introduction by Robert D. Cumming (Indianapolis: Bobbs-Merrill, 1956), p. ix.

56. Plato, p. 13.

Chapter 2

1. John Irwin, *Doubling & Incest/Repetition and Revenge: A Speculative Reading of Faulkner* (Baltimore: Johns Hopkins University Press, 1975), p. 55.

2. Several critics have commented on these weaknesses in the characterization of Bayard: Irving Howe, *William Faulkner: A Critical Study,* second edition, revised and expanded (New York: Vintage Books, n.d.), p. 34; Hyatt Waggoner, *William Faulkner: From Jefferson to the World* (Lexington: University of Kentucky Press, 1966), pp. 20–24; Melvin Backman, *Faulkner: The Major Years* (Bloomington: Indiana University Press, 1966), p. 7; Edmond L. Volpe, *A Reader's Guide to William Faulkner* (New York: Farrar, Straus & Giroux, 1964), pp. 71–72; Millgate, *Achievement,* pp. 80–81. All of these critics, of course, have discussed *Sartoris,* not *Flags in the Dust,* but their critical perceptions of Bayard's character are still valuable and relevant to this discussion, since Faulkner's treatment of young Bayard's character in *Sartoris* and *Flags* is essentially the same. Recently Kerry McSweeney, "The Subjective Intensities of *Flags in the Dust,"* *The Canadian Review of American Studies* 8 (1978):157–58 has commented that Faulkner "has no technical key to unlock the door of his [young Bayard's] consciousness."

 On the other hand, Arthur F. Kinney, *Faulkner's Narrative Poetics: Style as Vision* (Amherst: University of Massachusetts Press, 1978), pp. 123–39, apparently finds no difficulty in reading young Bayard's mind and interprets his actions far more positively than any other critic I know; similarly, John Pikoulis, *The Art of William Faulkner* (London: Macmillan, 1982), p. 5, pronounces young Bayard "a triumph of indirect portraiture." Donald Joseph Singal, "William Faulkner and the Discovery of Southern Evil," in *The War Within: From Victorian to Modernist Thought in the South, 1919–1945* (Chapel Hill: University of North Carolina Press, 1982), pp. 164–65, has offered the most coherent view of young Bayard's psychology so far. Singal concentrates on Bayard's obsessive and compulsive feelings which "stem not from normal grief, but from latent incestuous homosexual love" for his brother. Bayard has, for Singal, turned the glamor of the Sartoris affiliation with needless death and magnificent violence into a neurosis. His is a "classic case of secondary narcissism" since he has sought such a close attachment to his twin, who, I suppose, is a primary narcissist capable of living and dying by himself. In other words, young Bayard has borrowed whatever sense of power he wields from John III, and by extension, Singal believes, from his great-grandfather, the Colonel. The great-grandson must constantly test his Sartoris "omnipotence" in his great-grandfather's "presence" because young Bayard is never sure of his self-worth. Singal supports this point by noting occasions when young Bayard's driving incidents place him near the Colonel's statue and the railroad yards he built. But are we to assume this circumstantial linking of first and fourth generation Sartorises somehow substantiates Singal's view of "secondary narcissism"? Certainly young Bayard's psychology has been clarified, yet, as Singal, pp. 162–63, realizes, the novel suffers from "considerable confusion and ambiguity." Like John Irwin, Singal tries to bring a little too much organization, perhaps, to Faulkner's characters by recurring to a Freudian framework.

3. "Aviation sounds like the romantic side of the war... Like cavalry used to be." F. Scott Fitzgerald, *This Side of Paradise* (New York: Scribner's, 1920), p. 150.

4. F. Scott Fitzgerald, *The Beautiful and Damned* (New York: Scribner's, 1922), p. 54.

5. Cleanth Brooks, *William Faulkner: The Yoknapatawpha Country* (New Haven: Yale University Press, 1966), pp. 103–4; see also *William Faulkner: Toward Yoknapatawpha and Beyond* (New Haven: Yale University Press, 1978), p. 175.

6. *Faulkner in the University,* p. 23. See also Waggoner, p. 29; Millgate, *Achievement,* p. 80; Margaret Yonce, "'Shot Down Last Spring': The Wounded Aviators of Faulkner's Wasteland," *Mississippi Quarterly* 31 (1978):361, 366–68.

7. Volpe, pp. 71–72.

8. Backman, p. 7.

9. Adams, *Faulkner: Myth and Motion,* pp. 49–50.

10. Yonce, pp. 364–65, 367.

11. Yonce, pp. 367–68.

12. *Faulkner in the University,* p. 250.

13. Doreen Fowler, *Faulkner's Changing Vision: From Outrage to Affirmation* (Ann Arbor: UMI Research Press, 1983), p. 12.

14. Fowler, p. 11.

15. Fowler, pp. 11, 14–15.

16. Brooks, *Toward Yoknapatawpha and Beyond,* p. 11; Kreiswirth, p. 125.

17. Irwin, p. 59.

18. Irwin, p. 59.

19. In *The Sound and the Fury* (1929), Faulkner created a character, Quentin Compson, and a form, the interior monologue, which provided him with a way to clear up the confused relationship of past and present that marred *Flags in the Dust.* Unlike young Bayard, Quentin is not isolated from us; we see and hear his world through Faulkner's

precise evocation of imagery, of thought and speech patterns. The limitations of Quentin's response to past and present are revealed in the dialogue between himself and his father, in the comments of the narrator and other characters in the other three sections of the novel, and in the historical pattern which is implicitly developed in the structure of his section of the novel. See Chapter 7 for more discussion of *The Sound and the Fury*.

20. William Faulkner, *The Unvanquished* (New York: Random House, n.d.), p. 247. Page references to this photographic reprinting of the 1938 first edition are subsequently incorporated in the text within parentheses.

21. Vickery, p. 252.

22. Recently John Pilkington, "'Strange Times' in Yoknapatawpha," in *Fifty Years of Yoknapatawpha*, pp. 80–87 has made a detailed comparison of the carpetbagger episode in *Sartoris, Light in August,* and *The Unvanquished*.

23. Georg Lukács, *The Historical Novel* (Boston: The Beacon Press, 1963), pp. 36–37.

24. Blotner, *William Faulkner's Library*, p. 74. To some extent, Bayard, like Henry, receives his education from a family foe. In *Esmond* Dick Steele, one of the Williamites Esmond's family opposes in favor of the Stuarts, instructs Henry in the common interests of conflicting historical forces; in *The Unvanquished,* Colonel Dick, one of the Yankees against whom the family battles, shows by his gentlemanly example a side of the enemy remarkably similar to the Sartoris code of conduct. Faulkner, however, is not nearly so concerned as Thackeray to develop these relationships between adversaries, so that it is somewhat misleading to set the plots of the two novels side by side as if Faulkner is following a model of historical fiction. As always, his fiction resists facile categorization. In line with the precedent set by the Waverley novels, however, both *Esmond* and *The Unvanquished* reject fanaticism and narrow partisanship, and tend to suggest that underlying the disputes which divide men into opposing political parties or armies are the inherent contradictions in life itself, in the simple fact of being human. Thus it is not surprising that Henry's and Bayard's families are betrayed by their own servants, or that both heroes should have to acknowledge the deficiencies of "the Sartoris" and "the Stuart" by ultimately rejecting women who represent — as Sutherland, pp. 20–21, says of Beatrix Esmond, "a dangerous resurgence of the past which Harry can reject intellectually but not emotionally." Like Beatrix, Drusilla stands for those self-destructive aspects of a family cause against which the hero struggles to liberate himself with the aid of positive feminine examples like Aunt Jenny and Rachel Esmond.

25. On the historical novelist's choice of a hero, see Avrom Fleishman, *The English Historical Novel: Walter Scott to Virginia Woolf* (Baltimore: Johns Hopkins University Press, 1971), pp. 10–12.

26. G. Robert Stange, "On *The History of Henry Esmond, Esq.,*" *The History of Henry Esmond, Esq.,* ed. G. Robert Stange (New York: Holt, Rinehart & Winston, 1962), p. xiv.

27. Stange, p. xv.

28. Pikoulis, p. 132.

29. Millgate, *Achievement*, p. 169; for a contrary view see Pikoulis, pp. 118–19.

30. Brooks, *The Yoknapatawpha Country,* p. 86.

Chapter 3

1. John Hagan, "Déjà vu and the Effect of Timelessness in Faulkner's *Absalom, Absalom!*," *Bucknell Review* 11 (1963):33.

2. Hagan, pp. 41–42.

3. Hunt, pp. 120–21.

4. John A. Hodgson, "'Logical Sequence and Continuity': Some Observations on the Typographical and Structural Consistency of *Absalom, Absalom!*," *American Literature* 43 (1971):104. For a critique of this article, see Brooks, *Toward Yoknapatawpha and Beyond*, pp. 423–26.

5. Hodgson, p. 104.

6. Hodgson, p. 104.

7. Ruppersburg, p. 112.

8. Commentators on Chapter V's point of view detect several voices in Miss Rosa's narrative. Albert J. Guerard, *The Triumph of the Novel: Dickens, Dostoevsky, Faulkner* (Chicago: University of Chicago Press, 1982), p. 308, identifies "an interior voice, a stream flowing beneath full consciousness even, what the innermost spirit would say if it could"; Ruppersburg, pp. 86, 115, responds to "a fusion of what Miss Rosa says with what Quentin thinks and feels as he listens to her," and to the narrator who "intrudes into her mind, fuses her words, thoughts, emotions, and memories with Quentin's perspective"; John T. Matthews, *The Play of Faulkner's Language* (Ithaca: Cornell University Press, 1982), p. 121, concludes that "Chapter 5 is not Rosa's literal speech, nor is it the narrator's paraphrase or recounting, nor is it Quentin's remembered translation; it is more precisely some collaboration of all three. The effect produced by these interpenetrations of voice is of a variety of partnerships contracted on the common ground of Sutpen's story. That is, the hearing and speaking partners of each performance are seized by the intimacies of telling."

9. John Middleton, "Shreve McCannon and Sutpen's Legacy," *Southern Review* 10 (1974):116.

10. Arthur L. Scott, "The Myriad Perspectives of *Absalom, Absalom!*," *American Quarterly* 6 (1954):213. Scott's contention that the actual reconstruction took place at another time and Quentin and Shreve are only going over what they already know contradicts the obvious fact that Shreve is always catching up on what Quentin already knows right through their joint reconstruction of the past in Chapter VIII. It does seem true to say, however, that we never hear all that Quentin and Shreve said to each other in preparation for their cooperative effort.

11. Terrence Doody, "Shreve McCannon and the Confessions of *Absalom, Absalom!*," *Studies in the Novel* 6 (1974):463.

12. Donald M. Kartiganer, *The Fragile Thread: The Meaning of Form in Faulkner's Novels* (Amherst: University of Massachusetts Press, 1979), p. 88.

13. Doody, pp. 458–59.

14. Matthews, p. 157.

15. Magdalene Redekop, "*Absalom, Absalom!* Through The Spectacles of Shreve

McCannon," *William Faulkner: Materials, Studies, and Criticism* 5 (August 1983). Nan'un' Do Publishing Company, Tokyo, Japan.

16. Floyd C. Watkins, *The Flesh and the Word: Eliot, Hemingway, Faulkner* (Nashville: Vanderbilt University Press, 1971), pp. 216-23, explores in depth this distinction between the historical figures and their interpreters.

17. *The Compact Edition of the Oxford English Dictionary,* II (New York: Oxford University Press, 1971), p. 2064. Hereafter referred to as *O.E.D.*

18. Volpe, p. 212.

19. Volpe, p. 211.

20. Brooks, *The Yoknapatawpha Country,* p. 312.

21. Hagan, p. 47.

22. Brooks, *The Yoknapatawpha Country,* p. 433.

23. *Faulkner in the University,* p. 75.

24. *Faulkner in the University,* p. 274.

25. Redekop, p. 22.

26. Doody, p. 461.

27. *O.E.D.,* p. 2156.

28. Hagan, p. 47.

29. Vickery, p. 86.

30. David L. Minter speaks of the proliferation of designs in the novel, but he does not analyze Shreve's role in inventing the lawyer. See *The Interpreted Design as a Structural Principle in American Prose* (New Haven: Yale University Press, 1969), p. 216.

31. Joseph W. Reed, Jr., *Faulkner's Narrative* (New Haven: Yale University Press, 1973), p. 169.

32. John W. Hunt, "Keeping the Hoop Skirts Out: Historiography in Faulkner's *Absalom, Absalom!,*" *Faulkner Studies* 1 (1980):41.

33. Hunt, "Historiography in *Absalom, Absalom!,*" p. 44.

34. Quoted in Hunt, "Historiography in *Absalom, Absalom!,*" p. 47.

35. For another view of the importance of the New Orleans lawyer in Shreve's account, see David Krause, "Reading Shreve's Letters and Faulkner's *Absalom, Absalom!,*" *Studies in American Fiction* 11 (1983): 159, 165, 167.

36. Brooks, *The Yoknapatawpha Country,* pp. 302-3.

37. Recent criticism has begun to do justice to the subtlety with which the narrator arranges and characterizes historical interpretation in the novel. See, in particular, Richard Forrer, "*Absalom, Absalom!*: Story-Telling as a Mode of Transcendence," *Southern Literary Journal* 9 (1976):30-33, 45; Hunt, "Historiography in *Absalom, Absalom!,*" pp. 45-46; Thomas E. Connolly, "Point of View in Faulkner's *Absalom, Absalom!,*" *Modern Fiction Studies* 27 (1981):268-71.

38. Reed, p. 167, assumes that Henry provides Quentin with the information that is given in the passage on page 355.

39. Adams, *Faulkner: Myth and Motion,* p. 194.

40. For a provocative, but, I believe, inconsistent view of the italicized passage on pages 351–58, see Guerard, *The Triumph of the Novel,* pp. 334–36.

41. See, for example, Ilse Lind, "The Design and Meaning of *Absalom, Absalom!,*" *William Faulkner: Three Decades of Criticism,* edited with an introduction by Frederick J. Hoffman and Olga W. Vickery (New York: Harcourt, Brace, and World, 1963), p. 296.

42. M. E. Bradford, "Brother, Son, and Heir: The Structural Focus of Faulkner's *Absalom, Absalom!,*" *Sewanee Review* 78 (1970):81.

43. Loren F. Schmidtberger, "*Absalom, Absalom!*: What Clytie Knew," *Mississippi Quarterly* 35 (1982):257, strains nearly as much as the character-narrators of the novel to compel knowledge from Clytie that cannot be made explicit. Thus we have extremely oblique statements such as: "that Clytie may have known of her father's secret problems in New Orleans cannot be dismissed.... It does seem natural to suppose that in early childhood she [Clytie] learned from her mother of Sutpen's repudiation of his first wife and son...." John Hagopian, "Black Insight in *Absalom, Absalom!,*" *Faulkner Studies* I (1980):35–36, is certain "Clytie is the source of Quentin's insight...because she manifests in her posture and attitude the very status Bon sought," the status of being free and of being a Sutpen. Evidently for Hagopian, it is the moral theme of the Sutpen story — as Quentin has come to understand it — and not "any corroborative historical 'fact' or any explicit dialogue" that has convinced him that "it just has to be true that Bon, like Clytie, is a black Sutpen...." Hagopian's reasoning seems circular, yet the novel appears to invite just this kind of tautological argument.

44. For a different interpretation of "scion," see Brooks, *Toward Yoknapatawpha and Beyond,* pp. 324–25.

45. David Levin, *In Defense of Historical Literature: Essays on American History, Auto-biography, Drama, and Fiction* (New York: Hill and Wang, 1967), p. 137.

46. Waggoner, pp. 162–63.

47. Waggoner, p. 163.

48. James Guetti, *The Limits of Metaphor: A Study of Melville, Conrad, and Faulkner* (Ithaca: Cornell University Press, 1967), pp. 78–79.

49. Brooks, *The Yoknapatawpha Country,* p. 440.

50. Brooks, *The Yoknapatawpha Country,* p. 441.

51. Brooks, *The Yoknapatawpha Country,* p. 441.

52. Hershel Parker, "What Quentin Saw 'Out There,'" *Mississippi Quarterly* 27 (1974):323.

53. Parker, p. 325.

54. Parker, p. 325.

55. Parker, p. 326.

56. Given the tantilizing brevity of the dialogue between Quentin and Henry, it is unlikely

that any explanation of its place in the novel will prevail against the bemused comments of each succeeding critic. In *Toward Yoknapatawpha and Beyond,* pp. 321-22, Brooks shows again how there was time enough for Quentin and Henry to say more to each other than is indicated in the italicized dialogue. Brooks quite rightly notes, moreover, how "forthcoming" Henry is in answer to Quentin's questions. "Henry is far more circumstantial than he need have been ('Four Years') and more personal ('To die'). It is as if he were actually eager to talk. If Quentin had merely formed the words, 'Charles Bon was your friend—?', it is easy to imagine Henry's replying: 'More than my friend. My brother.' Faulkner has preferred to leave it to his reader to imagine this or something like it." Who better for Henry to confide in than Quentin Compson, descendant "of the only friend in Yoknapatawpha that his father ever had," Brooks points out. It strikes me that however the reader resolves this critical debate in his own mind, the historiographical design of the novel has been cunningly preserved by Faulkner's insistence that we move constantly from evidence to inference, from details of individual interpretations to patterns of meaning. Thus recent critics continue to ponder what Kinney, p. 213, calls the "peculiarly abbreviated and truncated" dialogue. "Ask the questions forward, backward, the questions ask...this is a rote catechism with foregone questions and foregone answers. Together Henry and Quentin merge, their roles interchangeable, coming back on themselves, their ends in their beginnings," Kinney suggests. James G. Watson, "'If WAS Existed': Faulkner's Prophets and the Patterns of History," *Modern Fiction Studies* 21 (1975-76):506, says "this conversation, like history itself, proceeds according to a pattern of recurrent cycles, and at the center are the prophetic words, *"To die."* Similarly, Stephen M. Ross, "The Evocation of Voice in *Absalom, Absalom!*," *Essays in Literature* 8 (1981): 147, calls the exchange between Quentin and Henry "a metaphor for all dialogue precipitated out of the narrative like a crystal out of solution.... The phrases form a palindrome, turning on the words *"To die?"* One is tempted, therefore, in the spirit of much contemporary criticism that seems cued by Jacques Derrida, to label the words between Quentin and Henry Quentin's "text," which withholds as much meaning as it delivers, so that we realize simultaneously how much and how little we learn from language. The language of the scene fulfills even as it exhausts Quentin's pursuit of the past. The language of the scene is ultimately his own, a language still pervaded with gaps he has done his best to fill in. Perhaps that is why Guerard, p. 317, speculates that the "dialogue with Henry [is] perhaps not spoken at all," for it is Quentin's retrospective view of his phantom, and it marks his departure from the present for a deeper level of consciousness, as have all of his italicized passages in the novel. Faulkner's use of italics is extremely complex. Stephen M. Ross, "'Voice' in Narrative Texts: The Example of *As I Lay Dying,*" *PMLA* 94(1979):308, indicates that each "change in type has its own 'reality' to explain it."

57. Richard Waswo, "Story as Historiography in the Waverley Novels," *ELH* 47 (1980):319.

58. Waswo, p. 321.

59. Waswo, p. 322.

60. For a more detailed comparison of these characters see my "Quentin and Quentin Compson: The Romantic Standard-Bearers of Scott and Faulkner," *Massachusetts Studies in English* 7 (1980):34-39.

61. James B. Meriwether, ed., *William Faulkner: Essays, Speeches, and Public Letters* (New York: Random House, 1965), p. 179.

62. *Faulkner in the University,* p. 135.

63. For a somewhat more detailed comparison of these two novels, see my "Faulkner and Historical Fiction: *Redgauntlet* and *Absalom, Absalom!*," *Dalhousie Review* 56 (1976):671-81. Karl Zender, "Reading in 'The Bear,'" *Faulkner Studies* I (1980):97, argues convincingly that "for Faulkner as for other writers in the modernist tradition, reading must struggle against reading"—that is, we reread the commissary books in *Go Down, Moses;* we reinterpret the past in each successive narrative in *Absalom, Absalom!*. Each narrative or, in Zender's terminology, "schema" destroys or (I would prefer to say) subsumes and advances beyond previous schemas.

64. Alan and Shreve typify the new order which seems to have no place for the outmoded Redgauntlets and Compsons: they come from the bourgeois class of professional men who take an increasingly active part in determining the course of the modern world.

65. Redekop, p. 26. On p. 27 she mentions that Quentin's name "echoes a Scott romance."

66. *Redgauntlet, A Tale of the Eighteenth Century, By the Author of "Waverley," In Three Volumes* (Edinburgh: Constable, 1824), I, 253.

67. Guerard, *The Triumph of the Novel,* p. 332.

68. Waswo, p. 312.

69. See Harry B. Henderson III, *Versions of the Past: The Historical Imagination in American Fiction* (New York: Oxford University Press, 1974), pp. 254-55, for a discussion of how Faulkner "reflects critically on historical idealism at the very time he appears to be embracing it."

70. Matthews, p. 16.

71. Guerard, *The Triumph of the Novel,* p. 333.

Chapter 4

1. Waggoner, p. 168.

2. Hyatt Waggoner, "The Historical Novel and the Southern Past: The Case of *Absalom, Absalom!*," *Southern Literary Journal* 2 (1970):70.

3. Levin, p. 118, mentions the articles he has read that touch upon his method of treating the novel, and he neglects to mention Waggoner's essay.

4. Levin, p. 137.

5. Waggoner, *William Faulkner,* p. 155.

6. Waggoner, *William Faulkner,* p. 168-69.

7. Brooks, *The Yoknapatawpha Country,* pp. 311-12.

8. Brooks, *The Yoknapatawpha Country,* p. 311.

9. R. G. Collingwood, *The Idea of History* (New York: Oxford University Press, 1956), p. 246.

10. Brooks, *The Yoknapatawpha Country,* p. 311.

11. Lind consistently uses the words "legend" and "projection" throughout her essay.

12. Lind, p. 282.

13. Lind, p. 282.

14. Joshua McClennen, "*Absalom, Absalom!* and the Meaning of History," *Papers of the Michigan Academy of Arts and Sciences* 42 (1956):357–69.

15. *Faulkner in the University,* pp. 273–74.

16. *Faulkner in the University,* p. 275.

17. Guetti, p. 73.

18. Margaret Uroff, "The Fictions of *Absalom, Absalom!*," *Studies in the Novel* 11 (1979):434.

19. Uroff, p. 435.

20. Collingwood, p. 60.

21. Lind, p. 282.

22. Herbert Butterfield, *The Historical Novel: An Essay* (Cambridge: At the University Press, 1924), p. 52.

23. Herbert Butterfield, *George III and the Historians* (New York: Macmillan, 1969), p. 205.

24. Patricia Tobin, "The Time of Myth and History in *Absalom, Absalom!*," *American Literature* 45 (1973):257.

25. Tobin, p. 257.

26. Tobin, p. 295.

27. Tobin, p. 257.

28. Tobin, p. 261.

29. Tobin, p. 266.

30. See Phillip S. Paludan's preface to his historical study, *Victims: A True Story of the Civil War* (Knoxville: University of Tennessee Press, 1981), p. xv, for an explicit linking of his methodology with that of the novelist's.

31. Martin Duberman, *Black Mountain: An Exploration in Community* (New York: Dutton, 1972), p. 13.

32. Collingwood, quoted in John Berger, *G: A Novel* (New York: The Viking Press, 1972), p. 52.

33. F. Garvin Davenport Jr., *The Myth of Southern History: Historical Consciousness in Twentieth Century Southern Literature* (Nashville: Vanderbilt University Press, 1970), p. 124.

34. Irwin, p. 157.

35. Irwin, p. 157.

36. Paddock, pp. 13–14.

37. Estella Schoenberg, *Old Tales and Talking: Quentin Compson in William Faulkner's Absalom, Absalom! and Related Works* (Jackson: University Press of Mississippi, 1977), pp. 4–5.

38. Forrer, p. 38.

39. Quoted in Hunt, "Historiography in *Absalom, Absalom!*," p. 38.

40. Hunt, "Historiography in *Absalom, Absalom!*," p. 39.

41. Gary Lee Stonum, *Faulkner's Career* (Ithaca: Cornell University Press, 1979), p. 25.

42. Schoenberg, p. 120.

43. Guerard, *The Triumph of the Novel,* p. 311, emphasis added on control.

44. Irwin, p. 157.

45. Irwin, p. 158.

46. See Schoenberg, p. vi, for her notes on the manuscript of *Absalom, Absalom!*. Like Irwin, she makes every effort to read the novel as if Faulkner had included a prominent reference to Quentin's death instead of his oblique one in the "Genealogy" appended to the novel.

47. Enrico Garzilli, *Circles Without Center: Paths to Discovery and Creation of Self in Modern Literature* (Cambridge: Harvard University Press, 1972), p. 57.

48. Hagan, p. 39.

49. Richard Poirier, "'Strange Gods' in Jefferson Mississippi: Analysis of *Absalom, Absalom!*," *Twentieth Century Interpretations of Absalom, Absalom!*, p. 17.

50. Levin, p. 131.

51. Collingwood, p. 163.

52. Hagan, p. 45.

53. Brooks, *The Yoknapatawpha Country,* p. 302.

54. Hagan, p. 43.

55. Floyd C. Watkins, "What Happens in *Absalom, Absalom!?*" *Modern Fiction Studies* 13 (1967):79–87, points out many inconsistencies in the narratives of all the characters. This particular example is noted on page 83.

56. Butterfield, *George III,* p. 41.

57. Collingwood, p. 118.

58. Ruth M. Vande Kieft, "Faulkner's Defeat of Time in *Absalom, Absalom!*," *Southern Review* 6 (1970):1108, mentions but does not pursue the resemblance between Mr. Compson's and Bon's letters.

59. Recently, a number of critics have speculated on the reasons for Shreve's interest in Charles Bon. See Kartiganer, p. 96; Doody, pp. 461, 465; Matthews, p. 144.

60. Lind, p. 292: "Nothing which is told or conjectured by the narrators, however distorted, is without thematic relevance." I would add that nothing they say is without historical relevance.

61. W. B. Gallie, *Philosophy and the Historical Understanding* (New York: Schocken Books, 1968), pp. 90–91.

62. Collingwood, p. 66.

63. Levin, p. 134.

64. Waggoner, *William Faulkner,* p. 151.

65. Martin Duberman, *The Uncompleted Past* (New York: Random House, 1969), p. 26.

66. Butterfield, *George III,* p. 250.

67. Butterfield, *George III,* p. 34.

68. Butterfield, *The Historical Novel,* p. 15.

69. Butterfield, *The Historical Novel,* p. 3.

70. Butterfield, *The Historical Novel,* p. 18.

71. Russel B. Nye, "History and Literature, Branches of the Same Tree," *Essays on History and Literature,* ed. Robert H. Bremmer (Columbus: Ohio State University Press, 1966), pp. 156–57.

72. Henri Bergson, *An Introduction to Metaphysics,* authorized translation by T. E. Hulme with an introduction by Thomas A. Goudge (Indianapolis: Bobbs-Merrill, 1955), p. 12.

73. Bergson, p. 22.

74. Waggoner, "The Historical Novel," p. 70.

75. Waggoner, *William Faulkner,* pp. 166–67.

76. Fowler, pp. 43–44. Tracing similar comments by Miss Rosa, Doreen Fowler concludes that the novel as a whole argues for a reality that can be reached only through the transcendence of fact.

77. Duberman, *The Uncompleted Past,* p. 31.

78. *Lion in the Garden,* p. 145.

79. *The Faulkner-Cowley File,* p. 89.

80. Butterfield, *George III,* p. 9.

81. Vickery, p. 84.

82. Vickery, p. 84.

83. John Lewis Longley, Jr., *The Tragic Mask: A Study of Faulkner's Heroes* (Chapel Hill: University of North Carolina Press, 1963), p. 210, writes: "In some ways, the discovery of what Sutpen was follows the classic pattern of thesis, antithesis, synthesis." But he does not develop this observation; see also Alan Holder, *The Imagined Past* (Lewisburg; Bucknell University Press, 1980), p. 63; Robert Con Davis, "The Symbolic Father in Yoknapatawpha County," *The Journal of Narrative Technique* 10 (1980): 49–50, speaks of the three phases of the symbolic father and proposes a scheme which seems Hegelian in nature, even though his subject is not history.

84. G. W. F. Hegel, *Reason in History,* translated by Robert S. Hartman (Indianapolis: Bobbs-Merrill, 1953), pp. xi–xii.

85. Butterfield, *George III,* p. 41.

86. Butterfield, *George III,* p. 41.

87. Volpe, p. 195.

88. Robert H. Zoellner, "Faulkner's Prose Style in *Absalom, Absalom!*," *American Literature* 30 (1959):499, has some interesting comments on the "abstract-as-most substantial" in Faulkner "which gives his prose the peculiar unreal quality so often criticized."

89. Waggoner, *William Faulkner,* p. 153.

90. Hegel, p. 75.

91. Conrad Aiken, "William Faulkner: The Novel as Form," *William Faulkner: Three Decades of Criticism,* p. 140.

92. Collingwood, p. 4.

Chapter 5

1. William Faulkner, *Go Down, Moses, and Other Stories* (New York: Random House, 1942), p. 3. Page references to this first edition are subsequently incorporated in the text within parentheses.

2. Brooks, *The Yoknapatawpha Country,* p. 257.

3. Dirk Kuyk, Jr., *Threads Cable-strong: William Faulkner's Go Down, Moses* (Lewisburg: Bucknell University Press, 1983), p. 70; see also Matthews, p. 244.

4. Vickery, pp. 126–27; Matthews, p. 245, calls "Was" and "The Old People" complementary stories of self-definition and points out the parallel use of "he" to refer to Cass and Ike.

5. Stanley Sultan, "'Call Me Ishmael': The Hagiography of Isaac McCaslin," *Texas Studies in Literature and Language* 2 (1961):55.

6. Leo Marx, *The Machine in the Garden: Technology and the Pastoral Ideal in America* (New York: Oxford University Press, 1967).

7. Cleanth Brooks, "Faulkner and History," *Mississippi Quarterly* 25 (1972):7.

8. Morris, p. 41.

9. Millgate, *Achievement,* p. 211.

10. Matthews, p. 219, argues: "The pain of undeniable loss, the yearning for forgetfulness and release from consciousness, and the horror of endless grief draw 'Pantaloon in Black' and 'Delta Autumn' together; each imprisons its cot-bound mourner in a shower of tears, of grieving rain."

11. "Go Down, Moses" was published in *Collier's* on January 25, 1941, which suggests that Faulkner set the story in July of 1940. Information on the publication date of this story is taken from James B. Meriwether. *The Literary Career of William Faulkner* (Columbia: University of South Carolina Press, 1971), p. 75. See Meredith Smith, "A Chronology of *Go Down, Moses,*" *Mississippi Quarterly* 36(1983):327, for a full discussion of the dating of this chapter.

12. Stevens's effort to see the funeral from Molly's perspective mitigates, somewhat, the argument advanced against him in Fowler, p. 51. She fails to distinguish between Ike and Stevens, calling both of them idealists who turn away from "the imperfect world of human interaction." For all his failings Stevens is not so absolutely alienated from the community as Fowler supposes.

13. Adams, *Faulkner: Myth and Motion,* p. 153.

14. Adams, *Faulkner: Myth and Motion,* p. 154.

15. Millgate, *Achievement,* p. 203.

16. Marc Bloch, *The Historian's Craft,* introduction by Joseph R. Strayer, translated from the French by Peter Putnam (New York: Knopf, 1953), p. 58.

17. See Walter A. Davis, *The Act of Interpretation: A Critique of Literary Reason* (Chicago: University of Chicago Press, 1978), pp. 30–31, 33, for a discussion of Ike's "scenic grammar" which leaves him "the victim of a complete defeat by the forces of modern history."

Chapter 6

1. *Lion in the Garden,* p. 260.

2. Matthews, p. 258, reacting to more than a decade of Faulkner criticism which emphasizes Ike's inability to act upon his political and moral principles, urges a fuller appreciation of the "eloquence" of Ike's "gesture," of his emulation of John Brown "whose action is more potent as a word than as a work." Throughout his provocative chapter on *Go Down, Moses,* Matthews stresses the power of language, as well as of action, to shape reality, thereby rectifying the balance between Ike and Cass that has been upset by recent critics like Davis, p. 22, who contends: "As so often in Faulkner, the profusion of words is a substitute for deeds. What his actions alone might not indicate, Ike's 'philosophizing' makes clear. The large amount of abstract quasi-philsophical and theological discussion in the commissary does not represent a wealth of reflection on Faulkner's part—as critics in search of 'meanings' and spokesman would have it—but rather the depth of confusion on Ike's part." Ike suffers from defects in character and in argument, to be sure, but it is simplistic and unfair to dismiss his ideas out of hand, as Davis does. The tension between Ike and Cass dissipates and the richness of response to history as word and deed is devalued in Davis's reductive remarks.

    Recently Warren Akins, "Providence and the Structure of *Go Down, Moses,*" *Southern Review* 18 (1982):497, has noted that "because a general providential view of history is less prevalent today than in the nineteenth century, Ike's reliance on it may seem more idiosyncratic than it in fact is."

3. Millgate, "'The Firmament of Man's History,'" p. 29.

4. G. J. Renier, *History: Its Purpose and Method* (New York: Harper Torchbooks, 1965), p. 103.

5. Ch. V. Langlois and Ch. Seignobos, *Introduction to the Study of History,* translated by G. G. Berry, with a preface by F. York Powell (New York: Henry Holt, 1925), p. 180.

6. Langlois and Seignobos, p. 212.

7. Volpe, p. 233.

8. Neal Woodruff, Jr., "'The Bear' and Faulkner's Moral Vision," *Studies in Faulkner,* ed. Neal Woodruff, Jr. (Pittsburgh: Carnegie Institute of Technology, 1961), p. 52; see also J. Edward Schamberger, "Renaming Percavil Brownlee in Faulkner's '[The] Bear,'" *College Literature* 4 (1977):92–94. For the significance of the curious surname, Brownlee, see A. J. Lofquist, "More in the Name of Brownlee in Faulkner's *The Bear,*" *College Literature* 10 (1983):357–59.

9. Langlois and Seignobos, p. 64.

10. Langlois and Seignobos, pp. 162–63.

11. Langlois and Seignobos, pp. 65–66.

12. J. C. Beaglehole, "The Case of the Needless Death," *The Historian as Detective: Essays on Evidence,* ed. Robin W. Winks (New York: Harper & Row, 1969), p. 286. Beaglehole's reconstructions of the events which led to Captain Cook's death provide a fascinating comparison with the method of historical reconstruction in *Absalom, Absalom!* and *Go Down, Moses.*

13. Beaglehole, p. 281.

14. Carol Ann Clancey Harter, "The Diaphoric Structure and Unity of William Faulkner's *Go Down Moses,*" (State University of New York at Binghamton, Ph.D. dissertation, 1970), p. 141.

15. Harter, p. 140.

16. Harter, p. 141.

17. John Lukacs, *Historical Consciousness or The Remembered Past* (New York: Harper & Row, 1968), p. 105.

18. Jacques Barzun and Henry Graff, *The Modern Researcher,* revised edition (New York: Harcourt, Brace & World, 1970), p. 116.

19. R. G. Collingwood, *Essays in the Philosophy of History,* edited with an introduction by William Debbins (New York: McGraw Hill, 1966), p. 102.

20. Collingwood, p. 102.

21. Collingwood, *The Idea of History,* p. 275.

22. Carl Becker, "Everyman His Own Historian," *The Historian as Detective,* pp. 19–20.

23. Liam Hudson, *Human Beings: An Introduction to the Psychology of Human Experience* (London: Jonathan Cape, 1975), p. 35.

24. Millgate, "'The Firmament of Man's History,'" p. 30.

25. Millgate, "'The Firmament of Man's History,'" p. 31.

26. Millgate, "'The Firmament of Man's History,'" p. 31; see also John Earl Bassett, "*Go Down, Moses:* Experience and the Forms of Understanding," *The Kentucky Review* 3 (1981):3–4, 19.

27. Reinhold Niebuhr, *The Irony of American History* (New York: Scribner's, 1962), p. 161.

28. See Warren Beck's defense of Ike in *Faulkner: Essays* (Madison: University of Wisconsin Press, 1976), p. 409.

29. Vickery, p. 133.

30. Herbert A. Perluck, "'The Bear': An Unromantic Reading," *Religious Perspectives in Faulkner's Fiction: Yoknapatawpha and Beyond,* ed. J. Robert Barth, S.J. (Notre Dame: University of Notre Dame Press, 1972), p. 178.

31. It has been suggested that Cass is out of character when he quotes Keats, but the critic

never explains why such a question should arise. See Lawrance Thompson, *William Faulkner: An Introduction and Interpretation,* second edition (New York: Barnes & Noble, 1967), p. 90.

32. Perluck, p. 178.

33. Blanche H. Gelfant, "Faulkner and Keats: The Ideality of Art in 'The Bear,'" *Southern Literary Journal* 2 (1969):45; see also Douglas J. Canfield, "Faulkner's Grecian Urn and Ike McCaslin's Empty Legacies," *Arizona Quarterly* 36 (1980):359–84; Joan Korenmann, "Faulkner's Grecian Urn," *Southern Literary Journal* 7 (1974):3–23.

34. Gelfant, p. 45.

35. Gloria R. Dussinger, "Faulkner's Isaac McCaslin as Romantic Hero Manque," *South Atlantic Quarterly* 68 (1969):379.

36. Millgate, *Achievement,* p. 207.

37. Bloch, p. 12.

38. Thompson, p. 81. His essay explores the thesis that *"Go Down, Moses* is built around different concepts of 'freedom' and 'bondage' (or 'enslavement')."

39. Millgate, "'The Firmament of Man's History,'" p. 30.

40. Arthur F. Kinney, "Faulkner and the Possibilities for Heroism," *Bear, Man, and God: Eight Approaches to "The Bear,"* eds. Francis Lee Utley, Lynn Z. Bloom and Arthur F. Kinney (New York: Random House, 1971), pp. 240–41.

41. Millgate, "'The Firmament of Man's History,'" p. 30.

42. Kinney, "Faulkner and the Possibilities for Heroism," p. 246.

43. Gelfant, p. 55.

44. Ursula Brumm, "Forms and Functions of History in the Novels of William Faulkner," *Archiv* 209 (1972):52.

45. See Kuyk, pp. 22–23.

46. Stange, p. xv.

47. Frederick R. Karl, *A Reader's Guide to Joseph Conrad* (New York: Farrar, Straus and Giroux, 1970), p. 65. I have benefited in a general way from Professor Karl's essay on "Time in Conrad," and more particularly from the connections he makes among twentieth-century historians, philosophers, and novelists.

48. David Daiches, *The Novel and the Modern World* (Chicago: The University of Chicago Press, 1965), p. 53.

49. See Guerard, *Conrad the Novelist,* p. 175.

50. Joseph Conrad, *Nostromo: A Tale of the Seaboard* (London and New York: Harper & Brothers, 1904), p. 6. Page references to this 1904 first edition are subsequently incorporated in the text within parentheses. Similarly, at the beginning of the novel, p. 1, Conrad places the town of Sulaco into historical perspective by referring to the present state of the orange gardens as "witness to its antiquity," as if to imply that the town's past and present must be seen simultaneously, so together they constitute an indivisible whole:

In the time of Spanish rule, and for many years afterwards, the town of Sulaco—the luxuriant beauty of the orange gardens bears witness to its antiquity—had never been commercially anything more important than a coasting port with a fairly large local trade in ox-hides and indigo.

51. Fleishman, p. 226.

52. Compare the circular "races" in "Was," and the chapter's ending to the ending of *Go Down, Moses* for evidence of a similar circularity in Faulkner.

53. Fleishman, p. 226.

54. Becker, pp. 246–47.

55. Becker, p. 251.

Chapter 7

1. *The Faulkner-Cowley File,* pp. 14–15.

2. *The Faulkner-Cowley File,* p. 53.

3. Stephen Neal Dennis, "The Making of *Sartoris:* A Description and Discussion of the Manuscript and Composite Typescript of William Faulkner's Third Novel" (Cornell University, Ph.D. dissertation, 1969). See especially Part One: "The Origins of Yoknapatawpha County and the Writing of *Sartoris,*" pp. 10–40.

4. James B. Meriwether, "The Place of *The Unvanquished* in William Faulkner's Yoknapatawpha Series" (Princeton University, Ph.D. dissertation, 1958), p. 13.

5. Elizabeth M. Kerr, *Yoknapatawpha: Faulkner's "Little Postage Stamp of Native Soil"* (New York: Fordham University Press, 1969), p. 7.

6. This quotation is taken from the cover of the paperback edition of Malcolm Cowley, ed., *The Portable Faulkner* (New York: The Viking Press, 1966). See *The Faulkner-Cowley File,* pp. 63–66, 69, for an explanation of the selection of the words which appeared on the cover of *The Portable Faulkner* and of Faulkner's reaction to them.

7. *The Faulkner-Cowley File,* p. 25.

8. *The Faulkner-Cowley File,* p. 25.

9. Joseph Blotner, *Faulkner: A Biography* (New York: Random House, 1974), p. 791.

10. Blotner, p. 791.

11. *The Faulkner-Cowley File,* pp. 90–91.

12. *The Faulkner-Cowley File,* p. 90.

13. William Faulkner, *The Sound and the Fury* (New York: Vintage Books, n.d.), p. 403. Page references to this photographic reprinting of the 1929 first edition are subsequently incorporated in the text within parentheses. The *Appendix* in this edition is taken from the Modern Library edition of 1946 which is slightly different from the *Appendix* in *The Portable Faulkner.* See *The Faulkner-Cowley File,* pp. 88–89.

14. Mary Jane Dickerson, "'The Magician's Wand': Faulkner's *Compson Appendix,*" *Mississippi Quarterly* 28 (1975):321,329.

15. Dickerson, p. 326.

16. Dickerson, p. 322.

17. See Dickerson, pp. 332–33.

18. Irwin, p. 112.

19. Dickerson, p. 329.

20. Lewis P. Simpson, "Sex and History: Origins of Faulkner's Apocrypha," in *The Maker and The Myth: Faulkner and Yoknapatawpha,* eds. Evans Harrington and Ann J. Abadie (Jackson: University Press of Mississippi, 1978), p. 63.

21. Simpson, p. 65.

22. Simpson, p. 66.

23. Lewis P. Simpson, "Faulkner and the Legend of the Artist," in *Faulkner: Fifty Years After the Marble Faun,* ed. George H. Wolfe (University, Alabama: University of Alabama Press, 1976), p. 94.

24. Simpson, "Faulkner and the Legend of the Artist," p. 95.

25. *The Faulkner-Cowley File,* p. 89.

26. Faulkner was reluctant to correct contradictory details in his trilogy even when he was specifically asked to do so. His editors were puzzled over the problem of reconciling the three volumes of *Snopes.* See Blotner, pp. 1729–30.

27. William Faulkner, *The Mansion* (New York: Random House, 1959). Faulkner's one paragraph introduction occurs before the pagination begins.

28. For other similar references to the immigrants see pp. 156, 158, 174, 178.

29. Richard J. Gray, *The Literature of Memory: Modern Writers of the American South* (Baltimore: Johns Hopkins University Press, 1977), pp. 198–99.

30. Through Quentin Faulkner pursues a use of the past similar to Scott's practice in *Quentin Durward.* Scott never shows us the age of chivalry which his hero so devoutly believes in and cherishes. Instead, the chivalric code is ridiculed by many characters, especially the soldiers and nobles whom Quentin Durward expects to be the very representatives of the tradition. Moreover, Lady Hammeline's pratings about chivalric tournaments are a parody of a code which has clearly degenerated into the fancies of a middle-aged woman. Perhaps the cruelest blow to Quentin's courtly pretentions is his uncle's rude but honest explanation that the Scots in France are mercenaries, not independent gentlemen; they are in the employ of a monarch who is trying to establish France as a modern national state. To talk of doing a "brave deed," as Quentin calls it, is, his uncle tells him, pure nonsense in a land where the king's policy is to achieve his goal of a united France by avoiding the necessity of battle. Men are judged by how they contribute to the king's plans, not by their personal courage and self-command. It is an unceremonious reign in which the king is likely to go about dressed little better than his subjects.

   Quentin Compson operates under similar chivalric illusions. In fact, the key to his character might be found in his failure to perform what Quentin Durward refers to as the "brave deed." Personal dignity and family honor count for as little in Quentin Compson's world as in Quentin Durward's. Quentin supposes he can protect the family's values and his sister's virginity by confronting and vanquishing Dalton Ames in the manner of a knight defending a lady. Ames treats Quentin as a novice, an immature young man who has not yet divined the less than pure motivations of the opposite sex. Furthermore, Ames's sympathy for Quentin makes it impossible for the younger man to maintain the aggressiveness and dedication to principle that inspires his challenge to Ames. The latter's cynicism is also rather like the cynicism Quentin Durward must endure every time he voices his clearly out-of-date and demonstrably out-of-fashion courtly sentiments.

Quentin Durward, however, is frustrated but not crushed by the discrepancy between his dreams and reality. His notion that men selflessly serve a code of conduct is mercilessly satirized by the presentation of a series of characters who clearly serve others only insofar as it is necessary in order to serve themselves. King Louis is engaged throughout the novel in carefully using men who might betray him if he were not clever enough to satisfy their own ends while he accomplishes his own. Quentin is deeply shocked by the king's devious, immoral maneuvers, but Scott shrewdly shows that Quentin has no choice but to become implicated in Louis's schemes. The only alternative is Burgundy, whose unruly, chaotic, and feudalistic ethic would make France ungovernable. If there is to be any coherence in this world, it will only be realized by Louis's plans—in spite of their grotesqueness to a person of fine moral sensitivity.

Perhaps it is a weakness in Scott's novel that his hero eventually triumphs in the very chivalric terms which the corrupt world of the novel rejected, for Quentin saves the heroine from many perils, wins her hand, and simultaneously preserves Louis XI's political policies. On the other hand, he lives in a world far different from Quentin Compson's. Quentin Durward is not carrying on a fight against his own family's decadence. The thrust of Quentin Durward's life is continually outward, so that he learns from several bitter experiences that he cannot remain aloof from life as it actually is if he expects to make his mark on it. Although the heroic past as Quentin dreamed it is dead, there is still the opportunity for individual acts of heroism. In this way, Quentin Durward is still able to define himself within the emergence of a powerful nation-state.

For still more commentary on Quentin Durward and Quentin Compson, see Dickerson, p. 325.

31. Quentin describes his shadow as "dragging its head through the weeds that hid the fence" on the immigrants' premises (165).

32. Ortega y Gasset, p. 221.

33. Paddock, p. 4.

34. Paddock, p. 1.

35. William Faulkner, *Requiem for a Nun* (New York: Random House, 1951), p. 112. Page references to this 1951 first edition are subsequently incorporated in the text within parentheses.

36. Beck, *Faulkner,* p. 591.

37. Ruppersburg, p. 135.

38. See Karl F. Zender, "Faulkner and the Power of Sound," *PMLA* 99 (1984): 100 and the entire article for a thorough treatment of this theme in several novels.

39. See Zender, p. 96.

40. Karl F. Zender, "Reading in 'The Bear'," p. 95.

41. Zender, "Reading in 'The Bear,'" p. 95.

42. Noel Polk, *Faulkner's Requiem for a Nun: A Critical Study* (Bloomington: Indiana University Press, 1981), pp. 19–20.

43. Ruppersburg, p. 134.

44. Ruppersburg, pp. 136–37.

45. Ruppersburg, p. 139.

46. Ruppersburg, p. 138.

47. Although Beck, *Faulkner,* pp. 583–635, does not concentrate on the narrator as historian, his detailed account of the narrator's shifts in point of view supports my analysis.

48. Polk, p. 54, observes: "The editor's decision, directly contrary to Faulkner's wishes and to the evidence in front of him, to have the drama begin on a separate page in the published book is a regrettable error in judgment, for Faulkner was clearly trying to emphasize the great amount of thematic if not narrative, continuity between the prologue and the drama (he handles this matter consistently on the typescript in all three acts)."

49. Blotner, p. 1387.

50. Brooks, *Toward Yoknapatawpha and Beyond,* p. 268.

51. Millgate, "'The Firmament of Man's History,'" p. 33.

52. Millgate, "'The Firmament of Man's History,'" p. 33.

53. Beck, *Faulkner,* p. 622.

54. Mary Montgomery Dunlap, "The Achievement of Gavin Stevens" (University of South Carolina, Ph.D. dissertation, 1970), p. 131.

55. Irwin, p. 140.

56. For a comparison of the dialogues in *Go Down, Moses* and *A Fable* see Millgate, *Achievement,* pp. 227–28.

57. Ruppersburg, p. 144.

58. Beck, *Faulkner,* p. 597.

59. See the discussions of Act II, Scene 2 in Polk, pp. 133–42, and Ruppersburg, p. 148.

Chapter 8

1. Daniel Aaron, in a chapter of *The Unwritten War: American Writers and the Civil War* (New York: Knopf, 1973), p. 311, has clearly shown that Faulkner read the Civil War's meaning "not in its heroes and battles but in the consciousness of a people."

2. Becker, pp. 233–55.

3. This quotation is from *The Idea of History,* but my source is a novel by John Berger, *G* (New York: The Viking Press, 1972), p. 311.

4. Fleishman, p. 14; see also Iser, p. 84.

5. Collingwood, *The Idea of History,* pp. 33, 36, 125–26, 143, 257–66, 269–70, 274–81, 319.

6. Butterfield, *The Historical Novel,* pp. 50–51.

7. Brooks, "Faulkner and the Muse of History," p. 268.

8. Blotner, p. 1426.

9. Blotner, p. 1426.

10. Brooks, "Faulkner and the Muse of History," pp. 270–71.

11. Morris, p. 17; see also pp. 61–62 for provocative remarks on historical and literary narratives.

12. Iser, p. 95; see also Waswo, p. 304, whose remarks on Scott are equally applicable to Faulkner even though Faulkner does not share Scott's concern with "presumed" actual events and people: "Both 'stories' and 'histories' consist in narratives. Recognizing this formal and etymological identity, Hayden White has argued with respect to nineteenth-century historiography that history itself is 'made' by the choice of tropological and narrative structures derived from literature. I wish to make with respect to Scott's fiction the same argument in the opposite direction: if formal history can be constituted by literature, so literature can constitute an historiography."

13. Iser, p. 96.

14. Morris, p. 62.

15. Martin Duberman, *The Memory Bank* (New York: Dial, 1970), p. 35.

16. Shelby Foote, *The Civil War, A Narrative: Red River to Appomattox* (New York: Random House, 1974), p. 980.

17. Paludan, p. x.

18. Paludan, pp. xiv–xv.

19. See, for example, Paludan, pp. 94–96.

20. Paludan, pp. 31–32.

21. See, for example, Paludan, pp. 24–36, 55, 86–88.

22. Paludan, p. 32.

23. Duberman, *Black Mountain,* pp. 110–19.

24. Vickery, p. 250.

25. Duberman, *Black Mountain,* p. 413.

Bibliography

Works by William Faulkner

Books

All items in this section are either first editions or photographic reprintings of first editions.

Absalom, Absalom! New York: Random House, 1936.
Flags in the Dust. Ed. Douglas Day. New York: Random House, 1973.
Go Down, Moses and Other Stories. New York: Random House, 1942.
The Mansion. New York: Random House, 1959.
Requiem for a Nun. New York: Random House, 1951.
Sartoris. New York: Random House, n.d.
The Sound and the Fury. New York: Vintage Books, n.d.
The Unvanquished. New York: Vintage Books, n.d.

Collections

Essays, Speeches & Public Letters by William Faulkner. Ed. James B. Meriwether. New York: Random House, 1965.
The Faulkner-Cowley File: Letters and Memories, 1944-1962. Ed. Malcolm Cowley. New York: The Viking Press, 1966.
Faulkner in the University: Class Conferences at the University of Virginia, 1957-1958. Ed. Frederick L. Gwynn and Joseph L. Blotner. New York: Vintage Books, n.d.
Faulkner at West Point. Ed. Joseph L. Fant and Robert Ashley. New York: Vintage Books, 1969.
Lion in the Garden: Interviews with William Faulkner 1926-1962. Ed. James B. Meriwether and Michael Millgate. New York: Random House, 1968.
The Portable Faulkner. Revised Edition. Ed. Malcolm Cowley. New York: The Viking Press, 1966.
Selected Letters of William Faulkner. Ed. Joseph Blotner. New York: Random House, 1977.

Other Works

Aaron, Daniel. *The Unwritten War: American Writers and the Civil War.* New York: Knopf, 1973.
Adamowski, T. H. "Isaac McCaslin and the Wilderness of the Imagination." *Centennial Review* 17 (1973):92-112.

Adams, Richard P. "At Long Last, *Flags in the Dust.*" *Southern Review* 10 (1974):878–88.

———. "The Apprenticeship of William Faulkner." *William Faulkner: Four Decades of Criticism.* Ed. Linda Welshimer Wagner. East Lansing: Michigan State University Press, 1973, pp. 7–44.

———. *Faulkner: Myth and Motion.* Princeton: Princeton University Press, 1968.

Aiken, Conrad. "William Faulkner: The Novel as Form." *William Faulkner: Three Decades of Criticism.* Ed. Frederick J. Hoffman and Olga W. Vickery. New York: Harcourt, Brace, and World, 1963, pp. 135–42.

Akins, Warren. "Providence and the Structure of *Go Down, Moses.*" *Southern Review* 18 (1982):495–505.

Altenbernd, Lynn. "A Suspended Moment: The Irony of History in William Faulkner's 'The Bear'." *Modern Language Notes* 85 (1960):572–82.

Angell, Leslie E. "The Umbilical Cord Symbol as a Unifying Theme and Pattern in *Absalom, Absalom!.*" *Massachusetts Studies in English* 1 (1968):106–10.

Aristotle. "On the Art of Fiction (from *Poetics*)." *Aspects of the Drama: A Handbook.* Ed. Sylvan Barnet, Morton Berman, William Burto. Boston: Little Brown, 1962, pp. 15–35.

Backman, Melvin. *Faulkner: The Major Years.* Bloomington: Indiana University Press, 1966.

Baines, Jocelyn. *Joseph Conrad: A Critical Biography.* London: Weidenfeld and Nicolson, 1969.

Barzun, Jacques and Graff, Henry F. *The Modern Researcher.* Revised Edition. New York: Harcourt, Brace & World, 1970.

Bassett, John Earl. "*Go Down, Moses:* Experience and the Forms of Understanding." *The Kentucky Review* 3 (1981):3–22.

———. *Faulkner: An Annotated Checklist of Recent Criticism.* Kent State University Press, 1983.

Beck, Warren. *Man in Motion: Faulkner's Trilogy.* Madison: University of Wisconsin Press, 1963.

———. *Faulkner: Essays.* Madison: University of Wisconsin Press, 1976.

Becker, Carl. *Everyman His Own Historian, Essays on History and Politics.* Chicago: Quadrangle Books, 1966.

Bedell, George C. *Kierkegaard and Faulkner: Modalities of Existence.* Baton Rouge: Louisiana State University Press, 1972.

Berger, John. *G.* New York: Viking Press, 1972.

Bergson, Henri. *An Introduction to Metaphysics.* Authorized Translation by T. E. Hulme with an Introduction by Thomas A. Goudge. Indianapolis: Bobbs-Merrill, 1955.

Blotner, Joseph. *Faulkner: A Biography.* New York: Random House, 1974.

———. Ed. *William Faulkner's Library: A Catalogue.* Charlottesville: University Press of Virginia, 1964.

Bloch, Marc. *The Historian's Craft.* Introduction by Joseph R. Strayer. Translated from the French by Peter Putnam. New York: Knopf, 1953.

Bradford, Melvin E. "Brother, Son, and Heir: The Structural Focus of Faulkner's *Absalom, Absalom!.*" *Sewanee Review* 78 (1970):76–98.

Braudy, Leo. *Narrative Form in History and Fiction: Hume, Fielding and Gibbon.* Princeton: Princeton University Press, 1970.

Brooks, Cleanth. "Faulkner and History." *Mississippi Quarterly* 25 (1972):3–14.

———. "Faulkner and the Muse of History." *Mississippi Quarterly* 28 (1975):265–79.

———. *The Hidden God.* New Haven: Yale University Press, 1963.

———. *William Faulkner: The Yoknapatawpha Country.* New Haven: Yale University Press, 1966.

———. *William Faulkner: Toward Yoknapatawpha and Beyond.* New Haven: Yale University Press, 1978.

Broughton, Panthea Reid. "*Requiem For a Nun:* No Part in Rationality." *Southern Review* 8 (1972):749–62.

———. *William Faulkner: The Abstract and the Actual.* Baton Rouge: Louisiana State University Press, 1974.

Brown, David. *Walter Scott and the Historical Imagination.* London: Routledge & Kegan Paul, 1979.

Brumm, Ursula. "Forms and Functions of History in the Novels of William Faulkner." *Archiv* (1972):43–56.

Brylowski, Walter. *Faulkner's Olympian Laugh.* Detroit: Wayne State University Press, 1968.

Butterfield, Herbert. *Christianity and History.* New York: Scribner's, 1950.

———. *George III and the Historians.* Revised Edition. New York: Macmillan, 1969.

———. *The Historical Novel: An Essay.* Cambridge: At the University Press, 1924.

Canfield, Douglas J. "Faulkner's Grecian Urn and Ike McCaslin's Empty Legacies." *Arizona Quarterly* 36 (1980):359–84.

Capps, Jack L. Ed. *Go Down, Moses: A Concordance to the Novel.* Ann Arbor: University Microfilms International, 1977.

Carlyle, Thomas. "Sir Walter Scott." *Scott: The Critical Heritage.* Ed. John O. Hayden. New York: Barnes & Noble, 1970.

Carr, Edward Hallett. *What is History?* New York: Vintage Books, 1967.

Cecil, David. *Early Victorian Novelists: Essays in Revaluation.* London: Collins, 1964.

———. *Sir Walter Scott.* London: Constable, 1933.

Chase, Richard. *The American Novel and Its Tradition.* New York: Anchor Books, 1957.

Cleman, John L. "'Pantaloon in Black': Its Place in *Go Down, Moses.*" *Tennessee Studies in Literature* 22 (1977):170–81.

Cockshut, A. O. J. *The Achievement of Sir Walter Scott.* New York: New York University Press, 1969.

Collingwood, R. G. *The Idea of History.* New York: Oxford University Press, 1956.

———. *Essays in the Philosophy of History.* Ed. William Debbins. New York: McGraw Hill, 1966.

Collins, Carvel. "Introduction." *The Unvanquished,* by William Faulkner. New York: Signet Classics, 1959.

Connolly, Thomas E. "Point of View in Faulkner's *Absalom, Absalom!.*" *Modern Fiction Studies* 27 (1981):255–72.

Conrad, Joseph. *Nostromo: A Tale of the Seaboard.* London and New York: Harper & Brothers, 1904.

Cosgrove, William. "The 'Soundless Moiling' of Bayard Sartoris." *Arizona Quarterly* 35 (1979):165–69.

Cowley, Malcolm. "The Etiology of Faulkner's Art." *Southern Review* 13 (1977):83–95.

Craig, David. *Scottish Literature and the Scottish People, 1680–1830.* London: Chatto & Windus, 1961.

Creighton, Joanne. *William Faulkner's Craft of Revision.* Detroit: Wayne State University Press, 1977.

Daiches, David. *The Novel and the Modern World.* Chicago: The University of Chicago Press, 1965.

Davenport, F. Garvin. *The Myth of Southern History: Historical Consciousness in Twentieth Century Southern Literature.* Nashville: Vanderbilt University Press, 1970.

Davidson, James West and Lytle, Mark Hamilton. *After the Fact: The Art of Historical Detection.* New York: Knopf, 1982.

Davie, Donald. *The Heyday of Sir Walter Scott.* London: Routledge, 1961.

Davis, Robert Con. "The Symbolic Father in Yoknapatawpha County." *Journal of Narrative Technique* 10 (1980):39–55.

Davis, Thadious M. "The Yoking of Abstract Contradictions in *Absalom, Absalom!.*" *Studies in American Fiction* (1979):209–19.

Davis, Walter A. *The Act of Interpretation: A Critique of Literary Reason.* Chicago: University of Chicago Press, 1978.

De Man, Paul. "Georg Lukács's *Theory of the Novel.*" *Modern Language Notes* 81 (1966): 527–34.

Dennis, Stephen Neal. "The Making of *Sartoris:* A Description and Discussion of the Manuscript and Composite Typescript of William Faulkner's Third Novel." Ph.D dissertation, Cornell University, 1969.

Dickerson, Mary Jane. "'The Magician's Wand': Faulkner's *Compson Appendix.*" *Mississippi Quarterly* 28 (1975):317–337.

Doody, Terrence. "Shreve McCannon and the Confessions of *Absalom, Absalom!.*" *Studies in the Novel* 6 (1974):454–69.

Duberman, Martin. *Black Mountain: An Exploration in Community.* New York: Dutton, 1972.

———. *The Uncompleted Past.* New York: Random House, 1969.

———. *The Memory Bank.* New York: The Dial Press, 1970.

Dunlap, Mary Montgomery. "The Achievement of Gavin Stevens." Ph.D dissertation, University of South Carolina, 1970.

Dussinger, Gloria R. "Faulkner's Isaac McCaslin as Romantic Hero Manque." *South Atlantic Quarterly* 68 (1969):377–85.

Early, James. *The Making of Go Down, Moses.* Dallas: Southern Methodist University Press, 1972.

Elton, G. R. *The Practice of History.* New York: Crowell, 1967.

Fitzgerald, F. Scott. *The Beautiful and Damned.* New York: Scribner's, 1922.

———. *This Side of Paradise.* New York: Scribner's, 1920.

Foote, Shelby. *The Civil War: A Narrative,* Volume 3. New York: Random House, 1974.

Forrer, Richard. "*Absalom, Absalom!:* Story-Telling as a Mode of Transcendence." *Southern Literary Journal* 9 (1976):22–46.

Fowler, Doreen. *Faulkner's Changing Vision: From Outrage to Affirmation.* Ann Arbor: UMI Research Press, 1983.

Gallie, W. B. *Philosophy and the Historical Understanding.* New York: Schocken Books, 1968.

Garzilli, Enrico. *Circles Without Center: Paths to Discovery and Creation of Self in Modern Literature.* Cambridge: Harvard University Press, 1972, pp. 52–60.

Gelfant, Blanche H. "Faulkner and Keats: The Ideality of Art in 'The Bear'." *Southern Literary Journal* 2 (1969):43–65.

Gold, Joseph. *William Faulkner: A Study in Humanism, From Metaphor to Discourse.* Norman: University of Oklahoma Press, 1966.

Goldman, Arnold. "Faulkner and the Revision of Yoknapatawpha History." *The American Novel and the Nineteen Twenties.* Ed. Malcolm Bradbury and David Palmer. London: Edwin Arnold, 1971.

Gordon, Robert C. *Under Which King: A Study of the Waverley Novels.* New York: Barnes & Noble, 1969.

Gray, Richard. "The Meanings of History: William Faulkner's *Absalom, Absalom!.*" *Dutch Quarterly Review of Anglo-American Letters* 3 (1973):97–110.

———. *The Literature of Memory: Modern Writers of the American South.* Baltimore: Johns Hopkins University Press, 1977.

Guerard, Albert J. *Conrad the Novelist.* New York: Atheneum, 1967.

———. *The Triumph of the Novel: Dickens, Dostoevsky, Faulkner.* Chicago: University of Chicago Press, 1982.

Guetti, James. *The Limits of Metaphor: A Study of Melville, Conrad, and Faulkner.* Ithaca: Cornell University Press, 1967.

Gross, Harvey. *The Contrived Corridor: History and Fatality in Modern Literature.* Ann Arbor: University of Michigan Press, 1971.

Hagan, John. "Déjà vu and the Effect of Timelessness in Faulkner's *Absalom, Absalom!.*" *Bucknell Review* 11 (1963):31–52.

———. "Fact and Fancy in *Absalom, Absalom!.*" *College English* 24 (1962):215–18.

Hagopian, John V. "Black Insight in *Absalom, Absalom!.*" *Faulkner Studies* I (1980):29–36.

Handlin, Oscar. *Chance or Destiny: Turning Points in American History.* New York: Atlantic-Little, Brown, 1955.

Harkness, Bruce. "Faulkner and Scott." *Mississippi Quarterly* 20 (1967):164.

Harold, Brent. "The Value and Limitations of Faulkner's Fictional Method." *American Literature* 47 (1975):212–29.

Hart, Francis R. *Scott's Novels: The Plotting of Historic Survival.* Charlottesville: The University Press of Virginia, 1966.

Harter, Carol Ann Clancy. "The Diaphoric Structure and Unity of William Faulkner's *Go Down, Moses.*" Ph.D dissertation, State University of New York at Binghamton, 1970.

———. "The Winter of Isaac McCaslin: Revisions and Irony in Faulkner's 'Delta Autumn'." *Journal of Modern Literature* 1 (1970–1971):209–25.

Harvey, Bruce Albert. "An Analysis of William Faulkner's Use of Quentin Compson in *Absalom, Absalom!.*" Honors Thesis, Honors Tutorial College, Ohio University, August 1980.

Hay, Eloise Knapp. *The Political Novels of Joseph Conrad: A Critical Study.* Chicago: The University of Chicago Press, 1967.

Hayhoe, George F. "William Faulkner's *Flags in the Dust.*" *Mississippi Quarterly* 28 (1975): 370–86.

Hegel, G. W. F. *Reason in History.* Translated by Robert G. Hartman. Indianapolis: Bobbs-Merrill, 1953.

Hemenway, Robert. "Enigmas of Being in *As I Lay Dying.*" *Modern Fiction Studies* 26 (1970):133–46.

Henderson, Harry B., III. *Versions of the Past: The Historical Imagination in American Fiction.* New York: Oxford University Press, 1974.

Hillhouse, James T. *The Waverley Novels and Their Critics.* Minneapolis: University of Minnesota Press, 1936.

Hodgson, John A. "'Logical Sequence and Continuity': Some Observations on the Typographical and Structural Consistency of *Absalom, Absalom!.*" *American Literature* 43 (1971):97–107.

Holder, Alan. *The Imagined Past.* Lewisburg: Bucknell University Press, 1980.

Holman, C. Hugh. "*Absalom, Absalom!:* The Historian as Detective." *Sewanee Review* 79 (1971):542–53.

Howe, Irving. *Politics and the Novel.* New York: Fawcett Publications, 1967.

———. *William Faulkner: A Critical Study.* Second Edition, revised and expanded. New York: Vintage Books, n.d.

Howell, Elmo. "Faulkner and Scott and the Legacy of the Lost Cause." *Georgia Review* 26 (1972):314–25.

———. "William Faulkner's Caledonia: A Note on *Intruder in the Dust.*" *Studies in Scottish Literature* 3 (1966):243–52.

Hudson, Liam. *Human Beings: An Introduction to the Psychology of Human Experience.* London: Jonathan Cape, 1975.

Hunt, John. *William Faulkner: Art in Theological Tension.* Syracuse: Syracuse University Press, 1965.

———. "Historiography in Faulkner's *Absalom, Absalom!.*" *Faulkner Studies* I (1980): 38–47.

Hutchison, E. R. "A Footnote to the Gum Tree Scene." *College English* 24 (1963):564–65.

Ingram, Forrest L. *Representative Short Story Cycles of the Twentieth Century.* The Hague: Mouton, 1971.

Irwin, John T. *Doubling and Incest/Repetition and Revenge: A Speculative Reading of Faulkner.* Baltimore: Johns Hopkins University Press, 1975.

Iser, Wolfgang. *The Implied Reader.* Baltimore: Johns Hopkins University Press, 1974.

Jack, Ian. *English Literature, 1815–1832.* New York: Oxford University Press, 1963.

Johnson, Edgar. *Sir Walter Scott: The Great Unknown.* New York: Macmillan, 1970.

Kantor, MacKinlay. "The Historical Novelist's Obligation to History." *Iowa Journal of History* 59 (1962):27–44.

Karl, Frederick R. *A Reader's Guide to Joseph Conrad.* New York: Farrar, Straus and Giroux, 1970.

Kartiganer, Donald M. *The Fragile Thread: The Meaning of Form in Faulkner's Novels.* Amherst: University of Massachusetts Press, 1979.

Keiser, Merle Wallace. "*Flags in the Dust* and *Sartoris.*" *Fifty Years of Yoknapatawpha.* Ed. Doreen Fowler and Ann J. Abadie. Jackson: University Press of Mississippi, 1980, pp. 44–70.

Kermode, Frank. "Novel, History and Type." *Novel* 1 (1968):231–38.

Kerr, Elizabeth M. *Yoknapatawpha: Faulkner's "Little Postage Stamp of Native Soil."* New York: Fordham University Press, 1969.

Kettle, Arnold. *An Introduction to the English Novel.* New York: Harper & Row, 1968.

Kinney, Arthur F. "Faulkner and the Possibilities for Heroism." *Bear, Man, and God: Eight Approaches to "The Bear."* Ed. Francis Lee Utley, Lynn Z. Bloom and Arthur F. Kinney. New York: Random House, 1971, pp. 235–51.

———. *Faulkner's Narrative Poetics: Style as Vision.* Amherst: University of Massachusetts Press, 1978.

Korenman, Joan S. "Faulkner's Grecian Urn." *Southern Literary Journal* 7 (1974):3–23.

———. "Faulkner and 'That Undying Mark'." *Studies in American Fiction* 4 (1976):81–91.

Krause, David. "Reading Shreve's Letters and Faulkner's *Absalom, Absalom!.*" *Studies in American Fiction* 11 (1983):153–69.

Kreiswirth, Martin. *William Faulkner: The Making of a Novelist.* Athens: University of Georgia Press, 1983.

Kuyk, Dirk, Jr. *Threads Cable-strong: William Faulkner's Go Down, Moses.* Lewisburg: Bucknell University Press, 1983.

Langford, Gerald. *Faulkner's Revision of Absalom, Absalom!: A Collation of the Manuscript and the Published Book.* Austin: University of Texas Press, 1971.

Langlois, Charles Victor and Seignobos, Charles. *Introduction to the Study of History.* Translated by G. G. Berry, With a Preface by F. York Powell. New York: Henry Holt, 1925.

Lehan, Richard. "Faulkner's Poetic Prose: Style and Meaning in 'The Bear'." *College English* 27 (1965):243–47.

Leisy, Ernest Erwin. *The American Historical Novel.* Norman: Oklahoma University Press, 1950.

Levin, David. *In Defense of Historical Literature: Essays on American History, Autobiography, Drama, and Fiction.* New York: Hill and Wang, 1967.

Levins, Lynn Gartrell. "The Four Narrative Perspectives in *Absalom, Absalom!*." *PMLA* 85 (1970):35-47.

Lewis, R. W. B. *The Picaresque Saint: A Critical Study.* New York: Lippincott, 1961.

Lind, Ilse Dusoir. "The Design and Meaning of *Absalom, Absalom!*." *William Faulkner: Three Decades of Criticism.* Ed. Frederick J. Hoffman and Olga W. Vickery. New York: Harcourt, Brace, and World, 1963, pp. 278-304.

Lofquist, A. J. "More in the Name of Brownlee in Faulkner's *The Bear.*" *College Literature* 10 (1983):357-59.

Longley, John Lewis, Jr. *The Tragic Mask: A Study of Faulkner's Heroes.* Chapel Hill: University of North Carolina Press, 1963.

Lukács, Georg. *The Historical Novel.* Boston: Beacon Press, 1963.

Lukacs, John. *Historical Consciousness or The Remembered Past.* New York: Harper & Row, 1968.

Lynen, John F. *The Pastoral Art of Robert Frost.* New Haven: Yale University Press, 1964.

Lytle, Andrew Nelson. "The Son of Man: He Will Prevail." *Sewanee Review* 63 (1955): 114-37.

Maclean, Hugh. "Conservatism in Modern American Fiction." *College English* 15 (1954): 322-25.

McClennen, Joshua. "*Absalom, Absalom!* and the Meaning of History." *Papers of the Michigan Academy of Science, Arts and Letters* 42 (1956):357-69.

McHaney, Thomas L. "Faulkner Borrows from the Mississippi Guide." *Mississippi Quarterly* 19 (1966):116-20.

McSweeney, Kerry. "The Subjective Intensities of Faulkner's *Flags in the Dust.*" *The Canadian Review of American Studies* 8 (1978):154-64.

Marx, Leo. *The Machine in the Garden: Technology and the Pastoral Ideal in America.* New York: Oxford University Press, 1967.

Matlock, James H. "The Voices of Time: Narrative Structure in *Absalom, Absalom!*." *Southern Review* 15 (1979):333-54.

Matthews, Brander. *The Historical Novel, and other Essays.* New York: Scribner's, 1901.

Matthews, John T. *The Play of Faulkner's Language.* Ithaca: Cornell University Press, 1982.

Memmott, A. James. "Sartoris Ludens: The Play Element in *The Unvanquished.*" *Mississippi Quarterly* 29 (1976):375-87.

Meriwether, James B. "Faulkner and the South." *Southern Writers.* Ed. R. C. Simonini, Jr. Charlottesville: University Press of Virginia, 1964.

————. "An Introduction for *The Sound and the Fury.*" *Southern Review* 8 (1972):705-10.

————. *The Literary Career of William Faulkner.* Columbia: University of South Carolina Press, 1971.

————. "The Place of *The Unvanquished* in William Faulkner's Yoknapatawpha Series." Ph.D dissertation, Princeton University, 1958.

————. "A Prefatory Note by Faulkner for the *Compson Appendix.*" *American Literature* 43 (1970):281-84.

————. "The Textual History of *The Sound and the Fury*" *Studies in The Sound and the Fury.* Ed. James B. Meriwether. Columbus: Charles E. Merrill, 1970, pp. 1-32.

Middleton, John. "Shreve McCannon and Sutpen's Legacy." *Southern Review* 10 (1974):115-24.

Millgate, Michael. *The Achievement of William Faulkner.* London: Constable, 1966.

————. "A Cosmos of My Own," "Faulkner's First Trilogy: *Sartoris, Sanctuary* and *Requiem For A Nun.*" *Fifty Years of Yoknapatawpha.* Ed. Doreen Fowler and Ann J. Abadie. Jackson: University Press of Mississippi, 1980, pp. 23-43, 90-109.

———. "Faulkner and History." *The South and Faulkner's Yoknapatawpha: The Actual and the Apocryphal.* Ed. Evans Harrington and Ann Abadie. Jackson: University Press of Mississippi, 1977, pp. 22–39.

———. "Faulkner's Masters." *Tulane Studies in English* 23 (1978):143–55.

———. "'The Firmament of Man's History': Faulkner's Treatment of the Past." *Mississippi Quarterly* 25 (1972):25–35.

———. "The Problem of Point of View." *Studies in The Sound and the Fury.* Ed. James B. Meriwether. Columbus: Charles E. Merrill, 1970, pp. 125–39.

Milum, Richard A. "Faulkner, Scott and Another Source for Drusilla." *Mississippi Quarterly* 31 (1978):425–28.

Mink, Louis O. "Collingwood's Historicism: A Dialectic of Process." *Critical Essays on the Philosophy of R. G. Collingwood.* Ed. Michael Krausz. New York: Oxford University Press, 1972.

Minter, David. *The Interpreted Design as a Structural Principle in American Prose.* New Haven: Yale University Press, 1969.

Moses, W. R. "Where History Crosses Myth: Another Reading of 'The Bear'." *Accent* 13 (1953):21–33.

Muhlenfeld, Elisabeth S. "Shadows with Substance and Ghosts Exhumed: The Women in *Absalom, Absalom!*." *Mississippi Quarterly* 25 (1972):289–304.

Neff, Emory Edward. *The Poetry of History: The Contribution of Literature to the Writing of History since Voltaire.* New York: Columbia University Press, 1947.

Nichols, Stephen G. "George Lukács: The Problem of Dialectical Criticism." *Criticism: Speculative and Analytical Essays.* Ed. L. S. Dembo. Madison: University of Wisconsin Press, 1968, pp. 75–92.

Niebuhr. Reinhold. *The Irony of American History.* New York: Scribner's, 1962.

Nye, Russel B. "History and Literature, Branches of the Same Tree." *Essays on History and Literature.* Ed. Robert H. Bremmer. Columbus: Ohio State University Press, 1966, pp. 123–59.

Ortega y Gasset, José. *History as a System, and other Essays Toward a Philosophy of History.* New York: Norton, 1962.

Otten, Terry. "Faulkner's Use of the Past: A Comment." *Renascence* 20 (1968):198–207, 214.

Paddock, Lisa. "'Sublimating the actual into apocryphal': The Case for Faulkner's *Collected Stories.*" Unpublished essay.

———. "Contrapuntal in Integration: A Study of Three Faulkner Short Story Volumes." Ph.D dissertation, University of Toronto, 1979.

Paludan, Phillip Shaw. *Victims: A True Story of the Civil War.* Knoxville: University of Tennessee Press, 1981

Parker, Hershel. "What Quentin Saw 'Out There'." *Mississippi Quarterly* 27 (1974):323–26

Parr, Susan Resneck, "The Fourteenth Image of the Blackbird: Another Look at Truth in *Absalom, Absalom!*." *Arizona Quarterly* 35 (1979):153–64.

Perluck, Herbert A. "'The Bear': An Unromantic Reading." *Religious Perspectives in Faulkner's Fiction: Yoknapatawpha and Beyond.* Ed. J. Robert Barth, S.J. Notre Dame: University of Notre Dame Press, 1972, pp. 173–98.

The Philosophy of Hegel. Ed. Carl J. Friedrich. New York: The Modern Library, 1953.

Pikoulis, John. *The Art of William Faulkner.* London: Macmillan, 1982.

Pilkington, John. "'Strange Times' in Yoknapatawpha." *Fifty Years of Yoknapatawpha.* Ed. Doreen Fowler and Ann J. Abadie. Jackson: University Press of Mississippi, 1980, pp. 71–89.

Pitavy, Francois L. "The Gothicism of *Absalom, Absalom!*: Rosa Coldfield Revisited." *"A Cosmos of My Own": Faulkner and Yoknapatawpha, 1980.* Ed. Doreen Fowler and Ann J. Abadie. Jackson: University Press of Mississippi, 1981, pp. 199–226.

Plato. *Euthyphro, Apology, Crito.* Translated by F. J. Church: translation revised, with an introduction by Robert D. Cumming. Indianapolis: Bobbs-Merrill, 1956.

Poirier, Richard. "'Strange Gods' in Jefferson Mississippi: Analysis of *Absalom, Absalom!.*" *Twentieth Century Interpretations of Absalom, Absalom!.* Ed. Arnold Goldman. Englewood Cliffs, New Jersey: Prentice-Hall, 1971, pp. 12–31.

———. *A World Elsewhere: The Place of Style in American Literature.* London: Chatto and Windus, 1967.

Polk, Noel Earl. "The Critics and Faulkner's 'Little Postage Stamp of Native Soil'." *Mississippi Quarterly* 23 (1970):323–35.

———. *Faulkner's Requiem for a Nun: A Critical Study.* Bloomington: Indiana University Press, 1981.

———. "The Manuscript of *Absalom, Absalom!.*" *Mississippi Quarterly* 25 (1972):359–67.

———. *Requiem For a Nun: A Concordance To the Novel.* Ann Arbor: University Microfilms International, 1979.

——— and Kenneth L. Privratsky. Ed. *The Sound and the Fury: A Concordance to the Novel.* Ann Arbor: University Microfilms International, 1980.

Raleigh, John Henry. *Time, Place, and Idea: Essays on the Novel.* Carbondale: Southern Illinois University Press, 1968.

———. "*Waverley* as History; or 'Tis One Hundred and Fifty-Six Years Since'." *Novel* 4 (1970):14–29.

Redekop, Magdalene. "*Absalom, Absalom!*: Through the Spectacles of Shreve McCannon." *William Faulkner: Materials, Studies and Criticism* 5 (1983):17–45. Nan'un' Do Publishing Company, Tokyo, Japan.

Reed, Joseph W., Jr. *Faulkner's Narrative.* New Haven: Yale University Press, 1973.

Renier, G. J. *History: Its Purpose and Method.* New York: Harper Torchbooks, 1965.

Robbins, Deborah. "The Desperate Eloquence of *Absalom, Absalom!.*" *Mississippi Quarterly* 34 (1981):315–24.

Rollyson, Carl E., Jr. "Faulkner and Historical Fiction: *Redgauntlet* and *Absalom, Absalom!.*" *Dalhousie Review* 56 (1976):671–81.

———. "Quentin Durward and Quentin Compson: The Romantic Standard-Bearers of Scott and Faulkner." *Massachusetts Studies in English* 7 (1980):34–39.

Ross, Stephen M. "The Evocation of Voice in *Absalom, Absalom!.*" *Essays in Literature* 8 (1981):135–49.

———. "The 'Loud World' of Quentin Compson." *Studies in the Novel* 7 (1975):245–57.

———. "'Voice' in Narrative Texts: The Example of *As I Lay Dying.*" *PMLA* 94 (1979):300–10.

Ruppersburg, Hugh M. *Voice and Eye in Faulkner's Fiction.* Athens: University of Georgia Press, 1983.

Sanders, Andrew. *The Victorian Historical Novel 1840–1880.* New York: St. Martin's Press, 1979.

Sartre, Jean-Paul. "William Faulkner's *Sartoris.*" *Literary and Philosophical Essays.* London: The Philosophical Library, 1955.

———. "On *The Sound and the Fury*: Time in the Work of Faulkner." *Faulkner: A Collection of Critical Essays.* Ed. Robert Penn Warren. Englewood Cliffs, New Jersey: Prentice-Hall, 1966, pp. 87–93.

Schamberger, J. Edward. "Renaming Perceval Brownlee in Faulkner's '[The] Bear'." *College Literature* 4 (1977):92–94.

Schleifer, Ronald. "Faulkner's Storied Novel: *Go Down, Moses* and the Translation of Time." *Modern Fiction Studies* 28 (1982):109–27.

Schmidtberger, Loren F. "*Absalom, Absalom!*: What Clytie Knew." *Mississippi Quarterly* 35 (1982):255–63.

Schoenberg, Estella. *Old Tales and Talking: Quentin Compson in William Faulkner's Absalom, Absalom! and Related Works.* Jackson: University Press of Mississippi, 1977.

Scholes, Robert E. "Myth and Manners in *Sartoris.*" *Georgia Review* 16 (1962):195-201.

Schultz, William J. "Just Like Father: Mr. Compson as Cavalier in *Absalom, Absalom!.*" *Kansas Quarterly* 14 (1982):115-23.

Scott, Arthur L. "The Myriad Perspectives of *Absalom, Absalom!.*" *American Quarterly* 6 (1954):210-20.

Scott, Sir Walter. *Redgauntlet, A Tale of the Eighteenth Century. By the Author of Waverley.* Edinburgh: Constable, 1824.

———. *Waverley Or, "Tis Sixty Years Since."* Ed. Edgar Johnson. New York: Signet Books, 1964.

———. *Quentin Durward.* London: Collins, 1954.

Walter Scott. Ed. D. D. Devlin. London: Macmillan, 1968.

Sir Walter Scott Lectures, 1940-1948. Ed. Sir Herbert Grierson. Edinburgh: Edinburgh University Press, 1950.

Sir Walter Scott Today: Some Retrospective Essays and Studies. Ed. Sir Herbert Grierson. London: Constable, 1932.

Sewall, Richard B. *The Vision of Tragedy.* New Haven: Yale University Press, 1959.

Simmons, James C. *The Novelist As Historian: Essays on the Victorian Historical Novel.* The Hague: Mouton, 1973.

Simpson, Lewis P. *The Dispossessed Garden: Pastoral and History in Southern Literature.* Athens: University of Georgia Press, 1975.

———. "Faulkner and the Legend of the Artist." *Faulkner: Fifty Years After The Marble Faun.* Ed. George H. Wolfe. University, Alabama: University of Alabama Press, 1976, pp. 69-100.

———. "Sex and History: Origins of Faulkner's Apocrypha," "Yoknapatawpha & Faulkner's Fable of Civilization." *The Maker and the Myth.* Ed. Evans Harrington and Ann J. Abadie. Jackson: University Press of Mississippi, 1978, pp. 43-70, 122-145.

Singal, Donald Joseph. "William Faulkner and the Discovery of Southern Evil." *The War Within: From Victorian to Modernist Thought in the South, 1919-1945.* Chapel Hill: University of North Carolina Press, 1982, pp. 153-97.

Smith, Meredith. "A Chronology of *Go Down, Moses.*" *Mississippi Quarterly* 36 (1983):319-28.

Stange, G. Robert. "On *The History of Henry Esmond, Esq.*" *The History of Henry Esmond, Esq.* Ed. G. Robert Stange. New York: Holt, Rinehart & Winston, 1962.

Stewart, J. I. M. *Joseph Conrad.* New York: Dodd, Mead, 1968.

Stonum, Gary Lee. *Faulkner's Career: An Internal Literary History.* Ithaca: Cornell University Press, 1979.

Strandberg, Victor H. *A Faulkner Overview: Six Perspectives.* Port Washington, New York: Kennikat Press, 1981.

Straumann, Heinrich. "An American Interpretation of Existence: Faulkner's *A Fable.*" *William Faulkner: Three Decades of Criticism.* Ed. Frederick J. Hoffman and Olga W. Vickery. New York: Harcourt, Brace & World, 1963, pp. 349-72.

Sullivan, Walter. "Southern Novelists and the Civil War." *Southern Renascence: The Literature of the Modern South.* Ed. Louis D. Rubin, Jr. and Robert D. Jacobs. Baltimore: The Johns Hopkins Press, 1965, pp. 112-25.

Sultan, Stanley. "'Call Me Ishmael': The Hagiography of Isaac McCaslin." *Texas Studies in Literature and Language* 2 (1961):50-65.

Sutherland, John. "Introduction." *The History of Henry Esmond,* by William Makepeace

Thackeray. Ed. John Sutherland and Michael Greenfield. Baltimore: Penguin Books, 1970.

Talon, Henri A. "Time and Memory in Thackeray's *Henry Esmond.*" *Review of English Studies* 13 (1962):147–56.

Thackeray, William Makepeace. *The History of Henry Esmond, Esq., A Colonel in the Service of Her Majesty Q. Anne, Written by Himself. In Three Volumes.* London: Smith, Elder, 1852.

Thompson, Lawrance. "Afterword." *Sartoris,* by William Faulkner. New York: Signet Books, 1964.

———. *William Faulkner: An Introduction and Interpretation.* Second Edition. New York: Barnes & Noble, 1967.

Thornton, Weldon. "Structure and Theme in Faulkner's *Go Down, Moses.*" *William Faulkner: Critical Collection.* Ed. Leland H. Cox. Detroit: Gale Research, 1982.

Tick, Stanley. "The Unity of *Go Down, Moses.*" *Twentieth Century Literature* 8 (1962): 69–73.

Tillyard, E. M. W. *The Epic Strain in the English Novel.* London: Chatto & Windus, 1958.

Tobin, Patricia. "The Time of Myth and History in *Absalom, Absalom!.*" *American Literature* 45 (1973):252–70.

———. *Time and the Novel: The Genealogical Imperative.* Princeton: Princeton University Press, 1978.

Trimmer, Joseph F. "*The Unvanquished:* The Teller and the Tale." *Ball State University Forum* 10 (1969):35–42.

Tritschler, Donald. "The Unity of Faulkner's Shaping Vision." *Modern Fiction Studies* 5 (1959):337–43.

Turner, Joseph W. "The Kinds of Historical Fiction." *Genre* 12 (1979):333–55.

Uroff, Margaret Dicki. "The Fictions of *Absalom, Absalom!.*" *Studies in the Novel* 11 (1979):431–45.

Vande Kieft, Ruth M. "Faulkner's Defeat of Time in *Absalom, Absalom!.*" *Southern Review* 6 (1970):1100–09.

Vickery, Olga W. *The Novels of William Faulkner: A Critical Interpretation.* Revised Edition. Baton Rouge: Louisiana State University Press, 1964.

Volpe, Edmond L. *A Reader's Guide to William Faulkner.* New York: Farrar, Straus and Giroux, 1964.

Waggoner, Hyatt. "The Historical Novel and the Southern Past, The Case of *Absalom, Absalom!.*" *Southern Literary Journal* 2 (1970):69–85.

———. *William Faulkner: From Jefferson to the World.* Lexington: University of Kentucky Press, 1966.

Walker, William E. "*The Unvanquished:* The Restoration of Tradition." *Reality and Myth: Essays in American Literature in Memory of Richard Croom Beatty.* Ed. William E. Walker and Robert L. Welker. Nashville: Vanderbilt University Press, 1964, pp. 275–97.

Warren, Robert Penn. "Faulkner, The South, The Negro, and Time." *Faulkner: A Collection of Critical Essays.* Ed. Robert Penn Warren. Englewood Cliffs, New Jersey: Prentice-Hall, 1966, pp. 251–71.

———. *Selected Essays.* New York: Random House, 1951.

Wasson, Ben. *Count No 'Count: Flashbacks to Faulkner.* Jackson: University Press of Mississippi, 1983.

Waswo, Richard. "Story as Historiography in the Waverley Novels." *ELH* 47 (1980):304–30.

Watkins, Floyd. "What Happens in *Absalom, Absalom!?*" *Modern Fiction Studies* 13 (1967):79–87.

Watson, James Gray. "'The Germ of My Apocrypha': *Sartoris* and the Search for Form." *Mosaic* 7 (1973):15-33.

――――. "'If *Was* Existed': Faulkner's Prophets and Patterns of History." *Modern Fiction Studies* 21 (1975-76):499-507.

Weinstein, Arnold. *Vision and Response in Modern Fiction.* Ithaca: Cornell University Press, 1974.

Welsh, Alexander. *The Hero of the Waverley Novels.* New York: Atheneum, 1968.

Wertenbaker, Thomas, Jr. "Faulkner's Point of View and The Chronicle of Ike McCaslin." *College English* 24 (1962):169-77.

Wheeler, Otis B. "Faulkner's Wilderness." *American Literature* 31 (1959):127-36.

Williams, J. Gary. "Quentin Finally Sees Miss Rosa." *Criticism* 21 (1979):331-46.

Winks, Robin. Ed. *The Historian as Detective: Essays on Evidence.* New York: Harper & Row, 1969.

Woodruff, Neal, Jr. "'The Bear' and Faulkner's Moral Vision." *Studies in Faulkner.* Ed. Neal Woodruff, Jr. Pittsburgh: Carnegie Institute of Technology, 1961, pp. 43-67.

Woodward, C. Vann. *The Burden of Southern History.* New York: Mentor Books, 1969.

Yonce, Margaret. "'Shot Down Last Spring': The Wounded Aviators of Faulkner's Wasteland." *Mississippi Quarterly* 31 (1978):359-68.

Zender, Karl F. "Reading in 'The Bear.'" *Faulkner Studies* I (1980):91-99.

――――. "Faulkner and the Power of Sound." *PMLA* 99 (1983):89-108.

Zink, Karl E. "Flux and the Frozen Moment: The Imagery of Stasis in Faulkner's Prose." *American Literature* 71 (1956):285-301.

Zoellner, Robert H. "Faulkner's Prose Style in *Absalom, Absalom!*." *American Literature* 30 (1959):486-502.

Index